TWO WHEELS
TWO COUNTRIES
ONE DREAM

Dear Norma

*I couldn't have
done it without
you! Thank you
so much Norma!*

Daniel Edward Murphy

Daniel Edward Murphy

Printed in Victoria, Canada

Editor: Norma Kennedy
Cover Design and Composition: VISU*TronX*
Front Cover Photo: Genevieve Steele
Back Cover Photo: Cecilia Munoz Aguilera

National Library of Canada Cataloguing in Publication

Murphy, Daniel Edward, 1963-
 Two wheels, two countries, one dream / Daniel Edward
Murphy.
 ISBN 1-55395-068-2
 1. Murphy, Daniel Edward, 1963- --Journeys--Alaska
Highway. 2. Alaska Highway--Description and travel.
3. Motorcycling--Alaska Highway. I. Title.
GV1059.522.A43M87 2002   917.11'87   C2002-904358-1

TRAFFORD

This book was published *on-demand* in cooperation with Trafford Publishing.
On-demand publishing is a unique process and service of making a book available for retail sale to the public taking advantage of on-demand manufacturing and Internet marketing.
On-demand publishing includes promotions, retail sales, manufacturing, order fulfilment, accounting and collecting royalties on behalf of the author.

Suite 6E - 2333 Government St., Victoria, B.C. V8T 4L7, CANADA
Phone   250-383-6864   Toll-free   1-888-232-4444 (Canada & US)
Fax   250-383-6804   E-mail   sales@trafford.com
Web site   www.trafford.com   TRAFFORD PUBLISHING IS A DIVISION OF TRAFFORD HOLDINGS LTD.
Trafford Catalogue #02-0782   www.trafford.com/robots/02-0782.html

10   9   8   7   6   5   4   3   2

Contents

Dedication

I dedicate this book to the brave war veterans—alive and deceased—of
World War II, who gave me the freedom to write this book.
I thank you from the bottom of my heart.

Dan Murphy

The author wishes to acknowledge:

My mother and my late father, for the love and support they have always
given to me, and my brothers and sisters who always
looked out for me.

Special thanks for the talents, patience, and friendship of Norma
Kennedy, who edited this book. I would not have been able to
complete it without her.

Dan Murphy

Part 1

It all started when ...

November, Year One of The Dream

I am operating an eighty-one-year-old elevator travelling down toward the bottom floor of the six-storey Elgin and Winter Garden Theatre Centre. Just part of my duties here at the theatre. My co-worker Kelly, (who recently got back from a three-month stay in Africa) asks me whether or not I'm going to keep a journal of my trip. I tell her that I was thinking of keeping one but that I hadn't decided yet. After she gets off the elevator, I decide that riding approximately ten thousand miles on a motorcycle might make an interesting book. At this point of my writing, I have nothing but questions—How much will such a trip cost? How long will it take? What should I take? What kind of motorcycle will I ride? How much will insurance cost in the United States? What happens if I wipe out in the middle of the prairies? Do I take still pictures, video camera, or both? I could go on, because the questions seem endless, but I won't. How stupid of me, I haven't even told you what the trip is yet.

My planned trip is a ten thousand-mile journey (approximately) from Toronto, Ontario, Canada to Alaska and back to Toronto via the United States. How did the idea to do this come about, you may ask. Well, I read an article in a magazine about the fiftieth anniversary of the Alaska Highway, which was built during World War II and is almost 1500 miles long. After reading the article, I thought to myself that it

1

would be great to drive the whole length of the highway from one end to the other and back again on a motorcycle. I later thought what a lot of trouble it would be to ship the motorcycle out to British Columbia. Why not just ride the motorcycle all the way there and back? At the time of this decision, I had not ridden a motorcycle in at least ten years. Nor did I have a lot of experience on a motorcycle. I had spent a brief time on an old on/off-road 125 Suzuki.

The trip was inspired by a number of events which happened a few years earlier. I was struggling in Toronto as an actor, trying to get parts, auditioning, doing plays, and doing the things struggling actors do. I was also reading adventure books and doing small walks. Small walks compared to Peter Jenkins, who walked across the United States and China. Another inspiration was Ted Edwards's book, *Fight the Wild Island*. And this is the book that got me started on my "I could do that, maybe" way of thinking and, to a certain extent, I did. I walked 19 miles, then 23 miles, and finally 26 miles, all on successive weekends. The last 26-mile walk I did was a bit of a disaster, because of my stupidity in walking the last 9 miles with torn tendons in my foot. I took a year off from walking trips. About a year later, I decided to test my hopefully healed foot by walking 40 miles. It was a success, only having to take four days off work with screamingly painful legs. Oh well, four days wasn't so bad compared to the two months I took off when I had torn my tendon on the previous walk. Two months without pay. I was a foot messenger at the time.

I think watching Jacques Cousteau TV specials, *National Geographic TV*, ABC's *Wide World of Sports*, and Mutual of Omaha's *Wild Kingdom* had subconsciously planted an adventure-loving seed which was to start seriously growing in my late twenties. What can you say about a guy like Jacques Cousteau, who, in 1943, along with Emile Gagnan, invented the aqua-lung? Jacques has always done what he loves to do—travelling to exotic locations all around the world, studying oceans, animals, and land. He seems to be happy; he's rich, successful, famous, a national treasure in France, respected internationally for his work, and he cares about the world in general. Cousteau would sound sad while narrating his specials or commenting on the destruction of the ocean because he could see first-hand what effect pollution was having on it. For my 40-mile hike I named my knapsack Cousteau One in his honour. That might sound dumb, but it's true. I take my hat off to you, Jacques-Yves Cousteau; you're a true gentleman explorer.

Anyway, just a little more about my walking trips. After telling friends of my past and future walking trips, they started saying things like, "You did what? You're crazy." The one question I could never properly answer was, "Why?" My friend Gina jokingly started calling me 'Madman Dan.'

The strangest reaction that happened just before my 40-mile walk (I hate metric measurements) was that some of my friends and family tried to talk me out of doing the trip. Even my most supportive friend, Nancy, didn't want me to do it. She didn't come right out and say it, but I could tell by how the conversation was going that she thought it might be too dangerous. I eventually promised Nancy and my mother that I would call from my first and only overnight stop, which I did. My first reaction to the "Maybe you shouldn't do it" was a bit of shock. Believe me, I'm not bad-mouthing my friends, family, or my mother. Their concern for me was quite touching and not altogether unpleasant. At the same time, I couldn't help but wonder how worried they would become in the future when I would walk 250 miles to Ottawa or 2000 miles across a country. Or even more importantly, how will they handle my current plan for this motorcycle trip? The walking trips taught me that almost anything is possible with the right preparation and planning. Now there was little doubt in my mind that I could walk to Ottawa starting in Toronto, which I may attempt sometime in the future. Who knows?

Am I mad, as my friend jokingly called me? The answer is, no. Am I afraid to die? Yes and no. I believe there are two kinds of death: 1. You are declared dead by a doctor because of illness or accident. That's it, you're dead. 2. The second kind of death is long and conscious, in that you spend your whole life not chasing your dreams or following a path that, deep down, you know you should take. To me, this is the worst death of all. You sit on your rocking chair at 70 or 80 years old, saying "shoulda, woulda, coulda." I realize that it's hard to live up to some of our dreams due to human nature itself and economic reasons. I hope that after reading my story you might try to fulfil a dream, whatever it may be. I really hope that happens. Oh well, let's move on to the motorcycle trip.

Why a motorcycle? Why not a car, as my father suggested? A car does not seem as much of a challenge to me. Besides, I've always liked motorcycles. I think some of them are as beautiful as the works of art you'd find hanging in an art gallery, particularly the old Indians and Harley-Davidsons. There is also nothing quite like the feeling of riding a motorcycle. Even with my limited experience, I feel qualified to say that.

Preparation:

Question: How do you prepare for a ten thousand-mile trip?

Answer: I haven't the slightest idea.

Problems:

Problem 1: I don't know a thing about motorcycles, especially how to fix them.

Big deal! Piece of cake. I'm only travelling a huge distance. If I should get a flat tire in the prairies, I'll just ...um...uh...quit! If I get an oil leak while I'm driving through the mountains, I'll...well...there's always...HELP! I suppose that taking a motorcycle mechanic's course is a must, which I dread, quite honestly, because I'm not mechanically inclined at all. I don't like fixing things, period! I used to get frustrated fixing my bicycle as a kid and not much has changed.

Problem 2: I am not an experienced rider.

Again, there are courses one can take, though I don't know if I will or not. I will have only one season of riding and will probably just have to learn as I go along. However, motorcycles, like airplanes, don't allow much room for error when it comes to accidents or lapses in concentration.

Problem 3: I hate cooking.

I hate it, and I don't mean that it's a pain in the neck that I do every day. I mean, I never cook, period. Every meal is bought in a restaurant or for take-out. My kitchen is never used. Cooking is something I loathe and detest. I'm afraid I won't make any promises in this area. (I hope that I will cook most of the time, but that would be a lie.) I will buy ultra-lite cooking equipment and all the other stuff that goes with it and try. But if I don't get at least one restaurant meal a day, I won't be responsible for my actions. If I don't eat in a restaurant over a three-day period, they will probably find me muttering and trying to order a chicken soft taco from a field of wheat in the middle of the prairies somewhere. There's an episode of the old *Dick Van Dyke Show* where Rob (Dick Van Dyke) gets a motorcycle and gets lost in the desert. They eventually find him trying to suck water from a rock. If you ever get a chance to see it, it's quite funny.

Problem 4: Up to this point in my life I have never been real camping.

When I say real camping, I mean the kind where you pitch a tent, cook your food, and everything else there is to know about camping. I have never done that. I came close to it a couple of times. What I know about camping can be written on the head of a pin. This is something I may practise, but will probably learn as I go along. It will be especially tough because of the incredibly limited number of things I can take. I'm assuming that everything must be ultra-lite, like tents, sleeping bags, GASP! cooking utensils, and a minimal amount of clothing. We'll see.

Problem 5: I'm lousy at handling money, budgeting, and saving money.

It's true as long as I've been handling money. The fact that all my meals are eaten as take-out or in a restaurant will give you an idea of how much I spend in a month. Saving money is the hardest thing for me. In all the years I've been working, I have saved exactly two hundred dollars. I will need a lot of money for this trip. I will be buying my first motorcycle in the spring, and hope to have three thousand dollars, but that won't happen. More like two thousand. I'm still paying off debts incurred when I was an actor. Although I work two jobs (at the theatre and as a foot messenger downtown), I still don't seem to be able to save and it's mostly my fault. After I have paid off the loans to my bank, which will happen this December, I will be able to save more each month. That's about all I can say on this subject. I don't seem to change much in this area. Another of my flaws.

Problem 6: I don't have a good sense of direction and can't read a map very well.

Let's face it, I have trouble folding a map, let alone reading one or understanding it. I'm not going to worry about it too much because the Trans-Canada Highway will take me practically right to the base or start of the Alaska Highway. As for coming back through the States, this could prove to be a problem, but so what. It will work itself out in the end. I hope.

Problem 7: Attitudes toward motorcycles and motorcyclists in general.

Potentially a problem, but the image has changed a lot since the Easy Rider/Hell's Angels movies of the late 1960s and early 1970s. Now people like Malcolm Forbes, Sylvester Stallone, and Jay Leno have all had their pictures taken on their Harleys. (Who else can afford one?) A brand new bottom-of-the-line Harley-Davidson (in Canada) starts out around $10,000. other Harleys can go as high as $30,000. I hope by now most people can tell the biker who is in a gang from the Harley-Davidson rider, or whatever make the person happens to be riding. From what I've read in magazines, I think I may have the most trouble from campsites that don't accept a motorcyclist on their premises. Maybe they have had bad experiences or for insurance reasons they can't take the chance. Whatever the reason, I'm not going to worry about it too much. Famous last words. I think while travelling through the United States I'll sew on one of those dual flag patches (Canada and U.S. flags) that kind of hints that we're in this together. Two countries side by side, blah, blah, blah. If I should encounter any gun-toting

Americans or Canadians, I'll do the time-honoured manly thing, which is to start crying and begging for my pathetic life. Or I'll launch into the "I know a martial art" routine, which is an absolute classic. Unfortunately, it's a classic that doesn't work, as I once found out.

November 11

A few hours ago I attended the Remembrance Day ceremonies at the Old City Hall in Toronto. I've attended it three years in a row and it never fails to choke me up. My Uncle Bill was a motorcycle dispatch rider in Europe during the Second World War. Another uncle of mine trained soldiers to ride motorcycles. Yet another uncle was a tail-gunner in British Columbia, during the war. My father and Uncle Sid were both in the army as well. My Uncle Bill risked his life, along with hundreds of thousands of others, so people like me would have the freedom to live our dreams. I honestly believe that had the Allied Forces not stopped Adolf Hitler and the military leaders of Japan, I would not be making this trip. I will be thinking about the veterans particularly on the Alaska Highway, which was built for the war effort.

I've decided to have a poppy painted on my gas tank as a tribute to the veterans, and to the people we lost (on both sides) in medicine, the arts, technology, and every other field of endeavour you can think of.

November 18

Something about the trip has been bothering me in the past couple of weeks and I now know what it is. I took a trip to an outdoor store in downtown Toronto and looked in their book section where they have great mountain-climbing expedition stories and cycle trips, covering thousands of miles in Siberia, no less. So what do you think slowly started to dawn on me as I looked at these fine books of incredible adventures? (Theme music from *Jeopardy* here.) Well, here goes. The trip's not going far enough. Sad but true. It's just not far enough. Another five or ten thousand miles ought to do it. If the trip only lasts a month, it won't be interesting enough. If I'm going to plan something two years in advance, it had better be worth it. Who am I kidding? We're talking four years from the time of the original idea to the trip itself. Now having decided this, all the same problems of the previous pages apply. It's just, now I can think of one more. Do I keep my apartment, sublet, or give it up?

November 23

I have now decided on a route for my trip. I will ride up to Ottawa, where my friend Dave Reid, his wife Pam, and their daughter Erica live. I will then cross the border into the United States and Maine, and drive down the coast to Florida. In Florida I will visit the Kennedy Space Centre. I will travel along the middle and bottom of the United States, to Memphis, through Texas and Nevada, then maybe up the other coast through California, into British Columbia, then Alaska and back through Canada. I don't know how many miles this will add to the trip (if any) but that is a rough outline of my trip.

December 10

It is roughly two weeks until Christmas. Christmas is looking good. The motorcycle trip is looking bad. I have saved a grand total of two hundred dollars. Far short of the projected fifteen hundred I ought to have saved by the end of December. On top of that, the theatre I work at part-time is closing for about a month and a half, and won't start really cooking again until the musical "Tommy" opens in February. The two hundred I did save will surely be gone by that time. But the completion of my loan this month will help. Still, I can't help but worry about money. I don't even have enough money for the bloody motorcycle yet! I'm still not cooking any meals. But I'll have to start, because I'm spending over four hundred dollars a month eating in restaurants and take-out joints, which is nuts. At least that's what my friends tell me. I HATE SAVING MONEY! ARGHHH!

Part 2 *Caution! Rider in Training!*

December 24

It's Christmas Eve day and I'm on a bus going to put a thousand dollars down on my first motorcycle. YIPPEE! YEEHAA! I'm giggling like a child and squirming in my seat. A life-long dream is only minutes away from coming true. I get off the bus, which stops practically right in front of the Bike Shop (not the real name of the store) in Scarborough, Ontario. I grew up in Scarborough, by the way. As I walk across the parking lot towards the showroom, I'm grinning like a Cheshire Cat and laughing. Even when I stop laughing, there is nothing in the world that could wipe the grin off my face that stretches from ear to ear. I walk in the showroom and there it sits—a 1983 YAMAHA MIDNIGHT VIRAGO. It's black and gold, 750 C.C. Even though it's twelve years old, it looks great, mainly because it has only three thousand kilometres on it. BEAUTIFUL! Oh sure, it has some scratches and rust here and there but, hey, who cares? I borrowed two thousand of the $2300 price tag three days after paying off my loan to the bank. You got it, three whole days being out of debt. To hell with it. I got the bike. Another good thing is that they will store it for me until spring. Now all I have to do is learn how to ride the great black beast and get insurance.

April 1, Year Two of The Dream

Today is a crisp, clear Saturday morning. It is April 1, three days before my thirty-second birthday. I have been looking forward to this day since the Bike Shop called and told me my motorcycle would be ready to be picked up. Time could not have gone by any slower than it has in the last couple of days. It's nine o'clock in the morning. I phone my friend Harlen and he says, "Come on over." We drive up to the Bike Shop and park the car. We go into the showroom and start to drool immediately, as there are about twelve brand new Harley-Davidsons right at the entrance. It is a sight to behold. They are beautiful. And all but two of them have SOLD signs on them, surprise, surprise. I look around some more and then spy my bike. It looks fantastic and is not shamed at all sitting near the Harleys. The gold trimmings against the jet-black are quite impressive and it reminds me of the gold trimmings you can get on a Cadillac. I was pleased that Harlen liked it too; after all, he was about to spend the next hour and a half riding up to Lindsay for me, where my brother Brian lives, as I don't feel quite qualified to ride in the city or on the highway yet.

After I sign the ownership papers, Harlen, the salesman and I sit down at the sales desk. The salesman says to me, "So where's your stuff?" (meaning my helmet and gloves). "I'm not riding it. My friend here is." I nod towards Harlen. The salesman frowns a little and says, "How come?" I look at him and say, "Well, I don't feel qualified to ride in the city and I've never owned a bike before." Dead silence. I can see the salesman is having an internal struggle and second thoughts now about letting me take the bike.

So quickly I say, "I've ridden bikes before. It's just that I have never owned one." Still undecided, he says, "Maybe you should take the riding course." I say, "I did." He says, "When?" I feel a little more confident when I say, "Last May. I'm getting my friend Harlen here to drive it up to Lindsay for me so I can learn how to drive it in a small town, then drive it back to the city when I feel ready." He says, "Good idea. It's a good bike to learn on. Not too small and not too big. If it had been

10

a four cylinder," (shakes his head) "no," and he leaves it at that. I can't say enough about the salesman at the Bike Shop and their policies, that they let me store my bike there free for four months. The salesman has arranged for my stickers and got my plate for me, saving me a lot of hassle. And he genuinely cared about my safety when I told him I had never owned a bike before. 750 C.C.'s is not a toy.

We take the bike outside and the salesman shows us a few things such as the fuel line levers and tool kit compartments. I shake his hand and we leave. After stopping and getting gas, Harlen and I are on the highway, me leaving in my mother's car, him following on the bike. I keep looking in the rear view mirror to make sure Harlen is still there and, as time goes on, I have an awful thought. What if something bad happens to him while he's doing me a favour? Even though he has had his own bike for five or six years, I couldn't help but worry. Not only is he a nice person, but his girlfriend Rene is a co-worker of mine at the theatre, and I would hate to make one of those, "Hello, Rene? It's me, Dan...um...uh...maybe you should sit down," type of phone calls. Before starting out, I tell Harlen to give me some kind of signal if he wants to stop for whatever reason. Well, about halfway there, he pulls past me and into a donut shop. He tells me outside that his hands are cold. "No problem," I say, "Let's get some coffee." I get the coffees. He goes to the washroom. When he returns, he wraps his hands around his cup and tells me that his hands are so cold they hurt. I look at his hands and they are a deep red, so cold they ache, and does that ever hurt! He grimaces in pain as he tries to warm up his hands on the cof-fee cup. The rest of the trip to Lindsay is pretty much without incident.

We get into Lindsay a bit earlier than expected, so I decide to pull into the government parking lot (ironically, where I got my driver's licence). Harlen suggests that I take the bike for a spin. I hesitate a sec-ond or two, then say, "What the hell." Finally, the time has come to ride MY motorcycle. I stall it, but get it going again and it is great riding around the parking lot. I wasn't as scared as I thought I would be, it being a 750 and all. Harlen then suggests I ride the bike through town and into the outskirts of Lindsay. This was a different matter altogether and, after hemming and hawing, I decide that I will. I stall at the first light and then stall it a couple of times at a stop sign. A pick-up comes around two cars that were behind me and by the time I get going, he is turning the same way as me on the outside lane right beside me! If that wasn't a "Welcome to the wacky AND dangerous world of motorcycling, kid," I don't know what is.

The next morning it is cold and cloudy. I take the bike out and it starts pretty good. Then it stalls. Oh well. I start up the bike and hit the road and it's great just riding it, but it's cold. Further up the road, I try a quick stop and it works pretty well. When I try to start it up again and let out the clutch, it stalls, then more stalling, hmmm... It seems to be stalling more today. I take the bike out a little later and as I'm riding I decide to go to town and try my luck among some real traffic. I'm doing ok until I stop on one of the side streets off the main road. I let out the clutch and stall, and then again. I stall about seven times. AGH! I take it back to my brother's house and I'm not too thrilled.

Later that afternoon, I decide to give it another shot by following my brother into town, as he has to pick up my sister-in-law, Sonja. My brother pulls away in his car, I intend to follow him. I let out the clutch and stall it. When I finally catch up to him, I signal for him to go, and I follow. I stall another five times, then catch up to him a second time. Again I signal. Again I stall. I stall so many times that I turn back, and after stalling some more, finally make it back to my brother's. I am now sitting on the motorcycle with the engine off and I'm cursing it and myself. I have stalled my own motorcycle about twenty times in only half an hour. After putting the bike away, and telling my brother why I never did catch up to him, I prepare to leave. As I'm getting ready to leave, a thought flashes in my mind, a thought that twenty-four hours ago would have seemed absurd. I'm actually looking forward to driving my mom's car, to driving an uncomplicated machine with an automatic transmission and power- steering. I say goodbye to Brian and Sonja. I hop into the car and can't believe how easy it is to drive, how ridiculously easy! Usually, I can find the humour in my failures, but not this time. There isn't an ounce of humour in me as I drive home stone-faced. I had looked forward to getting a motorcycle all of my life and now I don't even want to think about it. I am going up next weekend to try again. The joy I felt just twenty-four hours before is completely and utterly gone.

April 8

The weather will be cloudy and cold all weekend so I won't be going up to my brother's house. I call him on the phone and tell him I won't be up this weekend. He tells me that a veteran motorcycle rider friend of his took my bike out for a ride during the week and had the same problems I did. HA! VINDICATION! Boy, does this make me feel a lot better. YIPPEE! The fact that there is something really wrong with my bike doesn't dampen my spirits at all. I figure you can always fix a machine, but can't always fix confidence in yourself.

April 15

After getting lots of different advice and reasons why or what could be wrong with the bike and talking to the salesman at the Bike Shop, I am again heading up to my brother's house in Lindsay. This time I'm with my other brother, Mike. I decide while riding in the car that I am not going to try to fix it myself—to hell with that. If I have the same problems that I had before, then I'm taking it back. An hour after making that decision, I am sitting on the bike and it won't start. AHH! After trying some more, I get it started and decide to let my brother Mike have a go.

He takes off and, after waiting a few minutes, I start to walk in the direction he went, since he should have been back by now. Well, take a wild guess what happened. That's right. It stalled. What a shocker. He had to push the bike by himself because I was still looking for him. In fact, he pushed it all the way back to my brother's house, as I never did find him on my tour around the streets. Walking back, I spot my bike sitting exactly where Mike pushed it. I try and start it. No way. I come back to it ten minutes later and it starts first shot! Huh? It's running and idling well. I let out the clutch and it stalls, and won't start again. I get my brothers to push me on the bike and I pop the clutch (an old trick that works). It roars to life. To hell with it, I say to myself, I'm goin' to town!

I go through town with no problems so far. If I stall, it's going to be a long walk. I come up to a stretch of highway that has an 80 kph sign posted on it. ALL RIGHT! I take it to a 100 kph and I'm flyin', not in the air, no, all over the road. YEE HAW! At the other end of town, I stall. No, please start, please. It does. WHEW! I take it back to my brother's with no further incident. I let my brother Mike ride it again and I notice that he changes gears, especially off the mark, better than I do. I ask him to show me how he does that particular change, and he does. The more he shows me, the worse I get. Jeez! I'm not giving it enough gas when I let out the clutch, he says. I try it. It works a little better and I am slowly learning. That one good ride I had before doesn't change the fact that there is something wrong with the motorcycle and that it's going to be a pain getting it back to Scarborough from Lindsay. I leave the arrangements to my brother Brian. As we're pulling out of the driveway, I am looking at and cursing my bike. The salesman told me earlier in the day that if I had more problems, I should bring it back to be fixed. I will call him Monday.

April 22

It's a week later. I'm back in Lindsay. I'm pulling into the parking lot of a plaza near downtown Lindsay. I'm in a good mood. I pull into the spot. I shut off the engine. As I go to get off the bike, it just keeps on falling and falling. That's right. I have just dropped it. I forgot to put down the kickstand. JEEZ! I quickly pick it up, using every ounce of my strength. I turn around and through a slightly tinted window I can see people at the booths in a restaurant. The booths are flush with the window. I figure at least ten people, and possibly a quarter of a large restaurant, saw me drop my motorcycle. I do not take off my helmet as I sheepishly walk to the video store.

April 24

It's Monday. I call up the salesman and tell him that the bike keeps stalling. He tells me to bring it in. I tell him that it's in Lindsay and it will take a while to arrange transportation for it. I also tell him a veteran motorcycle rider said that the clutch was a little off, as well. He says, "No problem. We'll take a look at that too."

April 29

Have you ever felt really stupid? I mean really, really stupid? Much to my embarrassment, I had the choke wide open all the time when I thought it was closed. Of course it was stalling! After a cold start, I would leave the choke wide open thinking it was closed. I call up the salesman and tell him to disregard everything I said. Even the clutch didn't need adjusting since my brother had taken it to a local bike shop for that. The salesman was very understanding. Man, did I sound like an idiot. Won't be the last time, unfortunately.

May 6

Time to bring the bike back to Toronto. Finally. Kevin, who works with me at the theatre, has agreed to go up with me to Lindsay. I think I'll let him ride my bike home as he has more experience than I have. We pull into my brother's driveway. I feel bad but we have to leave almost immediately after the introductions are finished.

I decide to ride the bike to Toronto myself. Good idea, or bad? Because of a time factor (Kevin has to work that afternoon), I reluctantly agree that we'll take the highway back, instead of the country roads that we had discussed earlier. Kevin pulls away in my mom's car and I follow. I'm nervous. I'm still stalling the bike, but not as often. As I follow him, I can't help thinking about the 401 (a big, fast, busy, and sometimes scary Ontario highway). It scares you silly in a car sometimes. Who knows how scary it is on a motorcycle. I make it through the town ok. Now onto a small highway I go. You can go 80 kph. Oh well, so far so good. Big rolling hills and, man, does that wind hit you. The whistling in my ears is sometimes deafening. It's still cold, too. At 100 kph it's scary, exhilarating, and isolating. You feel cut off from the normal world as you enter a different one. A world of elements: wind, different temperatures, open sky, and road surface. All these have a direct effect on how you may feel and how the ride may go. You feel vulnerable. I guess it might be like one of those open cockpit planes they used to fly in the old days. You feel a part of nature, because nature also will dictate to a certain extent what may or may not happen. It's a feeling I like.

We are getting closer to the 401 and I'm feeling more confident now that I've gone faster for a long period of time. I approach the ramp leading onto the 401. Well, here goes. My god! The wind! With the wind and the speed I'm travelling, it's a wonder I don't get blown off the bike. Despite his assurance that he would do the speed limit, Kevin is doing 110 to 120 kph, with me staying behind him. At these speeds, things come up very fast. I have just barely missed a large, dead racoon lying in the middle of the highway. After about an hour, I'm starting to get cold. Twenty minutes later, Kevin starts to pull off the highway, and I don't know why. We stop at a parking lot just off the highway. Kevin says that maybe he should ride the rest of the way because the Don Valley Parkway is coming up (a lot of people in Toronto call it the Don Valley Speedway) and he feels it might be too much for me because of the sharp turns and crazy drivers. I agree. I follow him in the car. It turns out that there's a traffic jam on the Don Valley, however, and the rest of the trip goes smoothly. I now have my bike in Toronto. Yessssss.

June 30

I'm experiencing a curious side effect since I've been riding my motorcycle a lot. My left leg and hip joint hurt for a whole day after riding for long hours. When I go to stop the bike, I put my left leg down most of the time before it actually stops. WRONG! I have to cure myself of this, or get a hip and leg replacement before the summer is out. I also dropped my bike again a few weeks ago in a parking lot. That brings the total to four times I've done that. I have yet to go a day without stalling the bike at least once. Live and learn, live and learn, although I may not live long enough to learn more if I keep this up!

Now on to my financial picture. Unfortunately, the picture is pretty bleak. I am again way behind in the savings department. I told myself I would have to save about five hundred a month starting April 1st. Well, it's June 30th and I have only saved four hundred dollars for income tax, and I haven't given them a penny yet. I originally thought I would buy an old '82-'85 Honda Gold Wing, but I won't now because I don't want to get a hernia trying to pick it up after dropping it 50 million times. They weigh about 800 or 900 pounds. I will most likely be buying a Yamaha Virago 1100 for my trip. Hopefully, a late 1980s or early '90s model. The Virago 1100 that I'm thinking about buying most likely will cost around five thousand dollars. I can get a layaway plan starting in September, but it will have to be paid off by next May. There is no question in my mind now that I will have to get rid of my apartment about three or four months before the trip. Maybe I'll move in with my mom for that period of time.

July 1

I have yet to go on any sort of camping trip. I think that I'll learn the camping thing when I'm actually on the trip. Mistake? What do you think? I think the answer is: Yes, big mistake.

Part 3

The Summer of My Bike's Discontent

July 4

I have just watched the film Apollo 13. It was inspiring. At the end of the film my cousin turns to me and says, "Here's your helmet." When he said that and handed me my motorcycle helmet, I felt like he was handing me my astronaut's helmet, my piece of adventure, my ticket to something great, that he was perhaps handing me my destiny. Does that sound silly? Silly or not, I had such a powerful feeling that he was not just handing me my helmet, but a symbol of myself, of what I might become. I have always liked helmets, motorcycles, the space program, adventure stories, man against the elements and dreams of the so-called impossible. Now all of those likes have led me to this moment in time.

I said goodbye to my cousin, started to walk towards my motorcycle, and I started doing that piece of music "Fanfare for the Common Man" in my head. I swear I was getting chills. (This sounds crazy, right? I know, but it's true.) I stood beside my bike, helmet in hand, backpack on. I put the key in the ignition, switch it on, the green neutral light beams, I put both fuel lines on prime, open the choke a little bit, push the starter button and BOOM the bike roars to life. I have never felt that good going through the starting sequence for my motorcycle. Can you believe I just wrote the words "starting sequence" like it was a rocket ship? I begin to think that I'll have the Apollo 11 and 13 symbols painted on my gas tank (as well as the poppy) for inspiration. Maybe I'll name the bike I use on the trip A.A.L., for Armstrong, Aldrin, and Collins, but who knows. I do feel the bike should have a name. What would you call the bike?

July 15

It's literally about 90 degrees in the shade. I'm on the highway travelling about 70 mph. I'm following Christian and Rebecca in Christian's car and I have been doing so for about the last half-hour. Sometimes we do the speed limit, sometimes we don't. Still travelling at around 70 mph, I look down at the speedometer and it reads that I'm travelling at 0 mph. My first thought is, "Houston, we have a problem." I swear that's the first thing that came into my head. What now? My answer was to do nothing. So I didn't. I pull into the parking area and Rebecca points down towards the ground and says, "What's that?" I look to where she's pointing. There's a cable leading from the bottom of my front forks to about where I sit on the bike. Who knows how many miles I have dragged an approximately three foot long cable on the ground. After a few tries of trying to shove the top of the cable into a hole near the speedometer, I give up and tie it up with a piece of white string. I tie it to another cable, although I have no idea what function the other cable serves.

July 18

It's three days later and I'm leaving Huntsville. I pull into a gas station to fill up before a long ride home. The attendant points at my muffler and comments on the hissing sound that the water makes when it hits my already hot left tail pipe. I look down and see the muffler and the water drops turning to steam as they hit it. I also notice a hole where my tool kit used to be! The tool kit and its plastic covering are gone. I just shake my head and curse. It's about half an hour later and I'm going down the highway slower than normal because the road is still wet from an earlier rain and, besides, I can only guess at what speed I'm travelling. Something below me catches my eye and it's dragging on the ground. Can ya guess? It's my speedometer cable, all three feet of it, dragging along beside me. Yikes! I pull into the first gas station and do a bad job of tying it up again. After about two hours I hear a strange ticking noise in the engine. Hmmmm. I make it home with no further incidents.

July 20

I have taped up the speedometer cable with masking tape and it's not a pretty sight. I start the bike, put it into gear, and it stalls. I start again; it stalls again, and again. Now what? I leave it alone.

July 22

I call up the salesman and tell him there's a problem with the bike. He recognizes my voice. He groans and then laughs. "That's right, it's me again," I say. I explain the problem to him. He tells me to disconnect the cut-off safety switch on the side stand, the switch that makes sure I can't pull away from a stopped position with the kickstand down, preventing a potentially dangerous situation.

I say, "I'll try it, thanks." My motorcycle is coming back to haunt the salesman. He groans good-naturedly whenever he hears the words, "Hi, it's Dan Murphy. There's a problem with my bike." Anyway, I did what he said to do and it worked. I can now pull onto the street with the side stand still dangerously hanging down, which is perfect because I'm absent-minded as hell. Oh, and by the way, the ticking sound I told you about is getting worse.

July 30

I've just returned home after taking a long bus and subway ride. Why, you might ask yourself, when he has a motorcycle? Well, a couple of hours ago I had stopped to visit my old friend Dan Drummond and his girlfriend, Sherri. I sit down and we chat for a few minutes, then Dan asks me, "Have you ever dropped your bike?" "I said, "Yes, about four times now."

Sherri then asks me if I could move my bike so she can drive to the store. I go outside and look and curse as I see the kickstand has sunk two inches into the driveway. The combination of a very hot day and a five-hundred-pound bike will do this. I feel like an idiot. I pull it out, leaving a hole about the size of a small golf ball. I start the bike and move it a little and then for some reason the bike is falling again. I hear a snap as the handlebar hits the ground. I think it might be the clutch lever. It turns out that I'm right. Another freakin' bus and subway ride home. I have now dropped my bike a total of five times. Am I good or what?

August 2

My friend Dan has fixed my bike. He got a new clutch lever from the Bike Shop and replaced it himself. Way to go, Dan. It cost $10.80. My bike is still making that funny ticking noise. A bomb, perhaps.

August 8

Two Yamaha owners I know tell me the ticking noise that my bike is making is BAD NEWS. Uh, oh. They both agree that I should drive it straight home and add more oil. That night a guy named Jose had his bike stolen for the second time.

August 10

I add some oil to see if the ticking will stop. It doesn't. I will have to take the bike back to where I bought it. Another nightmare for the salesman.

August 12

It's Saturday. I pull into the back where the service centre is at the Bike Shop. I ask the guy behind the counter if he could come outside for a second and listen to my bike because I think there's something wrong with it.

He says, "I don't have to go outside. I heard it when you pulled up."

"Oh," I say. "Is it bad?" I ask, dreading the answer.

"Yeah, it's pretty bad. There's definitely something wrong with it," he says with a certainty I believe without a doubt. I tell him that I bought the bike here.

He asks, "How long ago?"

"December," I reply.

"Why don't you tell our manager. He's a decent guy and might give you a break on the price," he says.

"I'll do that," I reply.

I explain the situation to the manager and he says, "I'll give you a break on the parts. You're a customer and we want to keep our customers happy, but let's find out what's wrong with it first," he finishes. I leave and take the usual mode of transportation home.

August 16

I come back from a messenger run and I'm told that the Bike Shop has called me. I call, and an unfamiliar voice is at the other end. She tells me that they think they know what is wrong with it, but they want my permission to open it and take a look inside the engine. They also inform me that it will cost me fifty dollars. I tell them to go ahead. Not very exciting, is it?

August 23

Again I walk into the messenger room and hear that the Bike Shop has called. The person on the phone tells me a lot of semi-technical stuff, which I don't hear because I want to hear how much it will cost me. She goes on to tell me a lot of the parts are worn out. Still I wait for the cost.

Finally I ask, "How much?"

She begins, "Well let's see, with the labour and parts, we're talking about $975, and that's not including taxes. So we're talking over a thousand dollars; less if we get used parts," she finishes.

I say, "I bought the bike from your store for two thousand dollars not too long ago and now I have to pay a thousand to fix it? That's like buying a car for $10,000 and almost five months later bringing it back to the place where you bought it and they want $5,000 to fix it," I say, not too pleased.

"Well we might get another engine from the scrap yard. We might be able to save you some money, but not too much," she says.

"Maybe I should just take the bike to the scrap yard myself," I say.

"Maybe you would like to talk to our manager," she responds.

"OK, I'll talk to him, then," I agree.

"He'll be in on Saturday," she offers.

"I think I'll do that," I confirm.

After the goodbyes and the see-you-laters, I hang up. GIMME A BREAK! A THOUSAND DOLLARS! I say, to no one in particular. I call up the salesman who sold me the bike.

"I heard about the bike. Why didn't you tell me about your cousin?" he says. (My cousin works at the Bike Shop)

"I didn't want to get him involved," I reply.

"Well, Dan, sometimes in this world it's not what you know, it's who you know. You should have told the manager who your cousin was when you brought the bike in," he replies.

"Well I would hope that that shouldn't make a difference. I wanted to be treated like a regular guy," I say, giving him the "What happened to the common man" speech. Oh well. The salesman tells me he will also be in on Saturday. I tell him I'll see him then. I'm starting to feel like I've been ripped off and, although I hate to admit it, my feelings are slightly hurt. I'm thirty-two and this has hurt my feelings. What can I say? How would you feel?

August 26

I am not in a good mood. I'm sitting on yet another bus and also stuck in traffic. I shouldn't be on the bus at all, I think to myself. I should be riding my motorcycle. Finally, I get off the bus and walk into the showroom. I look at the row of brand new motorcycles with envy. The salesman is busy and so is the manager. After about ten minutes, the manager approaches me.

"Can I help you?" he asks. He does not remember me.

"My name is Dan Murphy and I came to talk to you about my bike. It's a 1983 Midnight Virago," I say, trying to keep my voice as non-confrontational as possible. "I was told it's going to cost me a thousand dollars, which seems like a lot of money considering I bought it here not too long ago," I say, not keeping the confrontational tone out of my voice.

"Let me pull the work order on that," he says, and walks away.

I wait. He comes back.

"Here we are. Yes, it's going to cost about a thousand dollars, but we'll cover the cost for half the total. That's the best I can do, given the fact that it's a used bike and you did ride it for five months before you brought it to us."

"Can I ask you a question?"

"Sure," he replies.

"Did you look at the engine when you bought it from the previous owner?"

"No. Here's how it works. My head mechanic will look at it, ride it and listen to the motorcycle. And based on that, we decide whether we'll buy it or not. We don't have the time to take apart and look at every engine we buy. We only buy about twenty-five percent of the bikes we see."

"Oh, I see. Well, thanks. I'll have to decide whether or not I want to get it fixed. I don't know if I want to spend any money on it right now." I say goodbye to the manager and leave it at that.

September 6

I decided after all to get the bike fixed. I call the Bike Shop and ask them when the bike will be ready. They tell me they're just waiting for the speedometer cable, and to call them next Wednesday.

September 13

It's now Wednesday. I call. It's ready! Pick it up on Saturday, they say. The bill comes to $536. The lady on the phone says that they have covered more than half the bill. If that's true, then it cost almost as much as the bike when I bought it.

September 16

    My bike is ready. I go to take my usual mode of transportation, and an idea pops into my head. I will take the silver monster (the subway) only part of the way, and taxi the rest of the way. I get off the subway, hail a taxi. I'm sitting in the taxi with my wad of bills I need to pay for the repairs, when to my horror I realize I'm about ten dollars, maybe twenty dollars, short of the $536 I need to get the bike back.

    I tell the driver to stop at the next set of lights, roughly four blocks short of the stop. I get out of the taxi. I count the money again, hoping I'm wrong somehow. I'm not. I'm nine dollars short. AAAAHHH! Wait a minute, I think I've got exactly nine dollars left in my account. I run to the nearest ATM. I check the account balance. I've got two dollars in my account. AHHH! I call up my mother, who lives in Scarborough. She's not home. I can't believe it. I'm nine dollars short and I live too far away to go back. My friends live too far away and, plus, it's nine in the morning. I decide to just go to the service department and tell them what happened.

    I walk in, dreading what I have to tell them. I feel like a first class idiot. I tell the lady behind the counter of my predicament and she, being a very nice and sympathetic type of person, loans me twenty dollars of her own money. I get on the bike and it feels great. It's been a long wait. The bike feels more powerful and responsive as I pull onto the main street. Oh yeah, definitely better. After about five minutes, I hear...no it can't be...no, no, no....it's still making the ticking sound! I just paid over five hundred bucks and it's still ticking.

    I get the money and bring it back to the shop. I thank the lady once again for her kindness and tell her that my bike is still ticking. Not as loud, perhaps, but I can still hear it. The mechanic who worked on the bike comes outside where I'm now standing near my bike.

    "What's wrong?" he asks.

    "It's still ticking. That's why I brought it in the first place."

    "Don't argue with me and I don't..."

    "It's still ticking..."

"Don't interrupt me, and I don't want you running into the manager's office, either. I..."

"I'm not going into the manager's..."

"I'm not going to argue. I spent a lot of my free time working on this bike, because of your cousin, and I want to wait and see if the ticking gets worse. If it gets worse, bring it back."

The guy is pissed off and I think I know why.

"I didn't want my cousin involved in this in the first place," I say, realizing that management must have put a little pressure on the mechanic.

"Yeah, well he doesn't want to be involved either. He's a pretty good guy and we did talk a little."

"I'm sorry if you got hassled because of who my cousin is. Everything from now on will be done between you and me. No cousin, and no management. Is that a deal? Sound good to you?"

We agree not to let any outside influences affect future repairs. My cousin wisely stayed out of it from the beginning. The mechanic tells me that he might have to replace one of the cams. He will reassess the ticking after two weeks. I leave. Despite the ticking, the bike still feels great.

I pull up to a stop light and I think there's smoke coming from somewhere, and it might be rising up through the front forks area. No way. I look to the left, forward, and under. Yep, there's smoke alright. Well, that's strange because IT WASN'T DOING THAT WHEN I BROUGHT IT IN! Well, that smoke has to be coming from somewhere. Oh, clever deduction, Dan, did ya think of that all by yourself? Nothing gets by me, I'll tell ya. More red lights, more smoke. I pull up to my mother's apartment building. I get off the bike. A-HA! There is definitely something leaking from the uh...uh...the thing-a-ma-jig onto the muffler thing. Ya know where the muffler is connected to the a...ya know...the do-hickey. I think it's oil. Let's see—hot oil dripping onto a boiling muffler ... that means um... KABOOM! Could it? Oh well. I won't tell them that. I want to ride it for a little longer. Maybe it won't explode. Hmmmm.

26

Part 4 *Money and Motorcycles*

September 23

At this point, I'm not going to fool myself anymore. I absolutely refuse to cook. Period. I'm moving into a cheaper apartment. I will save $160 a month in this new place. It has no bedroom and, are you ready? No kitchen. CACKLE! LOVE IT! LOOVVE IT. My friend Margaret suggested that I eat dried fruit and trail mix when I'm on the trip. Sounds good to me. Does that sound good to you? Well I really like the idea. Like that's a big surprise. Margaret is also putting all my notes on computer. I'm sure her dog, Mr. Puppy, is watching her the whole time. What a great name for a dog. It's hard to get mad at a dog while you're screaming, "Mr. Puppy! Mr. Puppy!" Oh well.

October 30

I call the Bike Shop to inquire about a 1993 Yamaha Virago 1100. I talk to the salesman who sold me my first bike. He tells me he will hold it for me and also go to bat for me to get a good price on it. I will, however, have to trade in my current bike to get an even better price. Well, I shouldn't have said I have to, but I will. The salesman will talk to the manager about the trade-in and the eventual price. The new (well reasonably new) bike is advertised at $5,999. I hope to get it for $5,000 flat. After work I ride to the Bike Shop. The salesman shows me the bike. It looks brand new. It's black and silver with lots of chrome,

It doesn't, however, look as good as my bike. Oh well. It has 13,000 kilometres (whatever that means) on it. As we look at it, he (the salesman) says to me,

"Do you have saddle bags?"

"No."

"Well you do now."

I open up one of the saddlebags. There's nothing in there. I look at the other one and it's buckled shut.

"Let's look in the other one," he says.

We look in the other saddlebag. Surprisingly, it has some stuff in it. He pulls out some plastic orange rainproof pants. I pull out something similar, only it's yellow. It's a crumpled yellow mass of plastic. I open it up and in big black letters it says KENNEDY SPACE CENTER. I stare at the words in disbelief.

"I can't believe it. The Kennedy Space Center."

The salesman looks at me.

"I'm going to the Kennedy Space Center on my trip. On my bike."

The salesman acknowledges the irony of it. You might be thinking now that this is either made up, or what else, I don't know. I swear on my life that it's true. What are the odds? It's like an episode of *The Twilight Zone*. This has got to be some kind of omen, if you believe in that sort of thing. Well, after that I put $200 down to hold the bike until more details can be worked out, even though it has a "sold" sign on it.

November 4

I wake up on a cold November morning, the coldest so far. I have mixed feelings about today. I will be riding my motorcycle for most likely the last time. I feel relieved in a way. My current motorcycle, as far as I can see, would have had even more problems than it has now (it's still ticking) and I would have had to put more money into it. I am a little sad because I had no intention of ever selling it. It was to be kept in a prominent place in a future motorcycle collection. Such is life sometimes.

I take the bike out of the garage. I'm riding down Danforth Ave. I look to my right and then straight ahead, as the big truck ahead of me suddenly comes to a complete stop. I jam on the brakes and the back wheel screeches. I stop about five feet from the truck. My heart is pounding. If I had looked a few more seconds to my right, I would have plowed into the back of the truck. It was close. It would have been ironic to get into an accident the very day I'm bringing the bike back. Everything I do on the bike has that "This is the last time" feel. I go to my mother's apartment. She takes some pictures of me on the bike.

I bring the bike back to the place where I bought it. Now my bike is a mere bargaining chip for a good price on the next one. What an awful thought. I hand the keys to the salesman who sold me the bike. That's it. He'll let me know how much they'll give me for it against the price of the new one. I remember when I was a kid, asking my father why he got rid of the great old cars he used to have. His first car was a Model T Ford. Now I know why he sold them. It wasn't financially practical to keep them. Plain and simple. If I could afford to keep the bike, I would, but I can't. I can't afford to be nostalgic. I have to do everything I can to make this trip a reality. The trip is seven months away and time is running out.

November 9

Well, since I've just about traded in my first motorcycle I guess I can say the riding season is over for me. Do you know what that means? I have survived my first season as a motorcyclist. Not such a big deal, you might be thinking, but I heard a lot of stories about men and women lasting only a couple of weeks or days, in some cases. When you become a motorcyclist (and some of you reading this are), you hear a lot of unbelievably gruesome stories about motorcycle accidents. Most people have heard, seen, or know someone connected with these sometimes truly horrifying tales. How did I survive, you might well ask? Well, I'll tell ya. Ready? Here goes. I survived by pure dumb luck. I should have been killed or injured a couple of times. It wasn't skill. I just got lucky. Period.

29

November 11

Another Remembrance Day ceremony. The war ended fifty years ago. It pours rain throughout the entire ceremony. Again, it never fails to choke me up. In a half century, we have not had a world war. I hope we are done with that particular brand of human madness. Now if we could only stop all the little wars that are going on in the world. As I write this, there are probably a dozen conflicts going on. How pathetic.

I call up the Bike Shop. I want to find out how much the new motorcycle will be with my trade-in. The salesman tells me that it will be a little over $5,800. I tell him I want a better price. I also tell him that we may be too far apart on our prices for us to make a deal, and that I will call him on Monday. I think the deal is now in jeopardy.

November 13

I call up the salesman and tell him I want it for $5,500. He says he doesn't think the manager will go for that, but he will try. I'm to call him in a few days.

November 17

I call. The salesman tells me the best he can do is a little over $5,700. Although I am disappointed, I accept. I would not get a better deal at another place because of the rough condition of my trade-in. With taxes, the newer bike would have cost $6,900. With my trade-in, and a little bit of haggling, I got the bike for $5,736.

January 20, Year Three of The Dream

It's a brand new year, and my situation is still pathetic. I have put down a depressingly small amount of money on the bike. A mere $1,200. With the $200 I originally put down on it, I still owe $4,500. With my new job came more money. I am now spending about twenty dollars a day on food. That's about $600 a month on food alone. I must be nuts. I am making more money than I have ever made in my life and I am still barely saving any. It has come down to this—if I don't get a personal loan of at least $5,000, there will be no trip and no book. I did have some good news today. Lori, my friend who also works at the theatre, told me there's some work coming up starting around February 10th, and it should last for about a month. That should help cover the cost of my twenty dollars a day food bill. Oh well, there are worse things I could be spending my money on.

February 15

I have just received a rejection notice from a second credit card company. Why, you may well ask? I think it is because of my new job and apartment. I haven't been at either long enough. I really think I need some kind of credit card for the trip. It will come in handy for a lot of things. Especially if the bike breaks down. I'll try some other credit card companies. I've got to get one.

February 16

I take my friend Mina to the Bike Shop with me. She wants to see the new bike. Mina, being an absolute whiz at making budgets and saving money, tried to get me (along with many other friends) to change my bad money habits. As hard as she tried, it just didn't work. I am hopeless in that department. We walk into the showroom. I introduce her to the salesman. I give him $700 towards the bike. All three of us go to a separate building where my newer bike sits. We stand around the bike. Mina comments that she likes it better than my old one.

"Do you know where your old bike is?" the salesman asks.

"The scrap yard?" I answer.

"No, it's in Germany. A guy came in, bought the bike, and took it to Germany with him."

We stand around the bike a little longer, then leave. The idea of my old bike being in Germany right now is strange to me. I had hoped it would stay in Ontario. Maybe I could have tracked it down one day to buy it back, or just to see it again. I can pretty well forget that now, I guess. Oh well, perhaps I will somehow find it again some day.

March 7

I tell my insurance company that I have bought a new motorcycle. It's 1100 C.C.s. The guy on the phone says there are no underwriters around (whatever they are), so he'll have to phone me back tomorrow. He asks more basic questions, then tells me he'll let me know.

March 8

I get a message on my machine saying they can't insure my newer vehicle. In other words, take a hike, pal. I didn't need this.

March 9

I walk (yet again) into the showroom of the Bike Shop. I hand the salesman $1,000. Because it's mostly in twenty-dollar bills, I have time to look around at all the gleaming new bikes. After he's finished counting, I mention that my insurance company dumped me. He hands me the card of an insurance broker who specializes in handling motorcyclists. I thank him, grab my receipt, and leave.

March 11

I call the insurance broker. Snooze-o-rama. I tell him the story about my last insurance company blah, blah, blah. He tells me that it will cost me $1,100 minimum. Say what? Now I'm awake. That's almost double what I paid last year.

"How much will it cost a month, about a hundred?" I ask.

"You can't pay in monthly instalments. The insurance company has to have the full amount within 60 days."

"I'll call ya back when I figure out some financial things." I thank him and hang up.

Groan. Double groan. This is extremely bad news. I had planned to pay a small monthly sum of money over the course of the year. While on my trip, it would have come right out of my account. It's like that old joke, "I'll pay for it on account, on account that I have no money!" Eleven hundred is a lot to pay within two months. Think loan, Dan, think LOAN.

March 13

I got a letter from a credit card company. They have given me a secret code number. Looks like I get a credit card. Phew! That was close.

April 2

It is two days before my thirty-third birthday. I'm sitting in a restaurant with my friends Lori and Kelly. It is Kelly's birthday. After the meal, Lori asks me how the plans for the trip are progressing. I tell her about Revenue Canada catching up with me. The crazy thing is that the government wants the tax money that I owe them. I know, go figure. Lori then asks if I've sat down recently and written out how much money I'm going to need and how much I owe.

"I'm afraid to," I reply.

The subject of calculating money is dropped briefly. Kelly, Lori and I talk about health insurance and the various states I'll visit. The subject comes back to money. I agree to let Lori write down how much money I'll need before I'm to leave on the trip. Here is a list. Please skip this part if you're getting bored of money talk.

Motorcycle insurance	$1,100.00
Chaps/new helmet/special motorcycle pack	800.00
Sleeping bag/tent/cooking stove (ha!)	450.00
Pair of good boots	200.00
Money still owing on the bike	2,000.00
Revenue Canada (taxes)	approx. 500.00
Health insurance	approx. 200.00
	approx. $5,250.00

So much for my plans to borrow $5000, stick some money in the bank and leave. Ha! My thoughts about leaving June 15th are suddenly and pathetically wrong. The numbers don't lie. I will now have to postpone the trip until early September. I feel numb. Instead of leaving in two-and-a-half months, I'll be leaving in five months.

33

There is some good to come out of all of this. What could possibly be good about any of this, you may well be thinking to yourself. Well, with my leave-on-June 15th plan, I would have ended up in the southern United States in the hottest part of the summer. Now, I'm a fair-skinned person. I don't tan, I burn, and I keep burning all summer long. I remember a Woody Allen movie once where he was talking about going to the beach in summer, and he said something like, "I don't tan, I stroke." I must admit, the thought of being in the deserts of Nevada in July never sat well with me. Lori tells me not to put a time limit on my dreams. She is right. To leave on June 15th would have been foolish and rash.

A strange number has been coming up in my life. The number is 1100. I bought an 1100 Virago. The government wants eleven hundred dollars. My motorcycle insurance is 1100 and something dollars. Hmmmmm.

Part 5 *Do you think this trip will ever happen?*

April 19

I have started dating a smart and pretty woman and I'm crazy about her. Uh, oh. What do you think of that? I can think of several reactions you might have.

     1. Are you nuts? What about the trip?!!

     2. She'll dump you. Or you'll dump her before you leave.

     3. Are you gonna take her with you?

     4. Don't do it, Dan. Just don't get involved.

     5. You'll be sorry.

     6. She'll convince you not to go.

     7. Dan, you'll use this as an excuse not to go

     ETC... ETC... ETC...

Well, for starters, we had been hanging out for a couple of months together before I told her I liked her. She knew about the trip and thinks that it's a great idea. She wants me to do it. Oh sure, you might say, she says that now, but wait until the time comes for you to go. Well, maybe you're right. Maybe not. I told you about her because it might affect the trip. What can I tell ya, I'm crazy about her.

May 11

My girlfriend and I ride the bus to the Bike Shop. I have $1,200 in cash and will put $850 on a credit card to pay off the balance. I know,

I know, I never learn. Oh well, in the eyes of the Bike Shop, this bike is paid for. They will let me know when I can pick it up. Donna declines an offer to go to the back of the building to see the bike. She says she'll see it when I pick it up. I don't think motorcycles thrill her all that much. I think she would rather ride around on the back of a bike than stand around and look at one. Oh well. A lot of people are like that.

June 5

My bike is ready to be picked up. I should be more excited, but I'm not. I was more excited last year, when I picked up my first bike. I haven't seen this new bike in months and still don't think it looks as good as the first one. As I sit on the bus, I am starting to get a little nervous just thinking of the size of this bike—a Virago 1100. Let's be honest here. I never got used to the first one, which was a 750 Virago. I just didn't get good at riding it. Now, I'm ten minutes away from picking up a heavier and more powerful one. Have I bitten off more than I can drop? I don't want to drop it. Groan. I don't want to drop this one. I don't think I'll be able to pick it up, if I do. Yet again, I step off the bus and walk into the showroom.

I say hello to the salesman and, after signing a few papers, we walk to the back and outside. WOW! It's stunning! There are miles of polished chrome. I take back what I said before about it not being as good-looking as my old 750. Everything gleams. It looks brand new.

I ask the salesman, "Are there any fundamental differences between this bike and the last one? I'm still nervous about the size of it."

"This runs better than the last one."

Well, that about says it all. He hands me the keys and suggests that I ride it around the parking lot a few times to get used to it. I agree. We shake hands and he leaves. I start it up. Sounds great. Click it into first and I'm off. I can't believe it but it handles better than the 750. I'm immediately more confident on the bike. My nervousness about its being bigger and meaner evaporates. After a few spins around the parking lot, I pull out onto the main road. It drives like a dream and I couldn't be happier. What a difference! This bike wants to go-go-go. It will take a little getting used to but, hey, I haven't dropped it yet. That's a good sign. For those of you who care, the 1993 Virago 1100 is shaft-driven. No chain. Why did I mention that? I haven't the slightest idea.

July 13

Most everyone seems to like my motorcycle. I'm sitting in the Golden Griddle. My bike is parked where I can see it. I do that so no one will try to steal it, but mainly because I like looking at it. There, I admit it. I will look at my bike a lot while sitting in a restaurant. People will stop and look at my bike. An older gentleman stops, looks, and cranes his neck to look at the speedometer and generally stares at the bike from every angle. I have never before owned anything that people will stop and stare at. It's kind of fun. At stoplights, people in cars will stare. Once a guy on a scooter said, "Hey, nice bike." I tip my hat to the designers at Yamaha. They have designed something that is beautiful, and a work of art. Oh come on, some of you might say to yourself after reading the previous sentence. Well, why not? Go to a motorcycle dealership or get a motorcycle magazine, look at the bikes and then go to a local art gallery. See if you can see anything that you find to be simple, or not particularly to your liking. Perhaps a piece of modern art that looks painfully simple and bleak. Then think of the motorcycles you saw. Could they not seem more pleasing to the eye than the art? Maybe and maybe not.

I'm coming out of one of the worst movies I have ever seen. Eight dollars and fifty cents down the drain. I walk to my bike. I start it and let her warm up a bit while I put a book in one of the saddlebags. I hop on and put the bike in gear. I go about eight inches and the bike stops dead. It starts to fall to the left. I jump off before it falls on me. I stand there for a few seconds in shock, looking at my bike lying on its side. I grab the handlebars and a thought flashes through my mind, "I can't pick it up; it's too heavy." A couple walk by and, sensing my embarrassment, don't stop. I grab the handlebars and somehow manage to lift it up enough for me to put the kickstand down. PHEW! Maybe I should have taken that lock off the front wheel before I pulled away from the curb.

Across the street is an apartment building. From about ten storeys up I can hear two guys laughing. I then go into this big performance of inspecting my front wheel, like I can't understand what happened. I try to make it look like it was something beyond my control. With my back turned to the two guys on their balcony, I try to unjam and pry the lock which is wedged between the front fork and the wheel. I finally unlock it and pull it free. Now I inspect the bike for real. I hope the brake disc didn't get bent. I don't see anything wrong with it, or the rest of the bike for that matter, as far as I can tell. Although, I find little comfort in this because it is nighttime. I hate to admit I've forgotten about the lock four or five times now. But this is the first time I've dropped the motorcycle. I'll look for damage tomorrow. The scary thing is that I'll probably do it again. Oh well, live and learn, live and—well so much for the second part.

July 26

I'm sitting across from the loan officer in one of Canada's largest banks. That's right, I didn't save any money.

"Have you ever seen your credit history, Mr. Murphy?" she asks.

Uh, oh. I don't like the sound of that question. I thought this was going to be a sure thing, that coming down here was a mere formality after being semi-approved over the phone by a new phone banking thing-a-ma-jig. I had hoped or thought that getting five thousand dollars would be relatively easy, considering I had two jobs.

"No, I haven't," I reply.

"Well, according to your credit history, you had trouble with some credit cards."

"You're talking about a department store credit card and a Visa credit card, right?"

"Yes."

"Well, that was three or four years ago."

"You missed some payments on them, didn't you?"

"Yes, I did."

Shocked that she's bringing this up now.

"How come you missed some payments?"

"I didn't have the money to make the payments."

Oh, good answer, Dan! Why don't you ask for $10,000?

"Well, I'm going to need two references and a fax of your current income from your company."

"Wait a second," I say. It starts to become clear that I will not get this loan. "Let's be honest here. If I'm not going to get this loan, let's not waste each other's time."

"Well, Dan, I appreciate your honesty."

"Does it look like I'm going to get the loan?"

"No, not really," she admits.

"Then let's leave it at that," I say. I shake her hand and leave.

I immediately go to the bank up the street where I got my last loan. I make an appointment with the loans officer. She will see me on Monday.

July 27

It's the next day. I'm trying to figure out a good story about why I need a loan. The truth simply won't work. Who am I kidding here? I'm going to tell a huge lie. When I think about that I get a case of the guilts. I met the loan officer very briefly and she seemed like a really nice person. I'll sit two feet away from her and tell a whole pile of out-and-out lies. Hmmm. It's almost noon the same day. An idea starts to worm its way into my brain. How about a layaway plan on $5000? I'll borrow the five grand, but ask the bank not to give it to me until the spring. Hey, that's not bad, Dan old boy. Just like the layaway plan I had with my motorcycle, only it will be a layaway for cash. I'll make regular payments on the five grand but I can't touch it until I have paid it all off. I'll pay interest just like a normal loan. How can the bank lose?

I'll pay interest on money they never really gave me. Then in the spring I'll pick up the five grand and everyone will be happy. The bank makes five or six hundred dollars for doing zilch. I think they'll go for that.

Hey, wait just one flippin' minute here, pal! If I do that, we're talkin' a-a-another P-P-P-POSTPONEMENT? To hell with that, Danny boy. Oh no, ya don't. You've told too many people that you're leaving SEPTEMBER 5th. Lots of people. In fact, you tell practically everyone you meet. It's true, when people ask me what I'm up to, I tell them about the trip. No, I can't postpone again. I'll look like an idiot. Again. It does make sense to wait, though. If I get the loan for the five thousand and then leave on September 5th, I'll be totally in debt with no money coming in at all. Then again, I can leave in the spring and not be in debt at all. Thing is, though, I don't think I can handle the "Hey, I thought you were going on a trip," or "How was the trip?" if they haven't seen me for a few months. In fact, I'm already getting those questions. This is not my first postponement, as you know. I don't think I can handle answering those two questions a million times over the next ten months. No way. I'm starting to sound like one of those guys who only talks a big story but never follows through. I'll get the loan.

It's about six o'clock the same day. I'm at the theatre. Who am I kidding? The idea of postponing the trip makes more and more damn sense the more I think about it. All the money I made, I totally blew. The trip, the money. I feel like an ass. I deserve to feel like an ass because I am one. I let myself down. I look like a big fool. I dread what people are going to say when I tell them I'm not going until the spring. I let a few of my close friends at the theatre know of my decision and they tell me not to worry about what people think. They also tell me to wait and go debt-free. Some of them wanted to know whom I was doing the trip for, them or me. A lot of people have had delays, they say. What are another nine or ten months for a dream? They are right, all the things that my friends said. It's just that it felt so good to tell people I was leaving on this trip and how great it was going to be. I still feel ashamed of myself despite all the things my friends just said.

September 8

I thought at this time that I would share an observation about myself. I'm sometimes way over-sensitive to other drivers' mistakes. I expect a little too much from the people in cars. Now having said that, I know some of you reading this (particularly motorcyclists and bicyclists) are howling in protest. In my first season as a motorcyclist I would freak out at a car driver if they made the slightest error anywhere near me. I would honk my horn, yell at them, and give them the finger. Sometimes I would just look at them and shake my head. I am not as bad this year. Although, if I'm in a bad mood I will revert to all my first year riding tactics. Sometimes a couple of incidents (other drivers' errors) will put me in such a foul mood that I don't enjoy riding the bike, and I realize it's just an over-reaction to a set of circumstances that weren't all that life-threatening. So what is the solution? I guess for myself, I'll have to calm down a little. I will say that I will still flip out if it is warranted if only to make the driver more aware that he or she ALMOST KILLED ME. When those things happen, my blood boils.

November 11

It occurs to me, as I sit in the Canadian Warplane Heritage Museum in Hamilton, Ontario, that this is the third time I will have written about Remembrance Day. My friend Audrey sits beside me as we wait for the ceremony to begin. I would like to take this opportunity to thank you (the reader) for sticking with me this far. This is my first book. Audrey is a teacher. She teaches autistic children. She will be helping me (as does Margaret) with grammar and will point out some of the areas I lack skill in. I hated school, especially grammar. "I'll never use this stuff," I used to say. Now I'm glad my parents always corrected my grammar when I spoke incorrectly. Which means I'm not totally useless.

After the ceremonies Audrey and I watch a Lancaster Bomber fly around the airfield. I believe the Lancaster flies over several ceremonies in the area. As far as I know, there are only a few Lancaster Bombers left that can still fly. As we watch the plane it begins to snow. Well, I guess it's time to put the old bike away.

November 14

I put the bike away for the winter. Pretty exciting, eh? My Canuckness is showing a bit in that last sentence. You know what that means don't you? I survived my second season as a motorcyclist. Thank you, thank you. Would you like to hear some good news about my finances? Okay, I have saved three thousand dollars as of this date. YIPPEE! YAHOO! No, I really did. I'm still with the same woman I started dating in the spring. Now I know you've read this before, but I'M GOING ON MY TRIP IN THE SPRING! See ya then. That is, of course, barring some major disaster.

Part 6 *Countdown to the Countdown*

January 4, Year Four of The Dream

Well, my girlfriend and I are at the largest (so they say) motorcycle show in North America. It's held every year at a huge place near Toronto International Airport. It's a great chance to see all the new bikes. I used to come to this show in the past when I didn't have a motorcycle. Come to think of it, I go to the big auto show every year, and I've never owned a car in my life.

We go in. Everything is here. New bikes, old bikes, clothes, helmets, travel junkets, and pretty much everything else you can think of. We are just making our way towards the exit when what should I spy but the Virago Owners Club of Canada booth. I talk to the people at the booth for a few minutes and then join up. They also tell me that there's a big Virago Club in the United States as well. Hmmm. Are you thinking what I'm thinking? When I'm going through Canada and the United States I can visit the different chapters and maybe hang out with them for a few days, if they're going on a small trip or picnic or something.

Early January

I have just finished watching Michael Palin's series called *Pole to Pole*. It was really, really good. On his way to the South Pole he meets Shinji Kazama, who will be riding a motorcycle from Patriot Hills to the

South Pole. This same guy has already ridden on a motorcycle to the North Pole and halfway up Mount Everest. Isn't that amazing? Next time you're at a party I want you (just for fun of course) to tell people you're going to ride a motorcycle to the North Pole. I would love to see the look on their faces. They will either

a) humour you

b) call you crazy

c) excuse themselves to go to the bathroom

It will be a rare person indeed who will ask serious questions or say they think you can do it. A couple of days ago the Thrust SSC broke the sound barrier. The Thrust SSC is a car. Can you imagine driving a car that can go over seven hundred and sixty miles an hour? So if you have a dream or goal in mind, please think about the two achievements I have just mentioned. It might not seem so crazy or harebrained after all.

January 13

I'm standing outside the motorcycle shop where my first meeting of the Virago Owners Club of Canada will take place. Unfortunately, I have the sometimes annoying habit of being half an hour early for everything. I especially hate this habit right now because it's about a ZILLION degrees below zero. I'm not in a nice neighbourhood, either. Two prostitutes are having an argument across the street. They are arguing in front of a coffee shop, which of course is the only place open. The prostitutes' boyfriend, or pimp or whatever has shown up. They are all arguing now. After a minute or two they all go into the coffee shop. I cross the street and walk into the coffee shop. What a mistake.

I pass the table where the prostitutes and pimp are sitting. They eye me suspiciously, especially the pimp. Oh great. He probably thinks I'm a cop or something. I'm about halfway to the back where the serving counter is (naturally it had to be at the back) when I notice a young girl about eighteen years of age. She has food all over her face and doesn't seem to care in the slightest. I get to the counter and wait my turn in line. As I look around the place I realize I'm probably the only sane one here. The pimp and his girls are still looking at me. The lady behind the counter, guessing I may have washed in the last few weeks, calls me sir about four times in just a short span of time. She seems relieved to see me, even though she has never seen me before. Although I feel sorry for her, and the rest of the people in here, I pay for the coffee and hastily get outta there. I cross the street and stand in front of the show-room window of the bike shop. It has to be one of the coldest nights of the winter so far.

I start walking again in search of some kind of shelter. I spot a pool hall and, after a few minutes inside, I am warming up. After about twenty minutes I decide to go back to the bike shop. This is not the same shop where I bought my bike, by the way. I try the door leading up to the space above the bike shop. It's open. I climb the stairs and enter a large room where there are four people sitting at a table. The walls have a lot of pictures on them. Most are of motorcycles, old and new, as well as pictures of the shop itself, which is pretty old, indeed. Some more people arrive.

The meeting begins soon after. After some introductions, they start to vote on some of the higher positions with the group. President, treasurer, plus event co-ordinator, that type of thing. Since I have just met all of these people about ten minutes ago, I don't participate in the vote. The newly re-elected president of our chapter starts to talk about future group activities with other Virago chapters and us. I must admit that I'm only half paying attention for the simple reason that I won't be around for about ninety percent of the activities that are planned for this year. I am interested, however, in the American Virago Owners Club. I get an application from the president. We talk some more. They usually meet once a month. They also meet for breakfast on Sundays when the weather gets better, if I heard correctly. Sounds good so far. I say goodbye and leave.

Part 7

Endings and Beginnings

January 19

Two weeks ago my girlfriend and I broke up. I waited two weeks to write about it because I couldn't at the time. It still hurts because it was her decision and not mine. These things happen. Some of you might be thinking that you knew it would happen, eventually, because of my trip and all, that maybe I should have expected this. As far as I know, it didn't have anything to do with the trip. However, this does change the trip. I will no longer have someone waiting for me to return besides friends and family. Which means I can take as much time as I want as long as the money holds out. Speaking of money, I have saved four thousand, three hundred dollars. That's pretty good for me.

March 20

I received my membership from the Virago Owners Club of America. These people are really organized. I got a plastic membership card, sticker for the bike, rental coupons, Virago pin and information on all the chapters in the US and Canada. They gave me a list of people's phone numbers and where they are located. There are even a couple of members in Alaska. Also there are shops that offer discounts to members as well.

March 22

I'm sitting in my mother's living room. My sister Marilyn is here as well. The topic we are discussing is money. I'm considering (out loud to my mother and sister) whether I should get a loan or not. I know what you're thinking. OH, NO. NOT AGAIN! I figure at this point I'll have six thousand of my own money by the time I leave, but that I should get another four thousand to make the trip longer. As I ponder the pros and cons of getting more money, I suddenly take a close look at the T-shirt my sister is wearing. Oh, COME ON! THIS IS JUST TOO MUCH! Another eerie coincidence? I ask myself. On the front of my sister's T-shirt is a military jeep in black with a gold circle around it. On the outside of all this it says in big black letters: ALASKA HIGHWAY ANNIVERSARY 1942-1992, WHITEHORSE. Don't you think that's kind of creepy? The whole trip started out as a trip to the Alaska Highway. I'm not sure what to think. My mother and I talk about money some more and out of the blue she tells me she will lend me the four thousand dollars. I make sure she can afford it before I accept. She says she can. I thank my mother a million times. I have more good news. My financial worries are over. I hope.

May 9

It's my last day at my full-time job. Quitting a job is a strange thing, particularly if you like your job and the people you work with. Everything I do today has that last time feel about it. Vanda, the owner of the company, makes a surprise visit to the office. I walk to the back to put something in the truck. As I re-enter the warehouse I see Vanda is holding a present. I start to blush immediately. It's a beautiful pen with my name engraved on it and a key-holder as well. Vanda and I walk toward the front of the print shop. At the front, all my co-workers are standing around a big cake. Now I'm really blushing. One of my bosses, Lynn Griffith, hands me an envelope. Inside the envelope is a gift certificate for two hundred dollars for an outdoors store and eighty dollars in cash. I'm stunned by their generosity. I thank everyone for this totally unexpected gesture.

It's a couple of hours later. I'm sitting in a bar with some of my co-workers and the owner of the company, Wayne Uttley. I tell them I'm writing a book about my trip. I ask Wayne how much it would cost to print a couple hundred copies of the book if I can't find a publisher. He tells me he would print them for free. I'm floored by this offer. I thank him profusely. In a way, though, I'm not surprised. The Graphicshoppe is the best place I have ever worked. The best pay, benefits, bonuses and fairest place I've worked of all the places I've been employed. I used to work for a brokerage firm that was partly owned by one of Canada's biggest banks. The combined wealth of these two companies was in the billions. The pay was lousy. I worked there for about four years and the way they treated some of the workers sometimes made me sick. The people I worked with were nice and they definitely deserved more money than they were getting. When you work for a lousy company, and then a really good one, it sure makes all the difference in the world.

May 16

I'm sitting in my insurance company's office. In a few moments I will hand over eight hundred and nine dollars for my motorcycle coverage. I've been handing over a lot of money lately for various things. I'll give you a brief list.

> $309.00—motorcycle shield and bike rack
> $300.00—C.A.A. medical insurance
> $150.00—new front tire
> $100.00—new camera

I sign some papers. I think it's worth a million dollars should something really bad happen. The woman who is processing the forms thinks my trip is a great idea. She tells me she would like to do something similar one day. I hope she does. The sad part for some people is that "some day" never comes. I shake her hand and leave.

May 19, T-MINUS 7 DAYS

Armed with my $200 gift certificate from the people at my old job, I enter the outdoors store. I should have done this a long time ago. I need a tent, most importantly. Unfortunately or fortunately, there are a million kinds of tents and they look complicated. I approach the counter person and tell him I need a tent. I tell ya, the sheer drama of it all! He shows me a two-person tent. I buy it. He shows me a sleeping bag. I buy it. Basically everything he shows me, I buy. Needless to say, there goes another three hundred dollars. Good thing I had the gift certificate. I leave, knowing I will not learn to set it up until I eventually have to use it. Strangely enough, I didn't buy any cooking equipment. My bike is in the shop getting the new tire, windshield, and bike rack.

May 20, T-MINUS 6 DAYS

I call the bike shop. My bike won't be ready for a couple of days. The new front tire didn't fit. I don't ask why.

May 21, T-MINUS 5 DAYS

Again I call the shop and it's not ready. The person on the phone apologizes for the bike not being ready. He says he'll call me. I go to another outdoors store. I buy some walking shoes, inspect repellent, sunglasses, and some thick socks. Well, there goes another two hundred dollars. I'll be lucky if I have eight thousand dollars by the time I leave. I thought I would have around ten or eleven thousand. As usual, my calculations are off. I have been in two outdoor stores in less than a week and have yet to buy anything even resembling cooking equipment. Why do I have such a deep aversion to all things to do with cooking? Am I just out-and-out lazy? I will be meeting three people (separately) for goodbye lunches today.

It's now five o'clock in the afternoon. I call the Bike Shop and my bike is not ready. At this point I'm not surprised because it's their busiest time of year. They tell me my bike is on the bench. They will call me when it's ready.

It's around 10:30 p.m. the same day. The end of my second-to-last shift at the theatre. My friend Lori hands me an envelope and a small purple bag. The bag contains a motorcycle-shaped chocolate. I open the envelope. It looks like almost everyone has given me a few lines of encouragement or a goodbye in writing. I'm choked. I start reading some of the things they have written. The Elgin and Winter Garden Theatre Centre is a great place to work and I have made a lot of friends there. I'm truly one of the luckiest people alive.

May 22, T-MINUS 4 DAYS

I have just completed my last shift at the theatre. I will truly miss the people and the theatre. We will go out tonight and celebrate, drink, and say goodbye. I suppose I will never see some of them again and this is a scary thought. It's one of those jobs where a lot of people come and go. I would recommend to anyone of any age to get a job at a live theatre because you meet so many interesting people.

I come home quite late and I check my answering machine. The bike is ready!

May 23, T-MINUS 3 DAYS

My friend Scott Gibbon and I go to the Bike Shop. My new windscreen and bike rack look okay. I thank the guys, pay my bill and leave. I immediately drive the bike over to my friend Kelli Ewing's house so she can paint the tank. I get to my mother's apartment a few hours later and see that Kelli has phoned me. She has left a message saying she won't be able to paint the bike until Monday the twenty-sixth. It is typical of me to have left things to the last minute. I have yet to put on the new nylon hard-framed bags that will replace my leather saddlebags.

May 24, T-MINUS 2 DAYS

I talk to Kelli Ewing again about the artwork that will be painted on my tank. The bike will be called The Spirit of Cousteau, in honour of Jacques Cousteau. Below that will be a red poppy in honour of

World War I and World War II veterans. Finally underneath, the letters A.A.C. for Neil Armstrong, Buzz Aldrin, and Michael Collins, who made up Apollo II. Armstrong and then Aldrin were the first humans to stand on the surface of the moon. I was only six years old at the time and don't remember. I was probably asleep. I have a medallion that commemorates that historic occasion which I found recently in a box of mine. I will keep it in my pocket from now on.

Kelli tells me she will have the bike painted on Monday. That will delay the trip a day. It is totally and utterly my fault for this latest development. T-minus two days and holding.

May 26, T-MINUS 1 DAY

I'm looking at the pile of stuff I will have to pack onto my bike and it looks impossible. Clothes, tent, sleeping bag, tools, books, insect repellent, rope, matches, hammer, first aid kit, maps, hats, flashlight, address book, fleece pullover, gloves, mini tape-recorder, paper, pens, camera, Walkman, transistor radio, spare watch, music tapes, batteries, self-inflating bed roll, spare shoes, bike cover, bug jacket, bungee cords, Tupperware with a knife, fork and spoon inside, Kleenex, bike lock, toothbrush and paste, shaving blades and cream, mini shampoo and conditioner, hair brush, two pairs of sunglasses, sun screen, deodorant, rain gear, plastic freezer bags, spare motorcycle key, and whatever else I can think of within the next twenty-four hours.

I will have my picture taken tomorrow with all this stuff packed on the bike. My friend Lori, who is an excellent photographer, will take the pictures. I realize now I will have to wear a knapsack on my back. The two side bags and backrest-knapsack will not be enough. I have yet to buy leather chaps. I hope to do that today. 'Mr. Last Minute'—oh boy.

Kelli calls me and says she should be finished by five p.m. Sounds good to me, I tell her. In the meantime, I'll go and get some chaps; I was given a card at the bike show for all kinds of clothes for motorcyclists so I decide to go there. After a half hour drive I arrive at the store. I go immediately to the section that has the leather chaps.

51

I find some brown chaps (I think they match my jacket) and try them on. They are too long. "No problem," the lady tells me. "We will alter them right now. Should only take fifteen minutes." I agree. While I'm waiting, I buy a nice pair of leather gloves. True to her word, the chaps are ready in a short time. I thank her and leave. There goes another two hundred dollars.

I'm again at my mother's apartment when Kelli phones. She says painting the bike will take longer than she thought. It should be ready by seven o'clock tonight. No problem, I tell her. I shall go take a nap. I can't wait to see what the artwork looks like, I think to myself, as I lay down to sleep. I'm also anxious to get the bike back so I can put on the new side bags. A few hours later the phone rings. It's Kelli and she tells me the bike is ready. Wha-hoo!

I walk to the main street and hail a cab. After twenty minutes or so I'm out of the cab and walking towards Kelli's backyard. I spot the bike, look at the tank and it looks great. Kelli did a fantastic job. I promised Kelli I would treat her to a nice dinner if she painted my bike. We will meet another mutual friend, Suzanne, there. After a great meal, I say goodbye to Suzanne. I drive Kelli home and also say goodbye to her. As I'm riding home I start to think about how I'm going to get the seat off the bike to put the new side bags on.

May 27, T-MINUS 7 HOURS

I wake up at five-thirty in the morning. I hope to be gone by one this afternoon. I can't wait to get going. I go outside to where my bike sits. I have to find a way to get the seat off. I check the owner's manual. I need an Allen key to get the seat off, according to the book. Guess what? I haven't got one. No surprise there, I guess. I go to a friend's house. I knock on his door. No answer. I get back on my bike and go to the Bike Shop. It's closed. Well, it is only seven-thirty in the morning. It opens at eight-thirty. I'll go have breakfast.

It's eight-thirty when I arrive back at the shop. My cousin tells me where to get a metric Allen key set. I thank him and leave. I go there.

I get it. I leave the store. I test the keys in the parking lot. I find one that fits. I arrive at my Mom's about half an hour later. I get the seat off and put on the new side bags. Everything seems fine. I may even leave today. Now I begin cramming everything in the backrest pack, the new side bags and a knapsack. I'll have to get a bigger knapsack. I leave for downtown soon to get my picture taken by my friend Lori. I'm standing behind the theatre and Lori is taking my picture. I feel self-conscious when people walk by. I hug Lori as we say our goodbyes. Lori has been very supportive and a good friend. I see tears start to well up in her eyes as I pull past her. I tell her not to cry, which is dumb because she already has started a little. I pull out onto the street. I turn and wave. I come to a stoplight a short way up the street and turn and wave again. My next stop is an outdoors store only minutes away. Inside the store I go directly to the knapsack section. I find one double the size of the one I've got, and buy it.

T-MINUS 2 HOURS

As I ride along towards my mother's apartment I cringe at the thought of having to say goodbye to her. I have visions of her crying and begging me not to go. I hope that doesn't happen. I am the youngest of five, the so-called baby of the family. I arrive home with thoughts of a hasty exit.

T-MINUS 5 MINUTES

I've got everything (I hope) crammed onto the bike and in the new knapsack. I am extremely impatient as I fiddle with my last minute things.

T-MINUS 2 MINUTES

I say goodbye to my mother. Although we don't say it, it could be for the last time. Who knows what could happen out on the road. I give my mom a hug and say goodbye. She's not crying. Perhaps she will later. To my mom's credit, she thinks the trip is a great idea. It could be that she is happier for me than she is sad.

T-MINUS 1 MINUTE

One minute, after years of waiting. One minute before a dream is realized.

T-MINUS 30 SECONDS

I start the bike. Sit for a bit.

T-MINUS 10 SECONDS

I look straight ahead.

T-MINUS 5 SECONDS

I put the bike into first. I start to let out the clutch.

T-MINUS 1 SECOND

Blast off! The bike starts to move. I pick up speed. I turn and wave. I make a right turn, but I don't go far, as I pull in behind a plaza. I had all this planned. I get off the bike and push the start button on my new Walkman. The music of Aaron Copeland's "Fanfare for the Common Man" floods my eardrums. It took five years to get to this moment. I look at the bike's painted gas tank, the bike itself, and I get all choked up. Tears are forming at the bottom of my eyelids, but don't fall. I notice a plastic piece on my bike ajar and smack it back into place. I rewind. I listen to this piece of music again and choke up a second time. It's time to go. Are you ready? I'll bet you're more than ready. I'm ready. LET'S GET OUTTA HERE!

It's a beautiful day. Perfect for riding, I think to myself as I go along with the traffic. Not too hot and not too cold. I'm on the highway now and the new windscreen really helps. With the bags and knapsack on my back I'm getting plenty of stares. As I buzz along the highway I keep looking in my mirror at the pack that fits over the backrest. It seemed flimsy and loose when I put it on. It doesn't move too much, but I keep checking it anyway.

After about an hour the countryside is rolling by and it's beautiful. Old farms and new ones sit to my right and left. I see a few people on their farms. I wonder what it's like to live on a farm. Forty-five minutes from now I'll be at my brother Brian's and his wife Sonja's house. They live in Lindsay, Ontario, about an hour and forty-five minutes' drive outside Toronto. Every once in a while I do a Homer Simpson, Wha-hoo! Out loud. I can't believe I'm actually doing the trip. Finally.

It's forty-five minutes later as I pull into Brian's driveway. I push the doorbell and wait. No answer. Oh well, I grab my new tent and decide this would be a good time to put it together. Or I should say if I could put it together. I pull the stuff out of the bag and, uh-oh this thing looks complicated. My brother picks this time to say, "Hi," from the bathroom window. I guess the doorbell doesn't work or he couldn't answer it for obvious reasons. My brother comes out into the backyard.

"The doorbell doesn't work," he informs me. "That tent looks more complicated than mine."

Great. I hate complicated things. I'm also not too good with instructions and maps. After trial and error we get the tent set up. It's a weird one, all right. The poles all go on the outside of the tent. Looks good, though. I think I'll sleep in it tonight.

"I should sleep in it tonight," I say to my brother.

"Are you sure? It's still pretty cold at night."

"I'm sure."

Oh brother, I think to myself. How cold can it get? Brian, Sonja, and I decide to go for a walk in a conservation area not too far away. We park the car and start walking. We come out of the woods to a lake and marsh. This is what I call big sky country. Above me, and to the right and left, my whole vision is taken up by sky. What a difference from downtown Toronto.

We turn around and start walking down a path that was once a railway line. Now the tracks are gone and in its place, a nice path. Why don't we turn a lot of the old railway lines into trails? My brother thinks he has just seen a porcupine up ahead and to the left. As we get closer to the spot where he saw the porcupine we hear a noise in the woods. We go towards the noise and after a few steps we see the porcupine near the base of a tree. We make some noise as we get even closer. It is now aware of our presence, but does not run away. I'm amazed. It starts to climb the tree but is taking its time. My first encounter with wildlife on the trip.

It's later in the night. As I prepare to go to bed my brother suggests that I wear long johns, sweater and pyjamas when I'm sleeping out in my tent. I take these items out with me, mostly to please him. I don't think it's going to be cold. This isn't easy, changing inside the tent. I go to sleep almost right away. I'm awake a few hours later and I'm FREEZING! I curse myself. I should have bought a warmer sleeping bag. I manage to get back to sleep. I wake up yet again and am still freezing. I put on the fleece pullover. There, that's a little better. The self-inflating bedroll isn't as comfortable as I thought it would be. I can still feel the lumps on the ground. Good thing I'm not going on a long trip. Duh!

May 28

It's the morning, and my brother and I are heading into town for breakfast. Ahhh, now we're talkin'. My territory, something I'm familiar with. Want to hear something interesting? Okay. I have yet to buy any cooking equipment. There's just no room for it. Now, that is a shame. I hope I don't cry myself to sleep tonight.

After breakfast, I decide to get a haircut. My brother recommends a place. We go. In no time at all I'm in the chair. What proceeds next could only be called a scalping. I guess the word "trim" was not in her vocabulary. I'm extremely impatient today. I keep looking at my watch. My brother picks up on this. We go into a store. I need long johns. My brother holds up a pair.

"I'll take 'em," I say.

"Or how about these?"

"I'll take 'em."

"These ones?"

"I'll take 'em." At this point I don't care anymore. I've done so much shopping lately I don't care.

We leave the store. We go back to my brother's house. I take the tent down and hang it on the clothesline to air out. We start re-packing the bike. My brother points out that the side bags are hanging a little too close to the back tire and are resting on the muffler.

"No problem," I say.

I then proceed to yank on the strap and it breaks. I can't believe it. Now what am I supposed to do? I look at the strap. The bags were poorly sewn where the bag and strap meet. Great, just flippin' great. I go into the house and phone Dave Reid and his wife Pam in Ottawa. I tell them I might be there later than expected. Ottawa, Ontario is my next stop.

We walk into the bike shop and, sure enough, they have bags all right, but not the kind I have. Nothing like mine at all, which are CHEAP PIECES OF CRAP! We go to another bike shop. No luck. We go back to the first shop. I will buy some leather saddlebags. A sales-person and my brother and I go outside to see if the new bags will hang too close to the back wheels. They sit on the muffler. The salesman suggests I mount an aluminium or steel plate on or above the muffler. When he says that, all I can think is—THAT'LL TAKE HOURS. I grow more impatient. I buy the leather saddlebags (which are just like the ones I left in Toronto) at a cost of two hundred dollars. I also buy a small piece of aluminium for three bucks. We go back to my brother's house.

I again call the Reids and tell them I will be further delayed. My brother takes the aluminium piece down to his workshop and makes the necessary cuts and bends. We take the rubber part of the back left foot peg off and, using the same screws from the peg, screw the plate on. The bag no longer touches the muffler. Way to go, Brian! Brian and Sonja had neatly rearranged the now useless side bags last night. Sonja is very good at packing, but unfortunately she is not around. As we start to repack, my brother and I realize the saddlebags are smaller than the other bags. I will have to leave some stuff behind.

A small plastic red gas can is the first thing to go, along with some books. A little more here and there, and I'm packed. As I start to put the screw back in the hole that holds the seat on, it drops into the abyss of the bike engine. It does not hit the ground. I don't care. I will leave it there. My impatience is really affecting my judgement now. My brother says he sees it, but doesn't know if he'll be able to get at it. I suggest leaving it there. I just want to leave. In ten minutes my brother has it out. It's almost five o'clock. We both run around looking for anything I may have forgotten. I hug my brother and say goodbye. I start the bike and he starts to fiddle with the bungee cords we've attached to the saddlebags to prevent them from getting caught in the back wheel.

It's still sunny out, which is good. I won't make it to Ottawa until after dark, however. I take a secondary highway, number 7. It's more of a scenic route than the bigger (401) highway. Maximum speed is 80 km an hour as opposed to 100 km an hour on the 401. The other drivers and I are doing 100 anyway. Beautiful green trees and homesteads roll by. I like the old ones the best. The best houses are usually on the main street.

Well it's later now and I'm getting closer to Ottawa. You know you're getting close to Ottawa when you start seeing the rocks and rock ledges at the side of the road. Some of the rocks had to be blasted to get the road through. A couple of cars are starting to ride my tail a bit, so I speed up a little more. I will wait until it becomes four lanes or we come to another small town and just wave them on to pass me.

A couple of hours later now and I see a sign saying Ottawa East right or Ottawa West straight ahead. It hadn't occurred to me where Nepean (the Reid family's home location) would be. I choose Ottawa West straight ahead. After about a half hour (it's pitch black now) I pull off the highway and arrive at a truck stop. I have a feeling something is not right and that I'm lost. I ask a man in the truck stop,

"Which way is Nepean, Ottawa?"

"About a half an hour down that way."

Of course it's the way I have just come from. He tells me I should have picked east instead of west. Not only am I lost, but I feel bad because I know Dave, Pam and their daughter Erica are holding off eating supper until I get there.

I call Dave and Pam and tell them I'm lost. I apologize for being late. Pam tells me I'm about a half-hour away from their house. Dave gets on the phone and gives me directions I'm too tired to understand. I tell him I will call when I get to Nepean. I hang up. I've been on the road for four and a half-hours now. The front of my bike is covered with dead bugs. Back on the highway I go.

It's about ten minutes later now and I'm on the highway. My fuel light comes on. Oh, man. Here we go. I ride with the fuel light on for as long as I can. I switch to reserve now as the bike starts to slow down. I seem to recall my brother saying that I have three litres of fuel in the reserve tank, or is it one? Hmmm. Like I know how much is in a litre anyway. I keep riding, expecting to hear that putt-putt sound. Twenty minutes later now and I see a sign for a Nepean exit. I hope to find a gas station. I stop at a traffic light and see a gas station about 300 yards ahead. Wha-Hoo! I pull in and ask a girl who's pumping gas if she knows where the street I'm looking for is. She tells me she doesn't know but that she's great at reading maps. I fill up my tank and go in to pay. There's the same girl with map in hand, trying to find the street for me. Eventually she locates it and gives me directions. I thank her very much and go outside. I get back on the road and find it fairly easily. I ride up their driveway at around 10:40 p.m. Five hours and ten minutes it took me to get here. It shouldn't have taken that long, but it did. Oh well.

Dave and Pam have a delicious chicken dinner waiting for me as I sit down in their kitchen. We all eat and have a few laughs. Their daughter Erica (who is five) has gone to bed. We have a few drinks and a few more laughs, then it's time to call it a night. Pam and Dave are great hosts and as generous as anybody you could hope to meet.

May 31

I haven't done much since I arrived except eat, relax and enjoy Dave, Pam, and Erica's company. Today Dave and I will go to some English pubs in downtown Ottawa.

We walk into the Earl of Sussex pub. They have a lot of good beer on tap. There's a male singer in the corner with a guitar strapped around his neck. It sounds like he's singing either Irish or traditional east coast songs.

"Are there any Newfoundlanders here?" the singer asks.

Dave raises his hand. He is the only one who does. The singer is glad to see a fellow Newf. He starts to sing again. After a few songs Dave tells me he's singing songs he hasn't heard in ten to twenty years. Dave and the performer banter back and forth between songs. It turns out they know some of the same performers in and around Corner Brook, Newfoundland.

The next song, Dave tells me, is called Barrett's Privateers. As far as I can figure out, it's about a young man (twenty-three, I think) who joins up to fight on the high seas on one of those old ships. Everyone, as near as I can figure, gets killed but him. It sounds depressing, but it's not sung that way. I like this song a lot. Perhaps it's because I have Irish blood in me and this sounds like a traditional Irish song. With a last name like Murphy, it's hard to be anything else. Dave and I order a pint of Murphy's Irish Stout (see what I mean?) which is very good, in our opinion. We leave there after a while and go to a much busier pub called the Heart and Crown. They too have a singer. Although he's older than the singer in the other pub is, he sings pretty much the same songs, including Barrett's Privateers.

I have decided I will leave on Monday.

Part 8

On the Road to Eastern Canada

June 2

It's Monday morning. I say goodbye to Dave, Pam, and Erica. They couldn't have been nicer to me. It occurs to me now that the next part of the trip will be a totally new experience. I had taken a driving trip with my parents to eastern Canada as a child but remember almost nothing. My chief concern, as I recall, was that my brother Mike stay on his side of the back seat. This time for my stay in Montreal I have picked an actual campsite. (That's right, ladies and gentlemen.) I'll have to use a map to get there and then pitch a tent and everything. I got the location for the campsite from a book that my friend Kelly gave me as a going-away present. The campsite is in a place called Dorion, Quebec. It's approximately two hundred kilometres away. As I set out from the Reid driveway it is a beautiful day.

I pull onto highway 417, heading east toward Montreal. As I travel down the highway I'm getting hit from all sides by tremendous winds. I sometimes have to lean into the wind to keep myself balanced. There are a lot of farms on either side of the highway. I see a hawk flying over a field.

June 3

It's about three o'clock in the morning. I have woken up a couple of times already. I think I heard something outside my tent last night.

To make matters worse, my throat is hurting and is swollen near my tonsils. If I eat too much food with sugar in it the back of my throat swells up. It happens about three or four times a year. Just what I needed. I'll have to gargle with salt water a couple of times a day for about a week until it goes back to normal. I get up. I get dressed. I go to the public washroom and gargle with salt water. YECCH!

I pull into the local restaurant and order breakfast. I have bacon and eggs. My favourite meal. After breakfast I gargle more. It hurts to eat.

Another beautiful day as I head out on the highway to old Montreal. After a couple of stops to check my map I drive to Old Montreal. Lots of narrow streets. It doesn't look just old—it looks really old. There are a lot of tourists. I don't look any different, with my white cotton hat and my camera in hand. I walk around a bit, looking at the signs, looking for the Notre Dame Church. I spot it. I walk up the steps. Hundreds of tourists. I walk into the church and I am stunned by its beauty. I have never seen a more beautiful church. There is a carved wooden spiral staircase to my left that must have taken (I'm guessing) years to build. No wonder people by the busloads come to see this place. I'm lucky everyone I have met so far has spoken both French and English. When I was in school they did not start teaching us French until grade six. I dropped French as soon as I got to high school. Consequently, I know only a few words and one or two phrases.

I sit down on one of the benches in the church near the back. I take a picture or two and then realize I have run out of film. Oh, great. I push the button that will automatically roll the film all the way to the end. Nothing happens. I push it again. Nothing. To hell with it. (Nice choice of words in a church.) I open the back and start trying to pull the film out. I think I just exposed the whole roll of film. You didn't want to see pictures of it anyway, did ya? OOPS. I leave. I retrieve my bike from the parking lot and go back to my campsite.

I'm writing postcards at my picnic table in the campground when a couple pull in on their motorcycles. They are both riding BMWs. A few minutes later they walk up to me and introduce themselves. (I forget their names immediately.) They are from Cape Cod. They start asking me questions about Montreal, my trip, the meaning of the words on my gas tank and things about the campsite. They've been on the road from about eight and said they were pretty cold. I give them as many answers to their questions as I can. After a few minutes they leave. It's a couple minutes later now and a strange and foreign idea starts creeping into my head. If I could find some firewood somewhere I could ... I could ... COOK! ...Ahhh!

Good God, man, have you lost what little you have left for a mind? As if some otherworldly power has taken over my feet, I start to walk towards the local store a mere fifty yards from my campsite. I walk into the store. I get hot dogs, a six-pack of beer, mustard, and a bag of kindling for the fire. I pay. I start walking back to the camp. Now to start the fire. It starts relatively easily. I shove a hot dog onto a stick. I put it into the flames. Thirty seconds go by and the hot dog falls into the fire. I get another one. After a minute or so, it's contorted and bubbling on its surface from the heat. It looks hideous. I put it in a bun anyway. Tastes great. I continue cooking and eat one after another until the whole pack is gone. I open a beer but don't want it. Well, that went pretty well, I think. I see a lot of hot dogs in my future. The couple ride by. I guess they're going to town for something to eat. For some reason I feel almost certain that tomorrow I will skip Quebec City and will try to make it to New Brunswick by the next day. I look at the map. There's a place called Edmunston, New Brunswick, I might be able to get to. It looks really far on the map, though. An eight or ten hour drive, perhaps. Yes, I think that's what I'll do.

June 4

I'm awake. My throat still hurts. It should go away soon. Again I am up at five o'clock in the morning. I went to bed at around nine o'clock, so I guess that makes sense. There's a cool breeze this morning as I start packing to leave.

63

After breakfast (no, I did not cook breakfast), I hit the road (Highway 20 east) at around eight o'clock. Correct that. I hit a morning traffic jam. I clear the downtown part of Montreal around nine o'clock. It's about ten minutes later when I get the feeling I'm not on Highway 20 anymore (The Trans Canada Highway). Although the scenery is beautiful, with old houses, and towns on the left side and water on the right side. I am actually on the wrong highway. The good thing is that I'm parallel to the one I should be on, which I guess is across the water. I pull off the road to look at my map. It is quite windy. I see I can cross at a place called Trois Rivières and get back on Highway 20.

I pass small town after small town as I head toward the crossing point I just mentioned. I see some spectacular (what I believe to be) Victorian homes and old churches. One of the things I've noticed about some of the small towns in Quebec is they have huge churches for such small places. I have decided at this point to ride all day if necessary and reward myself with a hotel or motel in Edmunston.

A few hours later I'm crossing the bridge at Trois Rivières. I get a nice view of the surrounding area from this bridge. I keep checking the pack that's on the backrest. It seems to be leaning a bit too much to the right. I check it. It seems secure enough.

I'm just outside the town of Eulaie when I see two wild deer just beyond the edge of the forest, deciding (I guess) whether to make a dash across the road. I have seen a lot of roadkill so I hope they make it. I see mostly racoons dead on the road, for some reason. The wind is really strong now as I approach Quebec City. I start to see more mountains now. I'm also seeing more and more moose crossing signs. It's getting colder the further east I go. I stop for gas.

Although the sun is still out, there is a storm brewing in the south and has been all day. I have been out-running it, so to speak, since I started out this morning. As I ride it's getting colder and colder. I stop for gas again a few hours later. That's twenty dollars in gas so far today. The gas pump guy hands me a $10 bill and some change. As I fiddle with my wallet and the change and other things, the $10 bill blows away. I chase after it, and every time I bend down to pick it up, it blows further away. I have on my knapsack and helmet and I feel like a bit of a fool. I finally grab the $10 bill. I turn to see the gas pump guy and a customer laughing at me. It is kind of funny. I smile, then laugh, and finally shrug.

I'm back on the highway now and, yes I am officially cold. I pull off the highway and put a sweater on. I leave the parking lot, and something doesn't feel right as I drive down the road. Maybe that's because YOU LEFT YOUR KNAPSACK BACK THERE! I turn around and roar back to the parking lot. It's gone. I left it for two minutes. I look around, look to my right. I notice there's a gas station. I walk over to the gas station to ask if anybody has turned in my knapsack. As I do, I spot it beside the ice machine. Whew. I thank the man (who is very busy with customers), "Merci."

Back on the road. Now my legs and hands are getting cold. I stop yet again and put on some heavy black leather gloves. No time to put on long johns as I am now obsessed with getting to Edmunston. I daydream about a warm bath.

It's a couple of hours later and I'm heading south. The landscape seems more rugged now. I worry about running out of gas sometimes. The wind is still quite strong as I'm being gently shoved from one side of the road to another. A Mercedes-Benz passes me from behind in my lane! A stupid thing to do. I blow my horn and give him the finger. My blood is boiling now. Not satisfied, I pass at 140 kph. I get in front of him and slow down to 100 kph. I'm so angry. I realize almost instantly that my move was even dumber. He could have run me off the road quite easily. When I passed him and gave him the finger, he didn't even look at me.

A little later now and my blood is simmering. The scenery is quite beautiful with huge, rolling hills. I arrive in Edmunston. It's around six o'clock. I accomplished what I set out to do. Edmunston is a pretty big place as towns go. I find a hotel. I walk around a bit, grab something to eat, and go to my hotel to sleep. Tomorrow I think I'll go to Fredericton, New Brunswick, and get a campsite.

Part 9

Tootling Through New Brunswick and P.E.I.

June 5

I wake up, get dressed and go for my complimentary breakfast. After breakfast I go and pack. I'm on the road again by eleven a.m. It's a little cool this morning but I'm ready this time. I'm wearing long johns and the matching undershirt beneath the usual get-up. Oh, something I forgot to mention. I have a dark brown suede biker-style jacket and dark brown leather chaps. When I have my knapsack on and all this other stuff, I feel like Chuck Yeager. I don't know why. It's just that when I have my helmet in hand, I'm wearing my jacket, chaps, boots, and backpack, and I'm walking along the pavement towards my bike, I feel like a jet pilot walking to his plane. When I'm walking around town with the jacket, chaps, boots, and gloves, I feel like a cowboy. I guess that sounds kind of silly, but it's true. It will probably wear off. When I was an actor I always said it would be great to have a role in a western movie.

The clouds are dark and it looks like it will rain. It's a good thing I dressed properly this morning because it's cold on the bike again. The desk clerk back at the hotel told me it would take three hours to get to Fredericton, New Brunswick. I'll take my time as long as the weather holds out. I see a sign that says Grand Falls. I'd like to see that.

I'm standing in front of the Grand Falls. It's not Niagara Falls by any means, but it seems very powerful, loud and beautiful at the same time.

I buy a tape of Stan Rodgers with "Barrett's Privateers" on it and some postcards. I write a lot of postcards these days. I leave.

As I ride along I spot a sign that says you can take a scenic route east instead of the Trans Canada Highway. I'll take the scenic route. It starts in Perth-Andover. I reach Perth-Andover and begin the route. It is scenic indeed. The St. John River is on my right side, and rocks and trees and houses are on my left. It's a blast driving along these winding roads. I pass through the town of Kilburn. Just up ahead is another town called Bath. I see a steel railroad bridge connecting the two banks of the river just outside the town of Bath. The rails have been taken out. As I ride along and watch the path the train used to take, I see that the train used to go right through the town. It actually ran behind the houses in between the two connecting backyards. I can't imagine having a train running almost through my backyard. It starts to rain a bit. It spits for a while, then stops.

I pull into Hartland, New Brunswick. According to the sign, it has the world's longest covered bridge. Or is it the largest? It's a biggie, all right. I immediately think of that movie, *Bridges of Madison County*. I follow a car through the entrance of the bridge and believe I should have waited because there's some kind of traffic light. Oops. Why don't they make covered bridges anymore? Or do they? Maybe it's a safety issue. I come out the other end and spy a gift shop. I buy some postcards and leave.

Back on the Trans Canada. The sky up ahead is black and I can see it's raining in the mountainous region up ahead. I don't know if they are mountains or not. When does something reach mountain status? I'm about an hour and a half from Fredericton. I don't think I'll make it too far without getting soaked. I spot a motel. I pull into the parking lot. I have mixed feelings. On the one hand I know I will get wet and then have to find a campground in the rain and set up as it rains; on the other hand, I feel like a cheater. What am I going to do, stop at a motel every time the weather gets bad? I'll be broke in a month or two if I do that. I don't really want to think about it right now. I guess I'll have to ease into roughing it. I check into the motel.

June 6

After breakfast I go back to my little room and prepare for the day's ride. It's overcast and cool this morning with a chance of rain. Along with the usual cold weather outfit, I will wear a fleece pullover and heavy leather gloves.

As I ride along, I realize after only a few minutes it is BLOODY COLD. It's not my imagination. The coldest so far. I hope to make it to Fredericton today. It's a dreadful day. I get to Fredericton and call my friend Dawn Murphy (no relation). She's glad to hear from me even though I have woken her up. We chat for a few minutes and I say good-bye. She lives in British Columbia. I'll be seeing her in a few months, I guess. I leave.

My hands and feet are freezing. Eighty kilometres from Moncton, New Brunswick I pull off to the side of the highway to put my smaller gloves on inside my larger ones. I pull onto the road again. Well, that's a little better for the hands, anyway.

I stop and look at my map and realize it would make more sense to go to Prince Edward Island now, instead of Nova Scotia, as I had planned. Although I have acquired a cold, I am in a "let's push on" kind of mood. It starts to rain a bit. I have been riding for about six hours now, with a few stops here and there. As I approach Moncton, the speed limit (according to the sign) is 110 kph, not the usual hundred. Oh, I forgot to tell you something. When I stopped to put on my extra gloves eight kilometres before Moncton, I could see my breath. Maybe you can imagine how cold that would be, going fast down a highway hour after hour on a motorcycle.

Anyway, as I make my way north to Prince Edward Island, it is drizzling a little harder now. At this point, though, all I can think about is the new bridge. The first of its kind in the world. It opened only a few days ago. It's raining as I approach the bridge. It is massive! The bridge does not go across in a straight line, that's for sure. Riding on this bridge is a blast. Just when you think it's about to end, you see how far you still have to go. Prince Edward Island still looks far away.

This bridge is a testament to human achievement. The surface of the new pavement is as black as night. The rain is getting more intense now, as I leave the bridge behind. I'm getting more soaked by the minute. So guess where I'm sleeping tonight? A motel, of course.

As I drive along I see the red earth of P.E.I. It's beautiful. That might sound odd, but the red soil against the rain-soaked green of the grass looks amazing. P.E.I. is famous for Anne of Green Gables (a book by Lucy Maud Montgomery), and potatoes. Unfortunately, the house Lucy Maud Montgomery's story took place in had a fire, but at least it was not destroyed. I want to see the house for myself, fire or no fire. It is still raining as I pull in to a motel in Disable, P.E.I. I walk in. The lady behind the counter is friendly. She tells me how to get to the Green Gables house. I will go tomorrow. She recommends the restaurant beside her motel. She tells me it's run by a couple from Newfoundland.

After a hot bath and a hot shower I amble over to the restaurant. I order a B.L.T. and a vegetable soup. The soup comes first, and it's awesome. Ditto for the B.L.T. I strike up a conversation with the waitress after a while and she tells me this house (the restaurant is actually an old house) used to be the home of Lucy Palmer's father. Lucy Palmer, it turns out, was a schoolteacher and one of her students was Lucy Maud Montgomery who wrote Anne of Green Gables. People from all over the world have called the government to volunteer to help repair the house. People from as far away as Japan have called the P.E.I. tourist bureau, crying, they were so upset. I thank her for the information and great food. If the weather's good, I'll find a campsite tomorrow.

June 7

It's a beautiful morning. The sun is shining and that makes a great amount of difference to me. After a delicious breakfast and more conversation with the owners of the restaurant, I venture off towards Green Gables. Highway 13 that I'm travelling on is in pretty bad shape. I'm in such a good mood I simply don't care. P.E.I. looked good in the rain, but it's a helluva lot better in the sun. I will definitely find a campsite today.

I pull into the parking lot of Green Gables. I walk towards some people who are talking to one of the girls from Parks Canada. The house, as I expected, is closed. I can see two men working to repair the roof. It still looks pretty good, though. Apparently, one and a half rooms upstairs were damaged. It's a nice green and white house, but nothing overly fancy. She also says the house won't re-open until around the end of August. That's bad news for this province. The whole island's tourism (as far as I know) is based almost entirely on the Anne of Green Gables story and this house. The licence plates on the cars even say "Home of Anne of Green Gables." I see a sign on the edge of the forest that reads Haunted Woods. Along the trail there are signs that explain the different stops while I walk through it. Anne thought the woods were haunted because of the eerie sound the wind made as it passed through the trees. I walk around a bit more and leave. I will find a gift shop.

I'm riding for maybe another minute when I spot a plaza with a gift shop. Naturally, I go there because I have to get more postcards. As expected, there are a lot of Anne of Green Gables gifts and cards. I buy some cards and a copy of the book. Although Mrs. Maud Montgomery wrote a lot of books, she is famous for the Anne stories, of which there are quite a few. Next I go to a government information station and look into possible campsites. I decide on the Prince Edward Island National Park. Before I go to the park I have to do something about my camera. I start by asking directions to Charlottetown. I think I can find it.

I'm in a mall in Charlottetown. I find a photo-developing place and explain that I can't get the film out of the camera. She looks the camera over, pushes a little button that winds the film and, presto, everything is fine. The pictures will take an hour to process, so I'll walk around a bit. I take a picture of a war memorial and generally just look around. I'm back at the photo place and, surprise, surprise, none of the photos of my stay in Montreal turned out.

I'm riding along when I realize I am lost. I thought I was heading towards the National Park, which is pretty close to the Green Gables house. Oh, well. I'm back on track after a while. I pull into the park and check in at the front gate. She tells me I can't have a campfire. That's okay. Despite the blazing sun, it is surprisingly cool today. I find my campsite, which is about twenty yards from the beach. I walk on the beach for a bit after setting up my camp.

I leave all my clothes on as I prepare for sleep. I can hear the wind coming off the Gulf of St. Lawrence. I am cold almost immediately. People I have talked to have told me the weather is normally warmer at this time of year, but they seem to be three weeks to a month behind. They aren't kidding. I'm freezing in this tent-turned-refrigerator. I wake up for the third time tonight. I'm trying to figure out a way to get warm. Curse this stupid sleeping bag. I will explore the island more tomorrow.

June 8

Two beautiful mornings in a row. I think I'll just explore the island today and take the ferry to Nova Scotia tomorrow morning. I like travelling by boat. It's not something I get to do very often, that's for sure. I'll go to the east first and then come back west.

I stop at a place called St. Peters. As you might have guessed, there is quite a big church there. I stop a short distance from the church and take a few pictures. Now I'm in the church graveyard. Some of these graves date back to the 1850s. More than one of the tombstones read that some of these unfortunate people were lost at sea. I take a few pictures of the older stones. (Is that a wrong thing to do?) I leave.

Not much time has passed before I'm in Charlottetown. I buy a paper and look it over, sitting on a bench. It says the H.M.S. Bounty, which was used in the 1962 movie Mutiny on the Bounty, is docked not too far from here. I'll start riding west again. I have to go back to the motel I stayed in the previous night because I left my watch there. I'm about halfway there when I see a sign that says ELVIS PRESLEY'S 59 CADILLAC. I have got to see this. It just so happens I hope to own a

'59 Cadillac one day. The biggest fins on a Caddy ever made, I think. I slow down and pull in. It's a car and farm equipment museum. I pay four bucks and start walking around. They have some really old classics here and, well, farm equipment too. Oh, yes, there is Elvis '59 Caddy. Definitely worth the four bucks. I look around some more and leave. If you're ever in P.E.I., check out that museum and see The King's Caddy. OK, on to the motel now where I will attempt to get my watch back.

I'm here and the motel looks kind of deserted. I talk to the woman about my watch and, yes, it's still in my room, in the bathroom. They have had to close the motel temporarily because of a water or electricity problem. I didn't catch which one it was. Maybe both. I think from here, I'll take another look at that huge bridge. It's not too far from here.

As I look at the bridge again, it's hard to believe the size of it. To cross it, it takes about fourteen minutes at a pretty fair speed. I wonder how much it costs to build something like that. I hear a couple of people died during the building of it. The ultimate price. I hope they are remembered somehow. A bronze plaque or something. I'll go back to my campsite now.

June 9

What can I say, another beautiful morning. At least there is no frost on my tent or the ground like yesterday. Did I mention that? I don't believe I did. To catch the ferry that leaves for Nova Scotia, I have to go to a place called Wood's Island. I pack up camp and leave.

It's a pleasant ride so far this morning. I arrive in Wood's Island just in time to board the ferry. The ferry-workers give me some canvas straps to secure my bike with in case the water gets rough. With that done, I go upstairs to the deck. It's awfully windy outside as the boat travels toward Nova Scotia. But I expected it would be. It's almost always windy on a ferry. I take some pictures and relax on the top deck for a while. The water is calm as we pass some fishermen. Before I know it, the time has come to go down below and get ready to leave. I don't think it took quite an hour to reach the shores of Nova Scotia. No doubt my friend Genevieve will be starting to worry, as I told her I would see her at the very beginning of June. I believe I told her the first or second of June. She is living in a place called Antigonish which, as I look at the map, is not too far from here. I ride off the ferry. I am now in the province of Nova Scotia.

It doesn't seem too populated once you get back on to the Trans Canada Highway. Anyway, I'm approximately halfway there and there are some railway tracks on my left and a stream on my right. I like the sight of railway tracks, for some bizarre reason. Is it because a lot of the railway lines are no longer in use? Maybe. I did travel to British Columbia and back twice by train. Maybe that's it. Hold the phone. I used to walk on railway tracks everyday going to and from high school. It was the only good part of going to high school at all, as I recall.

A half an hour has passed and I'm in Antigonish, Nova Scotia. Genevieve is acting in a play here, the title of which escapes me at the moment. I ask directions to the theatre where the play is being rehearsed. I'm really close. I park my bike and walk over to the theatre and ask anyone if they know my friend. No one does. I ask a lady coming out of the building if she knows Genevieve. She does. Her name is Jean. She informs me that Genevieve is in Halifax right now, but will be home tonight. She kindly offers to show me the house that Genevieve is staying in. We arrive and Jean introduces me to Genevieve's roommates, possibly other actors in the same show. I thank Jean and one of the roommates shows me to Genevieve's room, where I will put my stuff temporarily. First order of business is laundry. There's a small laundromat next door, I'm told.

I put my stuff in the washer, walk out the door and promptly lock myself out of the tiny laundromat. I go downstairs and around the front of the building. From what I can gather, this barbershop I'm standing in front of is a part of the same building as the laundromat. I sheepishly ask the barber if he has a key. He does. Well, to make a long story short, I locked myself out of the laundromat twice. Brother,

TWO WHEELS, TWO COUNTRIES, ONE DREAM

did I look like an idiot. I was also wearing a T-shirt with the Superman logo on it and the barber must have been saying to himself, or to his son (they look exactly alike), "Who is this dumbbell, anyway?" Oh well, they were kind to me, in a perplexed kind of way.

I'm riding around just checking out downtown Antigonish. Hmmm, that's strange. The bike doesn't seem to want to go from a high gear to a low gear. It won't go from second gear to first. I'm at a red light and can't get into first. UH-OH. I drive back to Genevieve's. I'll need to call a bike shop. I look in the phone book and, as far as I can tell, there is a bike shop in Truro. According to one of the roommates at the house, it is approximately an hour and a half's drive away. I'll test it again tomorrow and see if it's still acting up. Maybe it's something I'm doing wrong. Ha! What are the chances of that? Hmmm.

I'm sitting in a bar with some of Genevieve's friends and roommates. Here she comes! I give her a big hug. She tells me she got worried when I didn't show up earlier. I tell her about locking myself out of the laundromat and she laughs heartily. We have some drinks and talk some more.

Part 10

*Nova Scotia—
Friends, Whales,
and History*

June 10

As I awake today I wonder how long my stay will be now if there is indeed something wrong with the bike. I hope not too long. I don't want to over-stay my welcome. Well, I guess I'll go into Truro and see what happens.

Well, here I am at the bike shop in Truro, just a little bit outside the town proper. I walk into the shop and tell an older-looking gentleman what I think might be wrong with my bike. We talk for a bit. He leaves to go and talk to the mechanic. The mechanic arrives. Now all three of us are outside.

I tell the mechanic the same story I told the owner of the shop and he listens and looks at the bike. The mechanic starts the bike, puts it into gear and listens and repeats this several times. He rides it around the parking lot. He stops and changes from neutral to first, neutral to first. He turns off the engine and tells me it's not the clutch. He tells me the bike isn't running too good and it needs a tune-up for sure. The other man says they couldn't do it until the beginning of next week. I tell them it is too long to wait. He then gives me the name and number for a big motorcycle shop in Dartmouth, Nova Scotia. I thank them both and leave. I'll get the tune-up in Dartmouth. It will only cost a hundred dollars. I should have got it done before I left.

It's five o'clock in the afternoon. Genevieve says they need volunteers to usher at the Cape Breton Summertime Review. It's being performed at a theatre just up the street. Duty calls, my friends, duty calls. My friends back at the theatre will get a good laugh out of me ushering on my trip.

My usher duties are finished and now I'm watching the show. My god, there's a lot of talented people in this show. Multi-talented, I should say. It seems that everyone plays two instruments. There's lots of political humour, which I like. Some of the humour is local so I don't get all the jokes. There's lots of fiddle playing and step dancing, which some of the performers do at the same time.

Genevieve joins me after the show is over. I meet her friend Maura Lea, who was in the show tonight. I will stay in Antigonish one more day.

June 11

I will try and make contact with a Virago Owners Club member today. The woman I will try to contact lives in Cape Breton, Nova Scotia, about fifty-six kilometres from here. I call and there's no answer. Unfortunately, she doesn't have an answering machine.

Seven o'clock in the evening I try again. No answer. Oh well. I'll try again tomorrow.

June 12

I'll leave Antigonish today at around one o'clock in the afternoon. I hear Cape Breton and the Cabot Trail are beautiful.

It's one-fifteen in the afternoon. Genevieve and her roommates, Burgundy, Lorne, and Melanie, couldn't have been nicer to me. It's not far to Cape Breton. I leave. It's a pleasant ride and the weather is co-operating. I pull into Cape Breton without incident. I stop at the first information centre I see. They give me some maps and I decide I'll camp in a place called Inverness. It's a couple of minutes later when I ride by a dead deer in a ditch. I have seen a lot of roadkill so far, but nothing as big as a deer. It shocks me a little. I guess it's something you don't expect to see dead just off the road. I look in my right mirror only to see my sleeping bag about to fall off. I stop and fix it. I get going again. It occurs to me as I ride along that I don't feel confident taking corners today. I didn't ride the bike at all yesterday. Maybe that's it. I arrive in Inverness and keep my eyes open for the campground sign.

A half-hour goes by and I realize I'm lost. I stop at another information centre in Margar Forks. They inform me that I'm not too far away from the campground I'm looking for. They give me some pretty easy directions to follow. It's about ten minutes later and I am again baffled about where I am. I look at the map and still can't figure out which way to go. Looking at the map and reading maps doesn't seem to help me much. I feel stupid. Inverness seems very far away on the map.

Now it's three hours later and I honestly don't know where I am. I see business signs that say they are located in a place called Cheticamp, which is about a three-inch distance on the map to where I want to be. Well, I'm in Cheticamp now and in a mood most foul. Being lost for three hours drives me up the wall. I pull into a motel and the man who runs it tells me I am definitely in Cheticamp. I'm six miles from Cape Breton Highlands National Park. I book a room. Perhaps a bath or shower will lighten my mood.

June 13

I dismount my motorcycle in the parking lot of the Cape Breton Highlands National Park. I'm still somewhat of a curiosity to people as they look at my various backpacks, saddlebags, and riding get-up. It's around ten o'clock in the morning. It's cloudy and overcast. According to the guy at the information desk there's a chance it will rain today. After seeing how big the park is, I buy a four day pass. There's lots of short hikes and wildlife to see in the park. He also says there will be fog in certain parts of the park so I should be careful. I thank him and leave.

I pass through the gates. Almost immediately I'm riding in between two mountains. They look very powerful as they tower over me. It is a humbling experience. They have been here long before me and will probably be here long after I'm gone. Mountains are something I respect without question. I'm in motorcycle riding heaven as I drive on these beautiful roads. So pretty is the scenery that I find myself not paying much attention to where I am going in terms of traffic. This could become a deadly habit. It would be far too easy to wipe out. Oh, something I forgot to mention. This morning I booked a whale-watching excursion for six o'clock tonight. I can't wait.

I find my campsite pretty easily (for a change) and set up camp. I have a fantastic view of the—wait a second—a park ranger checks my permit—Gulf of St. Lawrence. I'm very close to the water.

Well, here I am at the dock where I will take the whale-watching tour. I enter the office to pay. The captain of the boat asks me where I'm from. I tell him I'm from Toronto. He raises his eyebrows in surprise. I pay the twenty-eight dollar fee and start walking toward the boat. The guide (I am now on the boat) introduces herself as Rene. She has lots of enthusiasm. She chats, laughs, and seems to genuinely like her job. Unfortunately, it is raining. There are nine of us watchers altogether, the captain and Rene included. I'm very excited as we pull out from the dock. I have always wanted to do this.

It's about twenty minutes later when I spot my first whale out of captivity. All I can say is—WOW. I repeat this one word yet again after spotting my tenth whale. It is quite a sight to behold as another whale comes to the surface. All the whales we have seen so far are of one kind. They are called Minkes and are about twenty feet long with a weight of around eight tonnes, if I heard correctly. The weather has turned a little nasty, although this nastiness only seems to last for around ten minutes. The whale-sightings aren't as numerous now. The captain and Rene still try as valiantly as ever to find us more whales as we stand in the pouring rain. Two hours into the trip the captain decides to call it a day. He graciously offers to let us come back tomorrow morning for free if we like. We are passing near the site of my camp and it is completely enclosed in fog. The thought of riding in the mountains in the rain and fog doesn't especially thrill me. I point out to Rene the location of my campsite. She says I might want to consider staying in town as it gets extremely windy where I'm staying. I thank her for the advice.

We are back at the point of departure and we all say goodbye to Rene and the captain. I will see them tomorrow. As I ride toward the park, my thoughts are returning to the foggy mountain roads. Now that I'm actually here in the park, the fog isn't as bad. The fog has pretty much lifted. I'm riding down the last hill before my campsite. There's a pick-up truck behind me now so I put my hazard lights on. Suddenly, out of the corner of my eye I see something move. A deer is scrambling up the bank of the road to my left and onto the road, not twenty feet ahead of me. In seconds he is in front of me.

I tense up and start putting the brakes on. He stops for a second and looks into my headlight, then actually starts toward me. I'm going to hit the deer. He comes out of his trance and just in time gets out of the way. My heart is pounding like a freight train. It all happened with blinding speed, a mere five seconds or so. But it seemed like forever. A few feet and a second or two of time averted a disaster. I'm still shaken as I pull into my campsite. I stop and get off the bike. I don't know what to do with myself, as my adrenaline hasn't quite calmed down yet. I'm shaking my head at the thought of what could have happened to me. The truck followed me into the campsite. He gets out of his pick-up truck. He's a Parks Canada Ranger, I think. He saw the whole thing, he tells me. I get the strange feeling he's going to give me proper hell, for some weird reason. He tells me that was a good idea that I put my hazards on. He advised me not to ride too much at night. He leaves. I was only going around thirty miles per hour at the time. I would have been writing this from a hospital bed, or not at all, if you know what I mean, if I had been going any faster.

I get ready for bed. I can't sleep. A big wind keeps flapping my tent all night. I sleep maybe two hours total all night as I realize it's early in the morning. I thought my tent and I were going to blow away last night such was the force of the wind.

June 14

Well, that was one of the worst nights I have spent so far. I couldn't sleep. This weather stinks. I get up and go to a place called Brigadoon's. A great place for breakfast and conversation. Soon I'll be going back to the docks for my free return visit.

Well, sports fans, here I am again on the good old whale-spotting boat. There's a lot more people on the boat this morning, I figure around twenty to twenty-five. It's colder and the water is choppier. We start out slow as Rene and the captain do their best to find us some whales. We begin to spot some whales, the same kind as yesterday, actually. In between seeing the whales we look at the National Park. I again see my campsite and take a few pictures. We come within, say, forty yards of a fishing boat. The fisherman waves and holds up a freshly caught lobster. Again the weather deteriorates and we head back to the docks. I am quite cold and my hands are hurting they are so cold. It has rained for most of the trip and the whales were few and far between. I still wouldn't have missed it for the world.

After lunch I don't know what to do with myself. The weather is still rotten, which would make a hike in the mountains a foggy and wet experience. I think I'll go back to my tent and have a nap. I'm in my tent now and sleep does not come easily. I'll listen to my radio my friend Lori bought me as a going-away present. Maybe I will hear a weather report. I eventually hear that the weather will be good the next couple of days. WHA-HOO! What can I say? When the weather is bad I get bored.

After my nap I decide out of sheer boredom that I will do some laundry. Actually, I'm looking forward to it. I'm about to pull onto the main road leading out of the park when I spot two motorcycles coming down the hill toward me. The first motorcycle that passes by me is exactly like mine. I can't get a good enough look at the second one as it passes by me. I will try to catch up with them. After about five minutes I am right behind the second rider. Hey! He has an Ontario licence plate. The bike that is the same as mine is too far up for me to see the licence plate.

In town they pull off the road. They are both from Ontario. I talk to the guy with the Virago first. It is the same year and colour as mine. The other bike is a Honda Magna 750. Roy owns the Virago and Wayne owns the Magna. I ask Roy if I can take a picture of his bike. He says yes. I start walking toward my bike and (pause) it was a good thing I left my camera back at camp. He takes a picture of my bike instead. They are on their way to Prince Edward Island. I warn them about the roads. Although they are kind of fun, I add. They wish me luck on my trip and leave. Well, off to do some laundry. Tomorrow if the weather is nice I'll move to a different part of the park.

June 15

What else can I say about the weather? It is still bad. I did sleep a little better last night. I guess it's because I'm getting used to (a little bit) sleeping in conditions that would have kept me wide awake a few weeks ago. I leave my tent and—hey!—the sky looks kind of, well blue, actually. I get ready to go to Brigadoon's for breakfast. Oh, something I forgot to tell you. I have dropped my helmet twice. It rolled off my seat in the parking section of the ferry and another time the same thing happened in a parking lot. Now, according to the experts, my helmet is useless in the event of my head hitting something. The helmet is designed to take one impact. It is supposed to spread the force of the impact to save your head from damage. It will not do this now because I have dropped it twice. As a motorcyclist, I am now supposed to throw it in the garbage and buy a new one. Let me ask you this: My helmet costs around $350 to replace. Should I buy another one? Well, maybe I should; maybe I shouldn't. Would you buy another one? Well, you might. I mean, this is our brain we're talking about. Right? If you say I should buy another helmet, you're right. Now think about this. I can almost guarantee I'll drop the new helmet at some point should

81

I choose to buy one. So what do I do? There isn't room in my budget for a new helmet. At the same time, I have no room in my financial picture for being dead, either. Here's something to consider. Some crashes are so bad it doesn't matter if you have the best helmet in the world, because the force of impact will be just too much for your brain to handle. I can't see myself buying a new helmet, knowing I'm going to drop it. So I will not buy a new one. It's something to think about, though.

Well, the fog and clouds have started to roll in, that's nice. I get my things in order and jump on my bike. As I approach Brigadoon's parking lot, I see two Harley-Davidsons loaded down with gear. They are identical Road Kings. Judging from their licence plates, I would say they are from Pennsylvania. We start up a conversation. The riders look like they could be part of a gang. But they are not. They are friendly. One of them asks me if I'm going on the Al-Can. Which, I'm pretty sure, means the Alaska-Canada Highway. I say, "I am, indeed." He tells me I have to watch the roads. He tells me of the time when his tires sank right into the dirt. Before they paved, they lifted the asphalt right off the road and just left the dirt underneath, then went over the earth with a steamroller, which didn't seem to help much. We talk a bit more and they leave. I'm riding back towards camp when the sun comes out. I will take my tent down when I get back.

As I start to take the tent down the sun is shining. I finish packing. I turn onto the road leading deeper into the park. I'm on one of the mountain roads when the bike engine begins to sputter and miss. I look at the fuel light and it's on. That means your intrepid adventurer started riding into the mountain roads with the main gas tank virtually empty. I flick the switch to reserve and drive back into town.

Now that I have some gas I think I'll take a second out to look at the map of the park. The clouds have begun their migration over my head. So guess who isn't staying in the park tonight? There's a place on the map called Meat Cove. As far as I can tell, it's the most northerly point I can go in Cape Breton. I get back on the bike again to ride on those beautifully scenic roads.

The scenery in the park is simply the best I have seen so far. Mountains and valleys fill the horizon. The roads are quite challenging to ride on. Some of the corners are quite sharp. I've been riding for about an hour, stopping now and again to take pictures. I would recommend that anyone see the Cabot Trail, whether by motorcycle, car, or bicycle. I stop and visit the sight of Cabot's landing. Cabot landed here June 24, 1497. It's a beautiful place with a long beach. It doesn't look like too much has changed here since he landed. I leave.

I'm zipping along when I see a sign that says Meat Cove eight kilometres. It's not long before the road I'm on turns into a dirt road. There are some long drops to my right, should I happen to make a mistake. I'm going very slowly now as I try to navigate through the sometimes-treacherous corners. It is definitely the most challenging riding I have done so far. A dog starts to chase me as I pass by him. He gives up. Most of the time I'm going no faster than 20 kph. I finally come to a clearing with a tent, some cars and a road up to the left. I stop for a few seconds to look around. I then go left up the road. Oh my god, this road is the worst. The rocks are the size of hardballs and I'm almost losing complete control of the bike. I manage to get to the top of the hill. There is a man standing in his driveway. He gives me a "turn around" gesture with his hand. Basically, the road or the end of his driveway is here. I go back the same way I came. I see a fox about to cross the road, then change his or her mind. I will carefully try to find a motel. Ten minutes later I have found one. I haven't had a shower or a shave in days. Let's just say, I'm due for both. The motel is in the Bay of St. Lawrence. The view from the front door of my motel room is like something off a postcard. The sun is setting behind the town, mountains, and water. I take a picture. I hope it turns out, although I will never forget it.

June 16

I'm up and the sun is shining. That figures, since I'm no longer staying in the park. I go down to the office. I make a reservation for the ferry that will take me to Newfoundland. It leaves from North Sydney, Nova Scotia. It will take about six hours to make the crossing from North Sydney to Channel-Port-aux-Basques, Newfoundland. I will still be travelling on the Cabot Trail today. According to the owner of the motel, there's a controversy about where Cabot actually landed. Nova Scotia and Newfoundland each claim to be the first place he landed. Now I know why I got confused when I saw advertisements from both provinces making the same claim.

I start off on the day's ride. I have picked Baddeck for my next destination. The scenery is much as before, only with slight variations of brilliance. The weather is still great as I pull up to a small open ferry that looks like it could hold maybe six cars. I pay $1.75 and it is such a treat to go this way across the water. I have only seen this kind of thing in books and on television. It takes only a few minutes and we are across.

I arrive in Baddeck, Nova Scotia, and it's around one o'clock in the afternoon. There's a national historic site here and it explores the life of Alexander Graham Bell. Mr. Bell had a home here outside the main part of town that he called Beinn Breagh. According to the brochures and whatnot, Alexander Graham Bell loved his home here (he had others). Although his achievements with the telephone are legendary, he had a lot of other interests as well. It might surprise people to know that he spent a lot of time working on solutions to problems for the deaf. There's a picture of him, Helen Keller, and her teacher Ms. Sullivan. He was also a pioneer in aviation, hydrofoils, and much more. Oh jeez, I forgot to mention that I'm in the museum but the public is not allowed to go to see his home. Anyway, I tend to zip through museums and places like it. I guess that's not a huge surprise. I leave.

I find a motel in North Sydney about ten kilometres from the ferry docks.

Part 11

Over to The Rock

June 17

The weather doesn't look too promising today. I will board the ferry bound for Newfoundland at eleven o'clock this morning.

Well, here I am waiting at the front of the line again to board the ferry. There's a big motorhome motorcade from America here. These motorhomes are huge. A couple of Americans come towards me and strike up a conversation. A big man from Florida asks me if I'm cold and I tell him that I'm not really. He says I can sit in his motorhome for a while if I want to warm up a bit. He also says today is like a winter day in Florida. I decline, but thank him for the kind offer. I'd start sweating in about three minutes in the big motorhome with all the stuff I've got on.

I ride to the very front of the ferry, as directed. The ferry workers tell me to strap my bike down with the thick canvas straps they have just handed me. I do my best to secure my bike so it won't fall on its side. I can't help but wonder how rough the five- to six-hour crossing will be. I shall now try and find a cafeteria or lounge. I find a lounge and park myself on a stool facing the windows of the ferry. The American I talked to and some of his friends approach me and stop. They ask me if I'm going to Florida. "I am indeed," I tell them. They suggest I go to Key West because of how beautiful it is. One of the ladies offers to give me her daughter's address in Kentucky. I'm sure the

85

daughter would love it if a total stranger pulled up to her house on a motorcycle and said, "Hi, I'm Dan Murphy. I met your mother on a ferry going to Newfoundland. So where should I put my stuff?" Would you have gone? Maybe, maybe not. I will not.

When I get to Newfoundland I will be contacting Pam Reid's mother. I spend my time on the ferry reading, looking out the window and watching a bit of television. I awake from a nap to hear that the cafeteria will be closing in fifteen minutes. I run down there. I get a burger, fries, and a milk. That was ten dollars.

I'm in the lounge again, reading. I put the book down and go to the washroom. I'm spending a long time in the washroom because I think the burger has given me Montezuma's Revenge. Over the public address system I hear that we will be in Newfoundland in half an hour. I go back to the lounge, gather my stuff and make a beeline for the car deck where my bike is. Well, my bike didn't fall over. Good thing I put the cover on because the bike was exposed to the elements the whole time. As I take the straps off the bike, I realize I can see my breath. After docking procedures are over with, I drive off the ferry onto Newfoundland soil.

Some people refer to Newfoundland as THE ROCK. Well, I'm riding along and am not two miles into my journey when I pass between two huge sets of rocks. Not too long after seeing the rocks I see large hills (mountains?) with snow still on them. Oh, by the way, my destination is Corner Brook, Newfoundland. The combination of seeing my breath and looking at snow does not fill me with a lot of confidence in the weather. I pass a sign that says GAS SAVING TIPS or HOW TO CONSERVE GAS. Something to that effect. Hmmm. I pass another that says STRONG WINDS NEXT 20 KMS. That's a strange sign. I'm still contemplating that last sign when the wind hits me full force. I'm being steadily pushed by the wind on my right side. Man, they weren't kidding. I'm leaning hard on the right. I'm doing an Ace Ventura with my head sticking out to the left of my windshield. If the wind were to suddenly die down, I would probably crash onto my right side. Never have I experienced such a substantial force of wind. As I make wide left turns, I almost feel like the bike and I will be lifted right off the ground soon. The combined weight of motorcycle equipment and me is about 700 pounds. I'm getting blown all over the road like I'm nothing. I've been riding for half an hour and have yet to see any kind of town. Which isn't too uncommon because I'm on the Trans Canada Highway. But still, I haven't even passed a gas station.

I see a gas station and pull in. I put as much gas in the tank as it will hold. I pay and start out again. The wind isn't as bad now. I still have another two hundred kilometres to go until I'm in Corner Brook. There are so many signs telling me how much farther I have to travel before I get to a place called Stephenville that it starts to become annoying. It's like watching a clock. Every four to ten kilometres it seems there's a sign telling you how far it is to Stephenville. The mountains to my right and left are about ten miles away with trees and flat plains in between the road and the mountains. I still don't see many towns or gas stations. It starts to rain and then quickly starts to pour.

Well, what do ya know, there's a gas station. Under the carport I begin to put my rain gear on. From inside, one of the gas station attendants comes out and offers me a green garbage bag for my backrest pack. I take it and thank him. I believe his name was Jeremy and this is an Irving gas station. I set out again, ready to tackle the elements. I look in the rear view mirror and see the long road behind me, also the mountains and my bright yellow raincoat, my very red knapsack on my back. I immediately think of National Geographic. The sight in my mirror looks like a National Geographic type picture. An adventurous-looking scene. It's still raining hard and getting dark.

I take a turn off the highway onto another (I think) secondary highway. That last turn didn't feel right for some reason, although it did say Corner Brook. There are almost no cars travelling on this road. No gas stations, stores or settlements. Nothing. I feel a bit like I'm on the moon, only it has trees. Nothing for miles and miles. I see a sign in a while stating how far it is to Corner Brook. I think that turn I made was wrong. I still keep seeing these signs telling me how close I'm getting to Stephenville. I stop and check the map. According to the map I'm going the right way. Why do I feel no comfort in that? It just doesn't feel right as I pass the first gas station I have seen in a while. It's getting darker and darker now. I turn around and go back to the gas station.

I ask the attendant if I'm heading in the right direction to reach Corner Brook. He points in the direction I have come from before I pulled back into the station. So, guess what? Good old Dan was going the wrong way. Good thing I have that map with me. Maybe I can use it to start a fire one day soon. He warns me that at this time of night the moose will be crossing the roads and highways. I ask him if there are any motels around. Again he points and, sure enough, there is one about fifty yards away. I'm soaked, tired, and don't care to ride anymore. I ride over to the motel. Check in. I call Pam's mother. No answer. I call Pam in Ottawa. Pam tells me her mother wasn't sure when I was coming so she is not exactly waiting for me. I'll try again tomorrow.

June 18

Someone knocking on the door wakes me up from a sound sleep. He tells me to call Dave Reid (Pam's husband). I call him. He tells me Pam's mother (my contact in Corner Brook) has had to leave for St. John's for an emergency. I will visit Corner Brook and move on. Since I'm up, I might as well go to town for breakfast.

I find a restaurant, pretty much in the middle of town. I talk to some of the people in the restaurant. They tell me how I can find the laundromat, photo-developing place, and the Arts Centre. I have a letter from Genevieve to a friend of hers and fellow actor, John Dartt. He's rehearsing a play there. I will try to find him today. I drop off the letter at the Arts Centre. John is not there right now, but will be at 5:30 p.m. I will come back then.

After doing some laundry and having a nap, I go back to the Arts Centre. I park my bike. I see a bunch of people at the back door.

Someone calls out my name. I walk over and introduce myself to John. He and some of the other actors appear to be taking a break. John tells me they usually go to a bar called Clancy's after rehearsals. I tell him I'll meet him there at 10:30.

I arrive at 10:30. John is sitting at the bar with some of the other people in the play, I'm guessing. I'll tell ya, Sherlock Holmes-like deductions just come naturally to me. I sit at the bar and everyone has a good tip or suggestion about things I should do or see. Again I am warned about the moose. We talk a bit more and I leave. I'm glad Genevieve got me to contact him. John and his friends were interesting to talk with.

June 19

I pull out of the motel parking lot under an overcast sky. I will go to Corner Brook today. The good thing is that it's quite warm today and so I won't need my long johns. Money is on my mind as I begin today's journey. I'm going through my money supply at a frightening rate. As you know, I have been staying in a lot of motels lately. I had originally budgeted for fifty dollars a day. Well, I'm spending around a hundred dollars a day and occasionally a little bit more than that. When I left Toronto I had around $3,000 in the bank. I have roughly $1,300 now. On top of that figure, I owe $400 on my credit card. If I pay off the credit card, that leaves me with $900. Wait, I have $500 in travellers cheques and another $120 in another account. $1500 is only going to last me another month and three-quarters. That's $1500 to last me for the rest of Canada and Alaska. Well, that should be easy, since I'm so good with money. Tragic, isn't it? The funny thing is that at the beginning of planning this trip I had no intention of coming out east. I'm so glad I did, though, and I wouldn't change the experience for the world. But at the same time, I'm spending my money at double the rate I thought I would. I'll keep you up to date.

I arrive in Corner Brook. I drive along the streets and just generally check things out. I see the golf course my friend Dave Reid used to play at all the time. He grew up here. Eventually I pull into a donut shop. Once inside, I pull out my trusty map. What a laugh that is. A man at the next table starts asking a few questions about where I'm going and what I plan on doing, stuff like that. I tell him (among other things) that I will be taking the Argentia Ferry to Nova Scotia. He tells me it will cost around $200 or more. Gulp. $200? I decide to cut my visit to Corner Brook, and the whole province for that matter.

It's a couple of hours later. I pull in to a gas station off the highway and there happens to be an information station beside it. After getting the gas, I decide to visit the old info place. I go in and ask about the ferry leaving from Argentia. It just so happens that the first voyage is to be on Friday night at 10:30 p.m. Which is the very next day. I reserve a spot on the ferry for tomorrow. Since the weather hasn't improved much, this has been a fairly easy decision. Oh, by the way, the ferry costs $100. Not $200, as the gentleman had told me. I decide I will ride to Gander, Newfoundland.

If you're wondering what the scenery is like as I ride along on my way to Gander, I will tell you. There are trees, mountains, lakes, and the usual, for mile after mile. I just thought I'd give you a kind of update.

I ride on into Gander. It's around four o'clock in the afternoon. I spot an aviation museum called The North Atlantic Aviation Museum. I'll check into a motel, get settled and then go to the museum. I find a nice modern one and check in.

I make a right turn into the museum parking lot. There are two big planes on either side of the building. The one on the right (I believe) is a water-bombing plane for fighting forest fires, and the one on the left is a fairly large World War II bomber, perhaps. I walk in and unfortunately I am the only customer. I say that because museums always seem to be in debt or close to it. I walk around a bit and look at the various artifacts. I chat a bit with a couple of the guys who work there and buy a T-shirt. I leave and take a few pictures of the planes outside.

June 20

My friends the clouds are with me again today. I'm getting restless. At the same time I'm feeling guilty about barrelling through Newfoundland. I ponder these things as I wait for my continental breakfast. The waitress arrives and I ask her if I have time for a couple of sight-seeing trips, go to St. John's, then back to the Argentia ferry leaving for Nova Scotia. She tells me I could visit Bonavista and then go to St. John's and back to the ferry. I thank her for her help, finish my breakfast and leave.

I pack up the bike and start out. I get some gas. I'm riding about three minutes on the highway when I see a sign that says Commonwealth War Cemetery, or something to that effect. I turn left onto the road that leads to the cemetery. I'm the only person here. There seems to be two groups of headstones. The headstones on the left, I see that all the stones are the same height and colour. The ones on the right are all different kinds, perhaps public or non-military graves. The first stone I read is of a man who served in the Royal Canadian Air Force. Most of the men who died were in their twenties. Some younger. What an incredible sacrifice to make at such a young age. Some of these graves are side by side with the same dates on them. Perhaps they were in training together. A lot of Air Force personnel were here during World War II, I understand. I take some pictures. To think that these men and their sacrifice are forgotten by a lot of people makes me sad. I don't mean these men specifically, I mean the veterans in general (living or dead). I know they have Remembrance Day in Canada and probably similar days in other countries, but maybe there is something else that could be done. I don't know, maybe people would rather not think about wars. As you have probably guessed, I personally feel extremely grateful to the veterans. I walk around a bit more. The sun is out. I will leave now and, as I do, I feel lucky and grateful. Well now I'm off to Bonavista.

I start seeing signs for Bonavista. I am going there out of sheer guilt. Not a good reason. I take a secondary highway now that will take me there. I'm riding along when I see some fog up ahead. Before I'm in the fog, the temperature drops suddenly. The swiftness of the change in temperature is incredible. I pull off the road and put on my heavy gloves and fleece pullover.

Well here I am, about to ride into Bonavista. It's more populated than I expected. The street that I'm on is narrow and the houses seem crammed together. I'm meandering through the town following the signs. I'm getting pretty hungry at this point. As I near a burger place just outside of the town proper, I realize that I'm being followed (though I can't be sure) by another motorcyclist. I pull into the burger joint overlooking the water and he pulls in right behind me. We exchange hellos and he asks me about the trip and the usual stuff. He tells me that he saw me go by him when I was about halfway through the town and followed me here. I would have probably done the same if I lived here too. I guess there aren't too many bikes in a town this size. We talk a bit more and he leaves.

I look out into the water and, hey, there are icebergs! They are a fair distance away and they look small, but they could be the size of a house or bigger, for all I know. I sit on one of the picnic tables to eat and look at the icebergs at the same time. I take a picture. The lady who served me lunch told me I could probably see some bigger ones from a look-out point that's farther up the road. I've got to see this. I finish my lunch and hop on my bike.

I'm not on the road long when I see a lighthouse with red and white stripes. I have already seen this lighthouse on postcards in some of the stores. I stop and go in. There are guides who will take you through the lighthouse or you can explore on your own. She tells a group of us that this is no longer a working lighthouse. She also says (if I heard her correctly) that the furniture and artifacts here are from the 1870s. I go up a very narrow set of stairs to an observation deck; this is also where the light spins around. A weight connected by either a rope or cable slowly drops from the top to the entrance level of the lighthouse down the centre and that is how the light would keep spinning around.

It would take about two hours for the weight to fall from the top to the bottom. I go downstairs again and outside. I spot a telescope mounted to the railing of the deck. I peer through and look at an iceberg. It's kind of a bluey-white as it sits in the water glistening in the sun. It's around three o'clock in the afternoon. Bonavista was the place John Cabot landed, according to the advertisements. There will be a huge celebration here soon. The Queen of England, no less, will be here. The Queen will be here, I will not. Well, time to start out to St. John's.

I arrive in St. John's after a few non-eventful hours. I call my friend Dave in Ottawa. He thinks I should stay here awhile but knows that I don't want to. I think he can hear it in my voice. I still have a lot of miles to cover and can only stay in one province for so long. Besides, I have a ferry to catch that I have already paid for. I tell Dave I'll see him in Ottawa in a week or so.

I'm now leaving St. John's after being there a grand total of twenty minutes. I've got ants in my pants (just an expression). Although, I literally did have an insect in my ear when I was entering the National Park in Cape Breton. I forgot to tell you that.

I'm on my way to Argentia. That's where I'll board the ferry that will take me back to Nova Scotia. It takes around 12 to 14 hours to travel the distance for the crossing. I've been on the road for about twenty minutes now and—oh wonderful—my fuel light just came on. Guess what I forgot to do in St. John's? Not only that, but I didn't get any money, either. I'll squeeze as much as I can out of the main tank. Great. I'm in the middle of nowhere.

The bike starts to slow down, so much for the main tank. I switch to the reserve. I'm on a highway and my reserve tank should last about twenty to thirty minutes. I feel a premonition of doom coming over me. The light of day is starting to fade. I envision myself walking mile upon mile to a gas station. The minutes go by without any signs that proclaim GAS UP AHEAD, More minutes go by and I'm simply waiting for the bike to start slowing down and then sputtering. Wait, there's a sign and it says—yes—GAS 2 KMS. I hope they take my ATM card, because I think I might have two dollars on me. I pull into the gas station and they do indeed take my ATM card. I ask directions for a bank machine. I will go get some money for my supper and the $111 for the ferry ticket.

I'm riding down the road leading to the ferry just at the end of dusk. What is it about this time of day that is so beautiful? Perhaps it's the colour, which is a spectacular shade of orange right now. Maybe the temperature has something to do with it, where the warmness of the day meets the coolness of the night. I think on a summer's day when there is no wind, this is a magical time to ride. I arrive at the ferry site and pull up to one of the wickets. I pay my money and again I am directed ahead of all the cars to the front of the line. There's another bike at the front of the line already. It's a Honda Transalp. I have only seen two of these bikes ever. The owner comes up. His name is Morgan. We get talking about his bike. He says he was in Germany and these bikes are all over the place. A 1987 Transalp 600. It looks to me like a combination of a dirt bike and a sport bike. Time to go aboard. We are directed on first. We strap our bikes down for the voyage.

It's 12:30 a.m. I can't sleep on the chairs, which are similar to the ones you get on an airplane. I look around and see that people are under tables, openly on the floors in some sections, and wherever they think of as a good spot to sleep. Because this ship is either exactly like, or indeed, the same ship I came to Newfoundland on, I remember a little-used lounge upstairs. I go up, to find it nearly deserted. There are people sleeping in a darker part of the lounge or on the floor between these airplane-like chairs. Looks good to me. I put my stuff on the chairs, lie on the floor and attempt to go to sleep.

June 21

There's an announcement over the P. A. system saying breakfast is now being served. It only half wakes me up as I have been tossing and turning all night.

It is sunny and calm on the water this morning. I was half asleep when I heard one of the five guys that were sleeping behind me among the chairs last night say that we have another biker on board. They have obviously seen my motorcycle helmet some time during the night or this morning. I rouse myself from the floor and start talking to them. They are surprised and envious of my five-month trip. They are travelling for twelve days through the East Coast. One of them asks me how I could afford such a trip and adds that I must have a good job. I tell them a little about my jobs and some of the adventures I've had so far. They wish me luck and I return the sentiment. I start to read my copy of *Shoeless Joe*, which I've read twice before.

I awake from a nap a little more refreshed. I get up and watch some episodes of *Mr. Bean*. I saw them already when I crossed from North Sydney. It makes sense because this is the exact same ferry, I have concluded. The ferry is a half hour ahead of schedule arriving in Nova Scotia. I have decided to visit a place called Louisburg. There's an old army fortress there that I want to see.

I arrive in Louisburg. Up ahead I see an old railway station with boxcars beside it. I pull into the parking lot. This place is an unexpected but welcome find. I walk in and discover that this is an information centre for the town and also a railway museum. They have all kinds of old railway uniforms, tickets, and pretty much everything else there is to do with railways. I walk outside and go into one of the antique passenger cars. There are two passenger cars from 1914. It's like walking into a time machine and coming out eighty-three years earlier. The seats look original. There's a wood-burning stove in the corner. I walk into the second car (they are connected), which was for first-class passengers. They got padded seats. They sure knew how to live, these crazy first-class passengers. Padded seats, can you imagine? My guess is that, first class or not, everyone on the train probably froze their butts off in the wintertime. My boots boom on the wooden floors. I take some pictures. I would like to have travelled on this train back in 1914. Perhaps with virtual reality, I will, sort of, one day. The way I'm dressed

95

I really feel like a cowboy now. I go outside and take a few more pictures. Well, off to Louisburg Fortress.

Without incident I arrive at the fortress. I walk into the building for paying my entry fee and information. The lady behind the desk informs me that it will close in less than an hour. Which is not enough time to see it properly. I leave. Perhaps I will come back here one day. I will go to Antigonish and re-visit Genevieve for a few days. She told me to stop by on my way back through Nova Scotia. I think from Antigonish I'll go to Halifax, then on to Yarmouth where I'll catch a ferry to the state of Maine. Once there, I'll go to Bangor and try to find a certain author's house. I'll give you a hint to his identity, he writes mostly horror books and his initials are S.K.

I arrive back at Genevieve's. My timing is great, she tells me, because they are having a party tonight.

June 22

I will relax and hang out with Genevieve today. Perhaps I will go and see a movie. There's one movie theatre in Antigonish; it's an older one with numbered aisles and seats. I'm restless to leave the east now. I don't know why, but I am. I'll probably be in Maine within the next two to four days.

June 23

It's cloudy and windy today. Yesterday was muggy and humid. By the time I get back to Ontario it will probably be very muggy indeed. I will, at that time, probably look back on the cold weather I sometimes experienced in the east with a certain longing. I am looking forward to going to the States, I must say. The exchange rate on the money is a little hard to swallow, though. I think a Canadian dollar is only worth 70 cents against the American dollar. Five hundred dollars Canadian will get me three hundred and fifty American. So I won't be lounging around too much in this small detour into the United States. Two or three days at the most, I would hope.

I'm committing a cardinal sin (for lack of a better term) worrying about my money situation already. I'm only twenty-seven days into the trip. I should have had a lot more money, I realize now but, well, you know the story. I haven't changed my habits much. It's pretty hard to change my old habits, and I guess my basic personality, when it comes to money and cooking and such. I should be thrifty and watching every penny. I would not be happy doing that. What if I tried to get another loan for, say, $5,000? Would it be so terrible if I were $9,000 in debt at the end of the trip? Would that be a tragedy? No, I don't think so. When I start working again (at the end of the trip), at probably two jobs again, how long will it take to pay off $7,000? I get another crummy apartment and pay everybody off at two or four hundred dollars a month until I'm out of debt. You might be cringing at the thought of all this debt. You might be getting frustrated with me and want to scream, WHY DON'T YOU JUST CHANGE YOUR WAYS!! I don't think it'll happen in the near future. How much I will owe at the end of this trip is anybody's guess. Perhaps you should make a guess now and see how close you get.

I'm getting ready to leave once again. I will be staying with Genevieve's parents in Dartmouth, Nova Scotia, which is about a three hour ride from here. I give Genevieve a big hug, as she is going swimming. I will be leaving in half an hour. Again she and her room-mates made me feel welcome.

I'm riding through Antigonish for the last time and I'm on my way to Dartmouth when I spot Genevieve and Burgundy walking along the street towards me. I stop. Genevieve takes a picture of me in front of the town sign welcoming people to Antigonish. I wish them luck on the opening night of the Agatha Christie play they are both appearing in. We say our goodbyes and I leave.

I'm approaching Sherbrooke, Nova Scotia. I decide to drive around a bit in Sherbrooke. I drive around for a minute or two and then spot a girl in a period costume. Behind her there is what looks like a village. I stop and talk to her. She tells me that the village behind her is the

Historic Sherbrooke Village. I park my bike and walk back to the same girl. I pay six dollars and she offers to store away my helmet in the little office behind her. She has beautiful red hair and a retainer on her teeth. Why did I mention that? I don't know. Anyway, it was nice of her to put my helmet inside for me. She gives me a map of the village.

There are thirty-three historic buildings here. A wealthy family of the village once owned the first house I walk into. They lived there in the 1890s. Inside the house it has the furnishings and decor of the period. I cross the street and go into the jailhouse. It really is a house. The jailer and his family lived in the house as well. The cell downstairs (street level) has bars on the door. I go upstairs and there is a cell with no bars. I ask the guide of the house why that is. The cell with bars downstairs is for the men, the cell upstairs with no bars is for the women. Apparently, if a man was in debt and could not pay, they would put his wife in jail until he could clear his debt. The first thought that came to me was what if he didn't like his wife or was out-and-out lazy? She could be in there a long time. What a weird law.

I then go to the courthouse, telephone exchange, print shop, blacksmith shop, etc., etc. What a great job they have done on this village to create a certain feeling and time. I don't mean that the buildings aren't authentic, they are, there's nothing fake about this place. It's the Real McCoy, alright. The scary part is that I almost kept on going without stopping in Sherbrooke. If you're ever in Nova Scotia, go and see this place because it is absolutely worth it. I leave. I get on the old bike and turn on to the main road. I'm just outside Sherbrooke when I see an old friend approaching me, and his name is Mr. Rainstorm.

I pull into Dartmouth around dinnertime. With the help of a map that Genevieve gave me I find her parents' house. I take off my rain gear before knocking on the door. I don't want them to think I'm some kind of demented fisherman on a motorcycle. Which, unfortunately, is how I look. Genevieve's parents, Mr. and Mrs. Steele, receive me warmly. We have chicken and pasta for dinner and it's delicious. After dinner they take me on a sightseeing tour of Dartmouth and then we head to

Halifax, which is not too far. As we drive along they point out some of the beautiful old homes and universities which Halifax seems to have a lot of. I have two people to contact while I'm here—a friend of Genevieve's named Julia and a friend of Pam Reid, Pitsy. I called them both earlier but did not reach them personally.

We pull into the driveway and go inside. There's a message that Pitsy called! I'll call her tomorrow.

June 24

I wake up refreshed and looking forward to getting some errands done. I have some banking to do and some pictures that need developing.

I arrive back at the Steele's residence. I call Pitsy and Julia and leave messages for them to call me. Genevieve's brother drops by for lunch. We have a few laughs about how many Tim Hortons Donut shops there are out east. I tell him that, as far as I can tell, I have seen a Tim Hortons in practically every city and town so far.

It's later on in the day. I get a call from Julia. We agree to meet in a bar downtown, downtown Halifax that is. It won't be too awkward because I have met Julia a couple of times already when she was in Toronto.

It's eight o'clock. I walk outside to clean up my bike. A few minutes later I look up into the sky to see the black clouds rolling in. It starts to rain before long and then it quickly turns into hail. The hailstones are a little bit smaller than mothballs, but not much. Mr. and Mrs. Steele offer to give me a ride downtown, which I accept gladly. They drop me off near the bar and I walk around a bit to put in a little time.

I'm not sitting at the bar too long when Julia comes in. She introduces me to her friends. We have a good time telling jokes and stories. Julia and her friends are quite humorous. After a while we leave. Julia helps me get a taxi. I bid her farewell.

99

Part 12 *Leaving the Country, Briefly*

June 25

I wake up at a reasonable time. I'm itching to get back on the road. Now when I stay in a place for a few days I start to get restless. I will go to Lunenburg, Nova Scotia first and then to Yarmouth. The ferry from Yarmouth leaves at 4:30 but you have to be there an hour early. I need to do some errands before I leave.

After getting totally and utterly lost doing those errands, I go back to Genevieve's parents' house to leave a note thanking them for letting me stay in their house. They were the perfect hosts. I leave the Steele household a lot later than I intended.

The drive to Lunenburg is uneventful. I pull up to an information centre just outside the town proper. I ask the woman about the old homes in Lunenburg that I heard so much about. I tell her I have to be in Yarmouth by 3:30. She regretfully tells me I won't have time to see the homes and make the ferry. I thank her and leave. I will drive around and see the old houses and some of the distinct architecture. I go downtown. The homes are pretty amazing, but I feel that I'm running out of time. I take a few pictures. I stop and get gas and also to ask for directions, then leave.

I'm about ten minutes out when I realize that my almost brand new sunglasses were on my seat when I left the gas station. I don't have enough time to turn back and, besides, they've probably been run over about fifty times by now. Oh well. I really have no time for deviations. I have to go or I'll miss the ferry.

It's almost three o'clock now (about 80 kilometres to go) when I realize I have made a wrong turn somewhere. I stop and ask a couple of guys if I'm on the wrong road. Figures. They advise me to stay on this road because it will eventually connect with the one I was on originally. It's now 3:13. I have sixty kilometres to go. I don't think I'm going to make it. I start driving a little crazy at this point. I take the turns a little too fast; on the straight parts (or straightaways) of the road I'm going way too fast. I'm going speeds and taking chances that are quite unlike me. I reach the speed of 160 km per hour, the fastest I have ever gone on my motorcycle. Not only dangerous but plain old stupid. A maniac has taken over my normal personality. I ease off the throttle slightly to 140 kph. Still 40 kilometres over the speed limit. I tell myself that if I can get to the ferry by four o'clock they might let me in.

It's almost four o'clock now and my fuel light is on. Oh, perfect. It's now five past four and I see the ferry terminal and parking lot and there are no cars in sight. I go to the ticket booth. She asks if I have a reservation. I tell her that I do and, to my relief she starts to print up my ticket. I'm directed toward the gate just in time to see three or four motorcycles drive into the belly of the boat. I catch up and follow them to our special parking area. We spend a few minutes or so strapping down our bikes and then, one by one, go upstairs to the main deck.

I spend my time eating and reading and not much else. When I look out the windows there is nothing to see but darkness. It occurs to me that this is my fifth ferry ride since the start of my trip. It takes around six hours for the ferry to reach the state of Maine. It will be approximately eleven o'clock when we get to Maine. I hope there is a gas station open.

Without further incident we dock in Maine. My fellow motorcyclists and I are not to be the first off the boat. Another unusual aspect of this landing is that I will have to go through United States customs.

After leaving the ferry I now wait my turn in line to be admitted into the U.S.A. After twenty minutes I ride up toward the officer and my helmet falls off my handlebar. The officer starts to chase after it and finally catches it. How do you like me so far? I apologize to the officer and thank him for retrieving my helmet. He asks me some routine questions and I'm allowed to go. I ask a younger customs worker if there are any gas stations around. He gives me directions and I leave. I begin following his directions but can't seem to find the street he was talking about. Instead, I try and find a motel because WELL SURPRISE, SURPRISE, it has started to rain. I find the gas station. I continue my search for a hotel or motel; they are all booked solid. Maybe I should try and drive to Bangor, Maine now instead of tomorrow. It starts to really pour now. I can barely see the lines on the road. I spot a motel to my right. I go in and get the last room.

June 26

I step out of my motel room and—hey, the weather's not bad. Partly sunny. I'll take it. Well it's off to Bangor, Maine to see that author's house.

The sun is fully out now as I drive among the trees, their shadows partly covering the road. Since my speedometer is in kilometres, I don't know how fast I'm supposed to go. I follow the signs to Bangor and I arrive there without getting lost. The first order of business is to get some breakfast.

I'm sitting in a tiny restaurant waiting for my breakfast when the waitress asks if I'd like to read a newspaper while I wait. I would, I tell her. On the front page is a picture of Jacques Cousteau and, oh my god, he's dead. How sad. The great man is gone. How I loved his television specials and his gentle voice. He was one of the great explorers of the world. I had hoped one day that somehow, somewhere I would be able to meet him. I don't know what I would have said; perhaps to shake his hand would have been enough. As you may remember, my friend Kelli painted THE SPIRIT OF COUSTEAU on my gas tank. Never again will I look at those words as before. We have lost one of the truly great men of the 20th century.

With breakfast over with, I now try and find a store I passed in downtown Bangor that had a picture of the author on it hanging outside flapping in the breeze. I find the store quickly enough and park around the corner. I walk in and look around a bit and ask the lady behind the counter a few questions. She is extremely helpful, particularly when I ask her how to find the author's house. My next order of business (hardly business) is to call my friend Dawn Murphy and tell her I'm in her favourite author's town. I find a phone booth and call her. She's glad to hear from me and is envious that I'm here. I don't tell her I bought her a T-shirt—I'll keep that as a surprise. We chat for a few more minutes and hang up.

Well now comes the time to find his house. With the directions given to me by the woman in the store I find it easily enough. I have seen pictures of it before so it wasn't hard to spot. It's a beautiful (Victorian?) mansion. It's red with nice big trees out front. The iron fence surrounding the house is just as impressive, custom-made for him by a Canadian, I believe. It has bats and cats worked into the design. I take a few pictures and leave. I feel I have intruded enough, although I stand across the street the whole time, the time spent there being about five minutes. I'll head back to the store now and buy a few postcards.

I leave Bangor after being hopelessly lost for around a half an hour trying to find the photo-developing store where I left my film. My ability to get lost even in a relatively small town is absolutely limitless. Was I born with no sense of direction? I have pretty much made up my mind that I'll try and get as far as Vermont today.

After a few hours I'm in New Hampshire. It shocks me every time I see a person on a motorcycle without a helmet on. I encounter both men and women riding with just sunglasses and sometimes a bandana and nothing else. I give them the wave, but few return it, probably because I'm not only wearing a helmet but a full-faced one at that.

I pull into St. Johnsbury, Vermont and it's around three o'clock in the afternoon. I find a motel that is clean and relatively cheap at $35 U.S. I ask the desk clerk and owner where I can get something to eat. He tells of a couple of good places, we chat about old cars (there's a 1940s sedan parked in front of the office) and I leave. I immediately am lost trying to find the restaurant. Sheepishly, I go back and ask him where the restaurant is again. Good-humouredly he tells me again. I start out again and find it.

After my dinner I hop on my bike and decide to take a look at the rest of St. Johnsbury. I'm driving along and I spot a movie theatre where *Batman and Robin* is playing. I turn right at the top of a hill and look to my right. It is a sight to behold: a row of what I think are houses built in the 1800s. One in particular catches my eye. The house is set far back from the street.

I'll go back to the motel now that I've seen most of St. Johnsbury.

I'm back at the motel now. There is a stream running right behind my room a few yards or so from my back door. I'll rest for a while and then go see the movie.

Part 13 *The Cross-Canada Tour Begins!*

June 27

After breakfast I go to the part of town where I saw those old homes. I take a few pictures and I notice that one of the bigger houses is for sale. If I had that kind of money, I would have bought it.

I'm packing my bike back at the motel. There's a young woman painting the lines in the parking lot. I strike up a conversation with her. She's from a lot bigger place than St. Johnsbury, Vermont, I believe. I ask if it was hard to adjust to a small town. She says that it is a big adjustment. I tell her that (or suggest that), "It must be tough filling your time and finding a job." I immediately regret saying the job part. She points to what she's doing and her gesture implies, "No kidding. Would I be doing this if there were a lot of jobs?" She doesn't do it in a mean way, though. She has a couple of kids, so it must be tough. I wish her good luck and leave.

I take Highway 5 north. Then onto 91. I go to the United States-Canada border. I'm asked routine questions and am allowed back into Canada. Soon I will be on fairly familiar roads and highways.

I'm in Montreal now near the place I camped a little less than a month ago. I pull in for some gas. After a slight communication problem with the gas attendant, I have a full tank again. I pull back onto the road. I'm only riding a few minutes when I realize I left my spare pair of Ray Bans on my seat, then pulled out of the gas station. Well, there goes another pair of sunglasses. Exactly how I lost the first pair.

A few hours later now and I'm in Nepean, Ottawa, riding up Dave Reid's driveway. Dave, Pam, and Erica aren't home. They weren't expecting me anyway. I'm comfortably sitting in the back yard when they come home around ten minutes later. They invite me to stay for four or five days even though they are expecting Dave's brother and his family soon. I ask them if they are sure and they say yes, indeed. Their kind gesture is typical of people I have met from the East Coast of Canada.

July 1

Today is Canada's 130th birthday. I have spent the last few days resting and relaxing. At this moment Dave, Pam, Erica and Dave's brother Steve's family—his wife, Mitch and their two boys, Michael and Dillon—and I are sitting on the grass. Along with thousands of others we are waiting for the Canada Day fireworks to start. Since we are in the nation's capital (Ottawa), I'm hoping that the fireworks will be good. It is an incredibly muggy and hot July 1st. The fireworks begin and I'm not disappointed. You could say the fireworks make up for the heat, which is a strange way to put it, but it's true. They are the best I have ever seen. There is one that shoots up, and then spreads out like a willow tree. It overwhelms me with its size and beauty. An immense golden willow in the sky. Like all the fireworks shows I have seen, it ends with a barrage of big booms, colour, and sparkling light. As we all begin to leave the grassy area, the smoke and the smell of smoke linger in the air.

July 3

I say goodbye to the two Reid families. I suppose at times Dave and Pam must have felt overwhelmed with five guests staying in their house. If they did, it didn't show. I could have stayed another day but decided it was time to go. I will visit my friend Jackie Hadley in

Sterling, Ontario next. I will be staying with either her parents or her grandparents; I can't remember which ones. Right now, though, I'm going to try and find the Canadian War Museum.

After being lost for an hour I finally arrive at the museum. I park my bike under the National Art Gallery. I have no intention of seeing the art gallery. I couldn't handle any modern art right now. The first almost blank canvas I saw with one coloured dot in the middle, or something like that, would drive me away. If I found out how much it cost, it would just piss me off.

I walk to the front of the war museum and see the sights. There are armoured vehicles, a canteen set-up, tanks, and some people demonstrating how some of the things work and answering questions. I go inside. One of the workers kindly lets me store my helmet and backpack. I stroll through the First World War section and look at the various weaponry, uniforms, medals, and stories of some of the heroes of that particular war. Next I make a beeline to the World War II exhibit. I'm more interested in the Second World War because of the movies I've seen, books I've read and veterans I've talked to. I have read four or five books on some of the escapes made by the allied prisoners. I approach an old Mercedes-Benz. Adolph Hitler once used this particular car. There is a picture of Hitler sitting in the passenger seat (behind the driver) in this car. I look at the passenger seat again, knowing that one of the most evil men in the history of mankind sat there. It's a strange feeling that I can't describe. (NO KIDDING, DAN, REALLY!!?) Anyway, after looking around some more I go to the gift shops. I look around a bit and decide that there isn't anything I can't live without. I'll leave now.

I don't know how much more of this I can take! I'm utterly lost again. How useless can I get? (I heard that!!) I've been trying to find the friggin' highway for an hour now.

Finally! Jeez. Well I'm back on the Highway 401 heading west towards Belleville, Ontario. There's not much to see on the old 401. It's still quite warm, although not as bad as the last couple of days. To a certain degree (ba-boom-bing), it's always a little cooler on the motorcycle.

It starts to rain as I arrive in Belleville. I stop under a carport at an abandoned gas station. It starts to rain quite hard as I rummage around my stuff looking for Jackie Hadley's hand-drawn map. She's appearing in a 1930s-style musical, as I recall, in her hometown of Sterling. I find the map. After studying it a few minutes, I realize I have taken the wrong turn-off. I put on my rain gear and head for Sterling.

After finding the right turn-off, it's not long before I find myself in the small town of Sterling. Just to make sure, I stop and re-check her map. So far, so good. Now all I have to do is find the theatre where she's appearing. I'm not on the road two minutes when I spot it on my left. I pull in front. All right! The show is already up and running (you know what I mean). It's six p.m. and the show starts at eight. My timing is almost perfect. Instead of calling her parents I might as well wait here and surprise her. I start talking to a guy outside the theatre. It just so happens he works at the theatre and Jackie will probably arrive around seven o'clock. I thank him for the info, buy a ticket for the show and go for a coffee.

It's seven o'clock now and I'm sitting outside at the front of the theatre. After waiting fifteen minutes, it occurs to me that Jackie will probably go in the back anyway. I'll go get something to eat, then come and see the show. I enter the theatre and leave word at the box office that I'm here and could they just pass that information along. I'll see her after the show.

The show was a lot of fun. They did songs and dances and jokes from (I believe) the 1930s and were all very good. Jackie is an excellent dancer and a strong singer.

I meet Jackie after the show and we briefly catch up on what's been happening in the last couple of months. There's a reception upstairs. We go up. There's lots of food and stuff. Jackie, of course, knows a lot of people because she grew up in Sterling. After the reception Jackie gives me a small tour of the backstage. For some bizarre reason there used to be prisoner cells down near the dressing rooms. I think the building once served as a community hall and was built in 1927. She calls her grandparents and asks if I can stay the night.

I'm following Jackie to the house. It's not long before I'm parked in her grandparents' driveway. The house is a beautiful older home with a nice porch. Jackie tells me the house and the farm are 125 years old. I meet her grandparents, Jeanette and Glen Morrow. I thank them for accepting me as a guest at such a late hour. The house is like the one I would have in my dreams. Large rooms, beautiful wood staircase, great furniture, and lots of large rooms upstairs on the second floor. Jackie shows me the room I'm to sleep in. I'm in the house ten minutes and I love it already.

July 4

I wake up at 7:30 a.m. and go downstairs. Jackie's grandfather Glen is up already and sitting in the kitchen, as she predicted he would be. He owns a farm, after all, and although he is no longer a dairy farmer, he still gets up really early. I join him at the table. He offers to make me breakfast but I don't want him to go to all that trouble, so I just ask for coffee and toast. We talk about all kinds of things. He tells me of some of the places he travelled to with his wife in a motorhome. Although Glen is 75 years old, he could pass for someone 60 or 65. He takes me on a mini tour of the main rooms in the house. There are framed letters on the wall from Canada's highest-ranking politicians congratulating them for having a farm in the same family for the last 123 years. He shows me photographs of his children, including a picture of one of his sons who had passed away. I could see by his eyes and his voice that it still hurt and that he still loved his son very much.

A few hours later now and Jackie and I are driving through town. We drive past some old homes on what seems to be the main street of Sterling. We go to a dairy and buy a milkshake for a buck and some curds. I had never tasted curds before but I like them, despite a kind of rubbery texture.

We drive back to the farm. I ask Jackie if she could give me a tour of the grounds. She agrees and we go to one of the barns and then to the other dairy barn. Some of the equipment for the dairy operation is still here. Next we go outside. What a place this must have been (and still is) for Jackie and her family to grow up near. With a creek running through the property, the open fields and lots of other children to play with, it sounds like an idyllic place to play as a child. Jackie tells me there was always something to do. They could play in the barns, swim or fish in the creek or just play and run around on acres and acres of land.

Back in the house Jackie and I relax. She tells me that her grand-parents have offered to let me stay another night. It is very tempting, but I don't think I will. I'm getting to a point now where I don't like hanging around too long in one place, although I spend the next two hours hemming and hawing about maybe staying for one more day. The Morrows' house is the kind of place you could stay for a long time and not get bored.

Jackie and her grandparents are standing on the porch to see me off. I thank them and as I pull out of the driveway I give a last wave goodbye. My next stop will be Algonquin Provincial Park. As I ride on highway 62 north there are huge black clouds on the horizon. Does this surprise me? Does it surprise you? It shouldn't. A little later on it starts spitting rain. There is a car RIGHT behind me and passes a little too close for comfort. I wave to the driver and open and close my fingers as if to say TOO DAMN CLOSE, BUDDY, but he pays no attention.

I pull into Algonquin Park. I park the bike and check the weather chart. According to the chart, it calls for showers. I talk to one of the Park Rangers anyway, who says it might not rain. It takes me a milli-second to decide that I'll get a motel.

July 5

It's beautiful this morning. I call my mother and tell her to put $500 into my account. I don't think I'll camp in the park today, or any day for that matter. It's such a nice day. I feel like riding a lot of miles today. I'll drive as far as I can. I intend to make the most of one of the few nice days I've had.

I'm about twenty kilometres from North Bay and it occurs to me that they had to blast through a lot of rock to make the Trans-Canada Highway. I have a contact name in North Bay but I decide not to use it. For some reason that I can't justify, I just want to keep going.

I'm in North Bay now and I had no idea how big it would be. There are lots of old motels. I'm basically just paying attention to keep from getting lost. I will continue on to Sault Ste. Marie. It will probably take most of the day.

As I pull into Sudbury, Ontario I have one thing I want to see. It's a huge nickel that I've been hearing about all my life. A giant replica of a Canadian five-cent-piece. Again I thought that Sudbury (like North Bay) would be a helluva lot smaller. Well, I'm not in downtown Sudbury twenty minutes (trying to find the big nickel) and I'm hopelessly lost. What happened to highway 17? I stop at a gas station and ask for directions. I pull away from the station feeling a lot better now that I have an idea where I'm going. That feeling evaporates almost immediately, as I'm lost again. At this point I couldn't care less about the nickel, I JUST WANNA GET OUTTA HERE! I see the signs that will direct me back onto the highway. As I go down the ramp to get to the highway, there's a bright shining object back and to my left. It's the friggin' nickel.

I pass by more lakes, trees and small towns. My right wrist is starting to get sore because of the throttle's constant need to be cranked for highway speeds.

I'm not far from Sault Ste. Marie and I have virtually no sense of body temperature. So perfect is the combination of what I'm wearing and the current temperature, I'm neither hot nor cold. I'm exactly in the middle. The last couple of hours the sun has been setting in front of me.

I pull into Sault Ste. Marie around eight o'clock and grab a motel.

July 6

I step out of my motel room and look up into black and grey sky. I put my rain gear on for the morning's ride. By the time I'm on the road

111

it's raining. Here I come, Thunder Bay. I pass a sign informing me it is 696 kilometres to Thunder Bay. Not that I know how far that is in terms of miles, but I do have a pretty good idea that it isn't exactly across the street. That distance will probably take the whole day. It's twenty minutes later now and I'm at the side of the road putting on my thick leather gloves. I can see my breath as I do this. I pull back onto the road to again fight the rain and the cold. It reminds me that I did this exact same thing a month ago in New Brunswick. A few minutes later I am again stopped by the side of the road to put on a second pair of gloves.

My hand begins to get sore as I struggle with the throttle. It's hard to keep a grip on it. It's really foggy now and I can't see too far ahead of me. This is when riding a motorcycle gets a little scary for me. It's the combination of rain, fog, poor visibility, and a steamed-up face shield that makes a motorcyclist think of his or her mortality. I click on my hazard lights to let the cars behind me know that all is not well in motorcycle land. Some of the drivers back off when I do this, others are either ignorant of my plight or simply don't care.

The fog lifts after a while but it's still cold and my hands are getting numb. I suddenly remember a silver waterproof pullover in a small zippered pocket at the top of my gloves. I get on the shoulder yet again to make the adjustment. It's designed (I believe) to keep the hands drier and warmer.

It's a little later now and the glove pullover is working to keep my hands a little warmer and drier. The only problem is that, with two pairs of gloves and the pullover, it is a huge effort now to keep the throttle cranked. My hand is slipping a lot. I'm having trouble keeping to the speed limit. I push on the throttle to try and keep it in place. This works to a certain extent but it takes a lot of energy. I'm getting tired. I stop to get gas and warm my hands. I will try and stop every hundred kilometres or so to get warm. At the halfway point to Thunder Bay I stop in Wawa. I have lunch and am back on the road by two.

It's three hours later now and I'm sitting in the gas station parking area doing nothing but warming my hands. Three hours of cold weather and sporadic rain. For two minutes I sit and do nothing. I'm exhausted. I will go no further. I'm in Terrace Bay. I'm still 270 kilometres away from Thunder Bay. I'll grab a motel and go at it again tomorrow.

July 7

It's cold but clear this morning. I put on the cold weather outfit. I will again wear the double gloves. My wrist hurts a little from yesterday. I once strained some tendons in my wrist and forearm working as a parcel-sorter. I believe I'm hurting in those same spots now. I pull out of the hotel parking lot. What a difference the sun makes even though it's still cold. I sing a song out loud that I heard on television last night. I finish my burst of song and laugh out loud. Am I cracking up? Perhaps.

I'm about an hour outside Terrace Bay. I turn around a corner and up ahead I see a construction site. To my right is about a five-storey-high rock face. Something catches my eye as I slow down for the construction crew. I look up to see a bald eagle soaring about halfway up the rock and fifteen or twenty feet from the surface of it. There's no mistaking the white head and tail from this distance. I'm still moving and trying to look up and behind me at the same time. Just an incredible sight.

I'm only a few kilometres outside of Thunder Bay (the downtown part anyway) when I see a sign that says Terry Fox Scenic Lookout. For those of you who don't know who Terry Fox is, I'll tell you. Few Canadians over ten years old in 1980 will ever forget watching the newscasts of Terry jogging with one good leg and one partial leg, which he lost due to cancer. To attempt to run the entire width of Canada is a huge undertaking, let alone for someone who is partially disabled. He inspired our nation and the people of other nations as well. He helped raise millions of dollars for cancer research. Unfortunately, he never made it across Canada and died not too long after his attempt ended in Thunder Bay, Ontario, after running 3,339 miles. He showed us what determination and sheer guts can accomplish. A true hero.

113

I leave the lookout and start in towards Thunder Bay proper. I'm in the downtown part now, just kind of riding around. I see an older theatre called The Paramount. I stop and take a picture of it and another theatre close by.

I'm now lost in Thunder Bay. I could have sworn that I took a simple route to get here and it would be a matter of going back the same way. After a while I give up trying to find the Trans-Canada Highway and look for Highway 102—at least it's heading west. I pull off the road for a consultation with my map. What a laugh that is. Well, according to the map, the road I'm on now will connect me with the Trans-Canada.

I'm sitting in a traffic jam of sorts because of construction up ahead. Whenever I stop now I immediately rest my right hand. There's a slight burning above my wrist towards my elbow. It has to be a tendon, I'm almost sure of that now. It is indeed the same sore spot I injured ten years ago. I'm given the signal to proceed. In the loose gravel and dirt it's a little tricky keeping the bike from sliding around. They wet the dirt to keep the dust down. It works, but now my legs and the bike have a lot of mud on them.

At times the scenery is breathtaking. The little waterfalls that come out of the hills and mountains are especially good. There are a lot of small bodies of water with little islands in the middle that seem almost at the same level as the usually calm water. As I get closer to Kenora I get the sense that I'm gradually coming down from the higher levels of the mountains. A levelling out is beginning to happen.

I pull into Kenora and I'm getting tired. My wrist is still burning and I have a slight headache. I start looking for a motel. As I drive through Kenora I can't decide on a motel. Before I know it, I'm back on the highway heading towards Winnipeg, which is in the province of Manitoba. I guess it won't be too long before I hit the border dividing Ontario and Manitoba. It will take an hour and a half to get there. I promise myself at this point that if I go all the way to Winnipeg I'll take a day of rest tomorrow. I have to give my wrist a break from the constant strain of maintaining highway speeds. I have pushed myself too hard the last couple of days. My lower back is pretty sore now and I can feel every bump as I cross the Ontario/Manitoba border. After a small bend, the highway is straight and flat. It's straight for as far as my vision will let me see the road; it seems to go on forever.

I stop for gas. It starts to rain. Once on the road again there's another small bend and it again straightens out. A long black line that disappears into the horizon. It's been flat and straight without change, it seems, for the last hour or so.

I'm approximately 30 kilometres outside of Winnipeg and the land has turned (if that's possible) even flatter. It's strange after riding in all those mountains, hills and twisty roads of only two or three hours ago. I spot a motel. I book a room for two nights. At some point I rode into a different time zone. I've ridden almost (except for gas and stuff) from 9:30 a.m. to 9:00 p.m. Why? I'll tell ya why. Because I'm nuts, that's why. I don't know what comes over me sometimes. I can tell ya this much, though. I have definitely done something to the tendons or muscles in my forearm. It's burning quite nicely now.

Part 14

Finally! Out of Ontario and Officially in Western Canada!

July 9

I spent yesterday doing nothing but sitting around. I'm not usually the type of person who can sit around and do nothing. Today is clear and warm. I wear my long johns just in case, though. I get back on the Trans-Canada and it looks, well, straight and flat. I pretty much just ride in the middle of my lane and point the bike straight ahead. It gives me a chance to look around, though, at the vast plains. The twists and turns are beginning now around Brandon, Manitoba.

I'm about 40 kilometres from Regina, Saskatchewan. New province, new time zone. One hour back. In the distance I can see a storm on the left and right of the road. The sun is shining in the middle onto the highway. I'm fortunately still headed into the centre of the storm. The eye, if you will. It's really interesting to watch a storm from such a long distance away. Lightning shoots down from clouds to destinations unknown. I'm heading toward the very middle of the storm now. There's an immense dark cloud directly over me. It's spitting rain now but nothing compared to what I see off to my left. As I pass the YOU-ARE-NOW-IN-REGINA-type sign, I spot a motel off to my left as it starts to rain even harder.

July 10

I walk out of the motel to see a whole mess of motorcyclists (around 5) parked near mine. They are from Simcoe, Ontario. As I start a conversation with them, the clouds are rolling in. I tell them I'm heading west to British Columbia. They respond by telling me to get my rain gear ready because it rained every day they were there. I didn't ask how long that was. I don't want to know. I pack up, wish them good luck, and leave.

I've been on the road about an hour now and, quite frankly, I'm bored. I can't even muster enough enthusiasm to do the speed limit. What do I think about, hour upon hour? You may well ask. I think about anything and everything. I think about old relationships, why some women dumped me and so on. The trip, the book. I sing a lot of songs in my head. I wonder sometimes if I'm cracking up. I think about what might happen if I had an accident or maybe that someone will steal my bike at night. I think about how lucky I am to be doing this trip at all. I'm free to pretty much do whatever comes to mind in terms of changing the trip. All that sort of stuff.

I arrive in Saskatoon and grab a coffee and a bagel. I'm still in the province of Saskatchewan. I think from here, I'll go straight to Edmonton in the province of Alberta. I have a contact there. He is a friend of my brother's and the rest of the family as well. He is Ian Russell. He and his wife recently had a child. I get back on the bike and resume the journey. The scenery is pretty much the same, as far as I am concerned. I stop and take a picture of some grain elevators, which are the symbol of the Canadian prairies. I'm in a bit of a melancholy funk. Is it me or is it the landscape?

I enter the province of Alberta at around four o'clock in the afternoon. The speed limit is ten kilometres higher here, (110). I seem to be pretty much out of my funk.

About an hour-and-a-half into Alberta, it starts to rain. I pull off the highway to put my rain gear on. Rain, rain, go away, and come back some other millennium. I'm almost in Edmonton now. To my left I see a small herd of buffalo. They are behind a fence so they aren't wild—some kind of park. I'm in Edmonton now, on the phone trying to get a hold of Ian Russell. I leave a message on his machine, telling him that I'm in town.

I have just spent the last hour and three-quarters being lost. It's a talent, really. I check into a hotel. I call Ian again. It turns out he is in Prince George, British Columbia. The same place I'll be visiting in two weeks or so.

July 11

It's sunny this morning. I'm taking the cover off my bike. Despite the sun, I can see my breath. It's pretty cool for July 11th. As I drive to the monstrous West Edmonton Mall, I can see the clouds not too far off in the distance. They are grey but are turning black.

Well here I am in the parking lot of the West Edmonton Mall. Normally I couldn't care less about a mall, really, but I've been hearing and reading about this mall for at least ten years. This is supposed to be the mall to end all malls. I walk into one of the entrances.

A little further on I can see a ship. Hey, it's pretty big, too. Looks like a pirate ship.

In another pool there are some dolphins. I walk a little farther and I come across a glass observation area. Below is an ice rink. Apparently, on certain days you can see the Edmonton Oilers hockey team practise here. I walk around a bit more and see a huge wave pool. This place is just so massive it boggles the mind. Another section looks like a re-creation of old New Orleans. I explore a little more and leave.

I'm in the mall parking lot preparing to leave. I put on my raincoat. As I pull back onto the highway, it starts to rain. You must be sick of reading about this, but I pull off the highway to put on rain pants and heavy gloves. I'm sorry that you have to read about the rain over and over again. I'm getting tired of the rain. It has plagued me practically the whole trip. I feel it is necessary to tell you about the weather. I think it's important because it is affecting me mentally. Riding in the rain sucks most of the time. Riding in it almost every day really, really sucks.

Later on that afternoon (here we go again) it's raining harder and it's getting cold. I'm freezing. My hands and feet are especially cold. I pull into a town called Edson. I go to a restaurant and have a bowl of soup. It makes me feel a little better, although I have one of those chills that go right to the bone.

Back on the highway now and it's raining even harder, if that's freakin' possible. I'm so disgusted with this weather. I will not make it to Jasper today. I'm becoming a little unhinged now. I want to scream inside my helmet! When my feet and hands are this cold, to the point where they hurt, I find it difficult to think straight. I can barely see, such is the strength of the downpour, and my helmet visor keeps fogging up. I'm involuntarily shivering now and all I can think about is getting a motel and taking a hot bath. I'm heading for Hinton, Alberta, which I believe is another half hour away. Another half hour of this and my sanity will surely slip a notch or two. It's only a few minutes later and Oh YESSS! There is the sign for Hinton. I was way off my estimate of a half hour. I was never so happy to be wrong.

I can barely sign my name at the motel, as my hand just doesn't want to function. A woman behind me tells me she pulled off the road because it was hailing. She came from the same direction I did. She was not on a motorcycle. Perhaps it started to hail just after I got off the highway. It must have. I would have known if it were hailing, wouldn't I?

July 12

What can I say? The clouds are rolling in at seven in the morning. As I walk toward the restaurant from my motel I stop and look at the clouds and—hey, wait a minute! There are mountains among those clouds and, man, are they BIG. Guess what direction I'm going after breakfast! That's right, I'll be going straight to those huge mountains surrounded by clouds.

After clothing myself with as much warm clothing as possible, I get on the old bike and get some gas. As I ride toward the mountains now, I realize they aren't like the ones I've seen so far, where I couldn't tell if they were mountains or giant hills. These look like the Mt. Everest kind.

I arrive at the entrance of Jasper Park and pay five dollars. I pull away from the booth and turn the first corner. Now I see three wild horses (I think they are) by the side of the road. There are no fences around them, no people, and they don't have saddles on their backs. Five minutes later and I see two cars pulled off to the side of the road. As I get closer one of the cars pulls back onto the road. I get closer and, oh my god, there's a moose, and a lady not fifteen feet away taking its picture. I don't think it's a mature moose (like I'm an expert) because it doesn't look that big and I know (hey, I've seen pictures) that they get a lot bigger. The best part is that I don't have any FRIGGIN' FILM IN MY CAMERA! Despite the rain and the cold, this is a great start. Real moose. YA-HOO! It's all I can do to keep the bike on the road, with the animal-sightings and my habit of looking up at the mountains instead of where I'm going.

I pull into the town of Jasper and it's quite busy. People are every-where. There are motorcycles, motorhomes, bicycles, campers, and people walking with big backpacks on. It feels like everybody is about to go on a great adventure. I call my mother and tell her I'm alive and well. After that, I buy some rubber gloves that are bright orange and some smaller cotton gloves to fit inside. I should have done this a couple of thousand miles ago. A fellow motorcyclist tells me about a big bike rally.

I'm entering the information centre for the park with the intention of asking about the rally. I'm in a small lineup and thought I heard the counter worker say something about snow. No, I must have heard wrong. See, she couldn't have said snow because it's FREAKIN' JULY 12th! It's my turn now and I ask if I overheard correctly.

"You heard correctly. We have reports that it's snowing in parts of the park between here and Lake Louise." She tells me a specific spot, but I instantly forget what it is. She notices the motorcycle helmet in my hand and says, "The snow isn't staying on the ground, but it might soon."

"Is there a different route I can take to Lake Louise to avoid the snow?" "No. I might recommend you stay in town for a couple of days and wait 'til it clears up a bit." I thank her for the help and leave. Will I do the smart thing and wait here for a day or two while the bad weather's in the park? Of course not. I'll take my chances and ride through the mountains.

I'm about halfway to Lake Louise and there's no sign of snow yet. Just one incredible mountain after another. I pull off the road to look at a glacier between two mountains. I can see cars heading down to the bottom of the glacier a couple of hundred yards ahead of me. I look at the glacier again and realize those little black dots that are moving up the glacier are people. I want to do that too.

I follow the road down to the base of the glacier. I park the bike and start to climb. I leave my knapsack on, for some reason. My rain gear as well. You have to climb a hundred or so feet to get onto the glacier. A man asks me if I'm going climbing. No. I stop just short of the glacier to sit on a cement block. I'm huffing and puffing. I'm sitting, trying to catch my breath, when a woman approaches me and asks if I'm on "foolish people" patrol. She has mistaken me for some kind of rescue mountain ranger kind of guy. "No," I reply. I get up and walk the last few feet to step onto an honest to goodness glacier. WHA-HOO!

I make it to the town of Lake Louise at around three o'clock. I get some gas and trot over to the nearest restaurant.

I arrive at the legendary Lake Louise and, as expected, it's kind of crowded. It is worth it, though. Mountains surround the green lake. It's kind of weird when you finally see something you've heard about and seen pictures of all of your life. There's a fancy hotel there that

121

probably starts at 500 bucks a night. I have my picture taken. I finally got some film. I look at it for a few more minutes. Well, time to go. As you'll notice, I don't linger much. I will push on into the province of British Columbia. That will be my ninth and final province. Which, if you include my home province of Ontario, will make it ten provinces, total. I will probably stay in Golden, B.C. tonight.

I'm about five kilometres outside of Golden when the traffic slows down, then comes to a halt. There's a person up ahead with a stop sign. Probably more construction. We're moving now and as I get closer to the sign-bearer I see the reason for the slowdown. There is a big eighteen-wheeler truck lying on its side in the ditch. We get moving again and I pass the truck. The section of the road the cars and I are on is a particularly tricky one. The truck serves as a reminder of just how dangerous these mountain roads can be. How I made it out of the mountains without getting creamed is anybody's guess. I did have one incident, though: A few hours back, the traffic was moving steadily but slowly and I happened to go a bit too far right in my lane. An idiot behind me saw a chance to pass me, which he did, IN MY FRIGGIN' LANE! He drove right beside me to pass. If I had swerved back into the middle of my lane at the wrong time, he would have knocked me into the side of the mountain, or worse.

The traffic starts moving at a normal pace again and I arrive in Golden, British Columbia.

I wonder if Jacques Cousteau ever saw the mountains that I have just seen. I hope so.

Part 15

Friends and Family on the West Coast

July 13

It's foggy this morning. In fact, the mountains are completely out of sight. I put on the usual gear. I'm not too far out of Golden when the sun comes out. The scenery hasn't changed much, except the mountains aren't as big.

Farther along now, and I spy a sign that says ghost town ahead. I eventually come close to the ghost town and turn into the parking lot. It looks like a real ghost town. All right then (are you ready?) I take off my rain gear. "Egads, man! Have you lost your mind?" I chuckle to myself, imagining an old British colonel saying that to me. Not only is it sunny, but quite warm too. There are some old railway cars as well as the town. I walk into the small motel to buy a ticket. The woman behind the counter tells me the ghost town is closed because of a lot of rain they've had lately (Really? No kidding!). I leave. I peek through the fence to see that indeed the place is flooded. I take some pictures and leave.

I'm going through a pass (unfortunately, I can't remember its name). It is quite the valley or pass. I had seen a postcard of it. I will be going to the Okanagan Valley today. I hear it is a very picturesque place. I am extremely eager to see my friends, Dawn, Gina, and Anne, and part of my family. My sister Pat lives in Burnaby, B.C. with her husband Don and their son Dan. My father lives in Nanaimo, B.C., which is on Vancouver Island. My friends Dawn and Gina went to the same theatre school as I did. Dawn is like a sister and great friend all in one.

I'm about to turn on to Highway 97A which will take me to the Okanagan Valley. There's a sign with the words 97A CLOSED on it in spray paint. I wonder if it is some kind of prank. More signs in spray paint. I'm approaching a woman who is dressed not unlike those I have seen on other construction sites. She informs me that indeed the high-way is closed. She suggests an alternate route to get there. I tell her I'll visit it another day. I use this piece of news as an excuse to go to Vancouver one day early.

It's not long before a highway sign reads that I can travel at 110 kph. I guess I'll make it to Vancouver a little faster, although it has been awhile since I travelled at these kinds of speeds (110, 120). As time goes on, my eagerness to see my friends grows considerably. I love to surprise people, I always have. I will visit Dawn first. The weather is perfect. I have in fact over-dressed. I'm still wearing my long johns.

As I get closer to my destination it occurs to me that there are still mountains almost everywhere I look. I spend my time (stuck in a traffic jam) devising a way to surprise Dawn. She won't be expecting me this early.

I'm in Vancouver now and, as you might expect, lost, with a capital L. I go to a gas station. The girl in the booth tells me I'm quite far away from downtown Vancouver. She gives me directions. I leave with a bunch of directions in my head. I come to the bridge she told me about, and a traffic jam. I ask a woman who is sitting in her car if I'm going the right way. I am.

The traffic is still heavy and we are all moving at a snail's pace or not at all. I'm roasting, with all the stuff I'm wearing. I have a pretty good idea where I'm going. I make it across the bridge. I make a left after the bridge. Well, I'm lost again, not having written down any of the instructions the girl gave me. I ask a cab driver for the street's location I'm looking for and he gives me directions.

I actually find Dawn's street and her apartment building. I buzz her apartment number but she's not home. I then get back on my bike and go to a casino where I think she might work. She doesn't. I go back to a gas station just around the corner from her place. I call her. She's home. At first I tell her I'm in Kamloops. I ask her if she's going to watch *X-Files* tonight. She says she is. I then suggest we watch it together. I can't bear it any more, and tell her I'm just at the gas station. It's been three years since we've seen each other.

I walk around the corner onto her street. She sees me and starts to run at me. I start to run at her as well, but I can't run because I'm still frying with all the road clothes on, and my knapsack to boot. We hug each other. The years melt away. I can't believe I'm seeing her in the flesh. We are kindred spirits, at times finishing each other's sentences and at other times reading each other's minds. She hadn't expected me this soon.

July 19

It's Saturday. I cruise into the bike shop in Port Moody, British Columbia. I want them to replace the back tire, and get a tune-up. Now in the shop and talking to the mechanic, I can't help but get a sense of deja-vu. I have this feeling because I'm asking him to listen to a knocking and ticking kind of sound reminiscent of my first bike, the Virago 750 I mentioned earlier on. He listens and says it's probably something minor that the tune-up will take care of. The taps or the washers or something like that. Whatever they are. I'm just happy it's not something major like the, the...um...oh, I don't know. I vividly recall the bike shop in Toronto wanting to replace the whole engine the last time I brought in a bike with that sound. Anyway, he will call me on Tuesday.

July 22

I'm at my father's house in Nanaimo, B.C. I took yet another pleasant ferry ride to get here. My sixth, if you are counting (I didn't think so). The phone rings. It's my sister, Pat, whom I'm staying with briefly. She says the bike shop has called and the news is NOT good. Apparently the ticking sound is something major. They think it might be the main bearing and it could cost $600-$700 for the parts alone. A feeling of doom comes on me as I call the bike shop.

A guy at the shop tells me the cost of fixing my bike, with parts and labour would reach $2,000. Let's not forget the new back tire and tune-up, ladies and gentlemen. I tell him I'm from Ontario and have no choice but to have the bike fixed. I also tell him I'm on a five-month trip. He says he'll call me back in a few days. I thank him and hang up. If he's right on his estimate, my trip is over. I will finish the trip next summer. Well, I'm pissed off, no doubt about that. IS THERE A DOCTOR IN THE HOUSE? I mean, just how many mirrors did I break when I was a kid, anyway? One year delay!

July 23

I'm sitting in my sister's home and I'm still cursing. I do that a lot these days. The phone rings. It's the guy from the bike shop. He tells me he's sorry, because it will take three weeks to get the parts for the main bearings. They have to send away to Japan. He asks me how long I'll be in town for. Oh...I don't know...a year. He apologizes again for the delay. I tell him not to worry and to take his time. I can't believe I said that. Well, the trip is officially over until next summer.

It's later in the day now and I'm with my friend Dawn. About once an hour I go through a kind of ritual of cursing, then groaning, followed by a shake of my head. Dawn, who has observed this ritual, tells me people will think I'm crazy. Would they be wrong? I think not.

July 24

I'm looking in a Vancouver newspaper at the want ads for a job. Man, this is depressing. I haven't had to look for a job without already having one for around ten years. I am an unskilled person. Oh sure, I can get lost anywhere at any time, but that just doesn't pay like it used to. I call a few courier places to see if they have people who pick up and deliver on foot. They don't. I will try and get a job as a brokerage firm messenger and an ushering job as well. Maybe I should go back to Toronto by plane and come back west next summer. I still can't believe the trip is over. One year. ARRRRGGGHHHHH!

August 20

My brother-in-law Don tells me that the bike shop has called as soon as I walk in the door. They have had my bike for a month now. Want to hear the funny part? It has rained only two times, tops, since they've had my bike. Which I find incredible for Vancouver, since it's very well known for its rainy weather. I call them. The bike is ready. WHA-HOO!

"How much?" I ask. He tells me to hold on for a second. I can hear him punching numbers on some kind of calculator or adding-machine. It comes to $1,600, he informs me. WHEW! I tell him I thought it would be a lot more. He says that under the circumstances it is the least they could do. I thank him and hang up. I will go tomorrow and get it. I check the paper for tomorrow's weather. It's supposed to rain, I kid you not. I do have some good news, though. I got a few days' work with a company that supplies ocean-going ships with food, cleaning stuff, boots and whatever else they need.

August 23

It's cloudy, as my brother-in-law, sister, and I drive along the high-way. We are en route to the bike shop to pick up my bike. I can't wait to get it back. I stand at the counter to pay the bill. It will be $1600 dollars. I pay a thousand with my credit card and $600 in cash.

Having finished with that nasty business, I go downstairs to collect my bike. It's been over a month now since I've ridden it. Maybe I'll be a bit rusty. Nah, did I not spend nearly two months riding it almost every single day? I start it, put it into first. My brother-in-law is in front of me (in his car) and I wait for him to start moving. I go to follow now and I...stall it. OOPS. Oh well. I catch up to him on the main road. He turns left and then a quick right up a small hill, into a parking lot. I do the same. Now there's a car in front of me going up the hill. I make a slow right turn up the hill and...my bike's on the ground.

I'm looking down at my bike lying on its side for a milli-second or two. I pick it up, not believing what just happened. One second I'm doing a turn, the next second the bike's on the ground. The mirror is bent. My sister Pat and her husband Don are oblivious to what has happened. They are already parked. I ride in the parking lot, trying to adjust my mirror at the same time. It won't go back. That was so weird. I was looking at the car in front of me. I turned right to go up the little hill, and the bike falls over. I must have taken the turn way too slow. I rode through mountain roads, dirt roads, construction sites, pouring rain, cold temperatures, and I didn't drop it then. It must be that I'm a tad rusty.

I worked for four days for the ship supply company and have more work next week as well.

September 8

I'm standing beside my bike just staring at it. Why am I staring and not riding, you may well ask. It won't start. It turns over a couple of times, then there is this strange clicking sound. Now, here comes the funny part. I just got it out of the shop two weeks ago. Ain't that a barnburner? Isn't that a killer? Laugh, I could die. The bike did get a tune-up when it was in the shop. I retrieve the work order and, aha! There's a note saying that the fluid or water level is extremely low. Now

I'm wondering did they just note it or did they note it and change it. I think they just noted it.

It's five o'clock in the afternoon now and Don and I fill the battery with fluid. It sure needed it. We put the battery back in and still it won't start. Fortunately, we live about halfway down a hill. Don suggests I try the old "pop the clutch while it's rolling and in gear" routine. It's worth a try. Our third try now and I pop the clutch and, bingo, it starts. Whew!

I got some good news today. I got an ushering job at the Ford Centre for the Performing Arts. I now have two jobs.

September 20

The last three mornings I have had to coast down the hill and pop the clutch. This morning I coast down the hill, pop the clutch, and JEEZ!—I almost got whiplash. I've had enough. I'll take it to the bike shop.

Well here I am in the waiting room of the service department. The mechanic comes in and tells me he's not sure whether it's the starter (GULP, KA-CHING, $$) or the battery. He suggests I come back in an hour.

I'm back. They have put a new battery in. They say only time will tell whether it's the starter or the battery that was the cause of the bike not starting. I leave $156 poorer. Oh, I forgot to tell you that I bought a new visor for my helmet while I had that hour to kill. It cost $59 for a clear shaped piece of plastic. It seems like a lot to me. I wonder what the profit margin is on something like that.

October 14

About two weeks ago the shipping company split in two. I worked for one of the partners two weeks ago. I have not been called since. I'll have to look for a new full time job. I have about $250 in the bank. I owe a $35 parking ticket and $170 on a credit card. Good thing I still have the ushering job, or else I would be flat broke right now. It's not all doom and gloom, however, because my friend owes me $1400. That will pay for motorcycle insurance and various other things when I start the trip again this coming summer.

October 26

Today I will be participating in my first charity toy run. Myself, and thousands of other motorcyclists, will donate a new unwrapped toy for thousands of underprivileged kids in the lower mainland. A lot of us take for granted that we'll get a gift for Christmas. I guess a lot of kids don't. I always did, when I was a kid. Let's face it, it will be fun for the motorcyclists as well. We'll all meet at a mall in Coquitlam, B.C. and from there we will ride approximately 30 kilometres to the Pacific National Exhibition. It's pouring rain as I take the cover off my bike.

I ride along the Barrett Highway and see only one other motorcycle up ahead. I thought I'd see a lot more. As I get closer to Coquitlam, I start to see more bikes. I'm waiting at a red light now, wanting to make a left turn, and I see about 30 motorcyclists go by, headed towards the mall.

I'm in Coquitlam now. I make the left turn and am now behind about ten motorcyclists. We are all waiting to turn left into the mall parking lot. I follow them into the parking area. It is here that my eyes are treated to a sight I have never before witnessed. There are motorcycles EVERYWHERE. Hundreds and hundreds of them. I spot three Virago Owners Club flags. I park beside them. As you might guess, there are a lot of Viragos here, including one the same year and colour as mine. I introduce myself to some of the Virago owners. I take some pictures, look around a bit, and there are motorcycles of every size, age, colour, and shape.

I'm standing in the mall drinking my coffee and generally just observing everyone, when I hear a loud rumbling coming from outside. It's 9:45 a.m. and the run is supposed to start at 10:00 a.m. People are getting ready to go. I'm walking toward my bike and the noise is getting louder and louder. There are quite a lot of Harley-Davidsons here and, well, you can imagine the noise they make. I don't say that in a bad way, though. It is music to my ears on this day.

I'm in a traffic jam now but hey—it's all motorcycles, for a change. After ten minutes or so we start moving slowly toward the exit of the parking lot. As we exit the parking lot there are people clapping and waving on the city streets. I did not expect this so soon. My sister told me there would be people at the coffee shop in Burnaby, but this is the very beginning and people are out in the rain, clapping and waving to us. We are riding two abreast now and there are whole families clapping and waving. I wave back like I'm in a parade, which I guess I kind of am. As far as I can see there are motorcycles in front and behind me. The police hold traffic lights as we cruise on through. This is a blast! Normally when I'm riding I encounter a motorcycle from time to time but today I'm part of something huge. There are no cars to worry about, no stopping, just riding. Today we are the majority on the streets, not the rare minority. We dominate the road and we number in the thousands. It is charity runs like this that allow us to unite for one day, and I for one revel in it.

I wave to more people. I see a hill quite far up ahead. From where I am and up and over is a solid double line of motorcycles riding side by side. It doesn't seem that a lot of time has passed when I see the now familiar grounds of the Pacific National Exhibition (PNE).

I turn into the parking lot of the grounds and spot the Virago people whom I had started out with but soon lost in the confusion of the start. I spot a 1983 Midnight Virago. Exactly like my first bike. I ask a guy who has a first year model Virago to take my picture. He does, and then we walk into one of the buildings to hand in our toys. Mine was a LEGO set, if you were wondering. I am given two pins for my jacket. It's shaped like a Christmas tree with Santa riding a bike. I walk outside and people are still arriving. I look upon a sea of motorcycles. I take some more pictures and leave. It was great.

November 11

In contrast to every other Remembrance Day I can remember, it's an absolutely beautiful day. Not a cloud in the sky. It feels really different. Not as solemn, somehow. In Toronto it's usually snowing or raining. The ceremony will take place in Confederation Park in Burnaby, a fairly short walk from my sister's house. I'm glad my nephew Danny is coming to the ceremony so he can get a sense of what sacrifices people made for each of our generations. There are a lot of wreaths to be laid. I still can't get over the strange feeling of the weather. It's so warm now I have taken off my jacket as the sun beats down on my back and head. There are an impressive number of Royal Canadian Mounted Police here, decked out in their traditional red uniforms. As one of the speakers talks, I can hear planes in the distance. They get closer and I look up into the blue sky to try and figure out which direction they are coming from. They appear and fly over the park. I can't tell what kind they are. They look old to me, but I'm not an expert.

It's later on in the ceremony and there is yet another speaker on the podium. More planes fly overhead. There sure are a lot of planes flying around to the different ceremonies. I don't think I've seen the same plane twice. I watch the veterans' eyes well up with tears and can only guess what is going through their minds as they remember horrific battles and events. Friends who died beside them, some at extremely young ages. As the veterans get older (I believe most of them to be in their seventies now) they must realize that their numbers get fewer and fewer every year. It must be particularly dramatic for the handful of World War I veterans who must wonder if anyone remembers the sacrifice that they made over eighty years ago now. I'm not sure if there are any here today, although I doubt it. There is a large crowd today, which I always like to see at these ceremonies.

It ends with a parade of veterans, police, firefighters, flag-carriers, and the like. I will think of them some more today and thank them again in my own thoughts.

Part 16

Time Out for
Regrouping
(and Refinancing)

December 27

Christmas has come and gone. My first Christmas ever that I was not in Ontario. I don't have a full-time job yet. I still work at the theatre and the ship-supplying job the odd time. It has been great working at the theatre. The show currently there ("Joseph and His Amazing Technicolor Dreamcoat") ends tomorrow. I have decided to call my former boss at the Graphicshoppe and see if they need me for six months or so. If they do, I will fly there A.S.A.P. Why the rush? I need money, plain and simple. If I want to continue the trip this coming July, I'll need three to five thousand in American funds. I also would like to pay my mother some of the money I owe her. With 5,000 Canadian dollars I will get 3,500 American after the conversion is complete. I will call the Graphicshoppe on Monday, two days from now.

December 29

I dread the call I'm about to make to the Graphicshoppe. I feel a little dumb, asking to come back after less than a year. I guess it makes me feel like a failure in a way. They had a cake for me, and presents, when I left. Jeez. Well, here goes.

I just hung up the phone. Good news! They will take me back. The best part is that I will be there for six months because one of the women at the Graphicshoppe will be on maternity leave until next August 1st.

That's perfect. I will be starting on January 19th. What a relief. I think The Elgin & Winter Garden Theatre might give me my job back as well. That means I'll have to tell the Ford Centre that I'll be leaving. I will miss them very much. They never treated me like an outsider. After my first couple of shifts they invited me out to a local pub. I started to hang out with some of the ushers and some of them (I think) will remain friends. The management and staff at the Ford Centre were a fun bunch. A small chapter of my life that isn't closed yet. There are too many of them to list all of their names.

I will leave my bike in British Columbia. I hope I can find somebody who rides. A bike that just sits for six months is not a good thing.

January 5, Year Five of The Dream

Well, I did get my job back at The Elgin & Winter Garden Theatre. I will have the same two places to work I had when I left. Is that lucky or what. A friend, Lisa, of a friend, Ruth, of my sister's who just sold her 1994 Virago 1100 has agreed to look after my bike while I'm in Toronto. More luck. I will be staying with my mother for a few weeks or so, then I will try and move downtown. I can't wait to see my friends again. My sister, her husband, and their son deserve a medal for putting me up for six months. I may have bad luck with the weather, but I have the best luck when it comes to family and friends.

January 13

I'm in the lounge in Vancouver's airport, killing time until I can board the plane bound for Toronto. Here's some financial stuff. If it bores you, skip down a bit. I have about $250 in cash. The Ford Centre owes me $140, which they will mail to me. I owe around $1,200 on my credit cards. I will pay my mother as much as I can for the first three months. I will then have three months to pay off bills and try and save some money. Talk about easy! Is that all? Should I kill myself now or later? Maybe the plane will crash. Jeez, why do I even joke about things like that? Do you think I'll be able to accomplish all that financial stuff in six months? Nah, neither do I but, hey, ya never know.

January 23

I'm walking toward the bus stop in a raging snowstorm, complete with swirling winds, small snowdrifts, and freezing temperature. I begin to reflect on my arrival in Toronto. After my brother Mike met me at the appropriate gate, we started walking toward his car. I commented on how cold it was. He then told me that up until the day before I arrived the winter thus far had been unseasonably warm. Imagine my surprise when I learned that the weather had turned bad just before my arrival. I look up now just in time to see my bus go by. That's nice. What's another fifteen minute wait at the bus stop in this brutal winter storm?

March 21

Well, here's what's been happening lately. I'm living downtown. I'm sharing a place with a friend of a friend at the theatre. Speaking of the theatre, they just lost a big show, "Forever Tango," to another theatre. I have paid my mother back a little over a thousand dollars. I will continue to pay her back as much as I can until the middle of April. My friend Dawn has agreed to lend me five thousand dollars. What a great friend I have. She will borrow the money and I will pay her back as soon as I get settled again. I will take that $5,000 and convert it to American funds. I will, hopefully, have a few thousand of my own, which will make it a tidy sum.

I hope to take a helicopter ride when I'm in Alaska. I have always looked up into the sky whenever I heard one. So I have always wanted a ride on one. Why not do it in Alaska?

June 9

I found out last night that my friend Dawn couldn't get the $5000 loan. It is completely and utterly not her fault, I might add, just something neither of us counted on. As the saying goes, "NEVER SAY DIE," so we are both scheming and pondering ways for me to still go this July. One of my plans is to go and just use my credit cards to the absolute maximum. Would you do that? Or maybe you would wait another year? Keep in mind that I have already given my notice at work for July 24th. I'll keep you posted.

Part 17 *Go West Again, Young Man!*

July 25

Well here I am at Pearson International Airport. I'm in the waiting area looking at the Trip Tik provided by the Canadian Automobile Association. It tells me what kind of road conditions I might expect, among other things. I glance at it and see the ROUGH ROAD stamp at various locations in B.C., Yukon, and Alaska. Maybe this will be the most challenging riding yet. When I arrive in British Columbia I will again stay with my sister and her family in Burnaby. I hope to begin my trip as soon as I can upon arrival.

July 27

The weather in British Columbia has been beautiful so far. I'm walking toward the bike shop where my bike was put in for an oil change and tune-up. Lisa chose this bike shop (I think) because it's in Burnaby, or maybe it's because they're very reasonable, I forgot to ask her. I have not ridden my bike in 7 months.

I get to the entrance and see my bike sitting in a row of many others. I walk into the showroom, passing a new Honda Aero, which is a great-looking bike, in my opinion. I get the bill for work done on the bike. It comes to $174. I get talking with the woman. She already knows I'm going to Alaska. She has a pleasant accent (Australian, perhaps) and asks me if I have a tire repair kit. I tell her I don't. She gets a surprised look on her face and asks what I'll do if I get a flat tire in the middle of nowhere. I get a dumb look on my face and shrug. I'll call CAA, I think to myself, but that doesn't sound good enough all of a sudden. I then look at some leather gloves with her help but they are all too big. We talk a little more and I leave. I hope to be on my way to Dawson Creek in three days. The weather is supposed to be sunny and warm all week.

It's later on in the day and I'm with my friend Dawn. I'm so glad to see her again. I have already seen my friend Gina. Dawn has $530 in American funds for me, and the rest she owes me in Canadian funds. We have decided to see a movie called *Saving Private Ryan*. I believe it's about getting a soldier out of the war and back to his mother because he is the only son left out of four.

It's the end of the movie now and I think I'm going to lose it. My hand is covering my face. I could really start crying hard any second. My eyes are already filled with tears. The lights come up. Hardly anyone gets up to leave. I think I'm going to really start crying hard but the moment passes. *Saving Private Ryan* is one of the best movies I have ever seen. Steven Spielberg, the actors and everyone else connected with this film have done a brilliant job. When the credits started rolling everyone just sat there, too emotionally drained to get up, like me. I hope Steven Spielberg wins an Academy Award. I think about the red poppy painted on my gas tank and how the Alaska Highway was built for the war effort. Again I silently give thanks to the veterans.

July 29

I stand and stare at them. They mock me. I can't decide what to do. They sit there patiently as they have all the time in the world. I mean, how many kinds of bread can there be, anyway? Loaves upon loaves of bread. I am definitely in foreign territory. I'm in some place called Save-On-Food. My friend Christine works here, but she is off today. I decide on 60% whole wheat, a kind of beige colour. I have in my food basket a package of those tiny boxes of cereal, peanut butter and now bread. Will I actually eat this stuff? Who knows? I have also purchased (earlier on) a tire repair kit, motorcycle oil, freezer bags, travel-size bottles of shampoo and conditioner. I will leave tomorrow.

July 30

It's sunny right now and warm in Burnaby, B.C. this morning. After over a year of waiting I will be resuming my trip in about ten minutes. My sister Pat takes my picture. I pack up the remaining gear and say goodbye to my nephew. I leave. Ten minutes later or so I'm riding on the good old Trans-Canada Highway, travelling east. I try and think to see if I've forgotten anything.

It's quite warm in Hope, B.C. Maybe because I'm sitting on my motorcycle, writing a postcard. The engine is still hot. I promised the Graphicshoppe lots of postcards. I leave.

As I ride past a place called Boston Bar I can't believe how hot it is outside. The mountains are a light brown with (looks like) a scattering of pine trees here and there. It almost looks like a desert with trees and mountains. There's not a lot of grass to speak of, just short stump-like bushes. Well, there ya go, there's a small forest fire up ahead on the side of a mountain. Vancouver and most of British Columbia are having a heat wave right now. I guess it's no different here. I begin to notice more than the usual number of fruit stands as I approach a place called Spences Bridges, B.C. I will stop here for lunch, in a restaurant or take-out, naturally.

I turn in to a gas station in Williams Lake, B.C. I stop beside the pump and try to put the bike into neutral. It won't do it. I keep trying, waiting to see the green light come on to indicate I've hit neutral. I try and change the gear with my hand instead of my left foot, nothing is working. The bike's engine must be incredibly hot right now. I push the bike away from the pumps. I'll let it cool down. After ten minutes or so, I try again. No luck. I push it back to the pumps. I try again and, hey, it went into neutral.

139

I tell myself that I will stop in Quesnel, B.C. because the bike is really acting up now. It absolutely refuses to go any lower than third gear. When I'm stopped at a traffic light, I have to start out in third gear when it turns green. I have to let the clutch out extremely slowly or I will stall it.

I'm in Quesnel now and I'm going to keep right on going. Outside Quesnel I pull off the highway to put on my jacket. It's getting cool and late. I get back on the highway (in third gear) and begin to think about all the warnings I've heard advising not to ride at dusk. There are plenty of deer-crossing signs. Perhaps I will go to Prince George. I look upon the stretch of highway before me as the shadows get longer. Still looking ahead, I see (a hundred yards or so) a deer crossing the road and it appears to be in no hurry as it hesitates at the sound of the approaching motorcycle. I'm in no danger as it goes into the forest on the other side of the road. It gets me thinking, though. There are more where it came from.

I'm about 70 kilometres from Prince George when the fuel light comes on. Here we go again. I don't switch to reserve right away as I'll see how far I can go on the main tank. I switch over to reserve a little later, with about 50 kilometres to go. I forget how long the reserve tank will last; it's been awhile.

Thinking that I must be riding on fumes by now, I spot a gas station just outside Prince George. I phone my friend Rod Drummond but don't have the right number. I get some gas and decide to go to the City Centre of Prince George. My bike is still not gearing down below third.

Inside Prince George I spot a huge YAMAHA sign. I turn into the street to a large fence. It's closed. Oh well, it's here, that's the main thing. I walk across the street to a gas station and ask the woman when the Yamaha dealership opens. She thinks it opens at 8:30 a.m. I also ask her for directions to a motel if she knows of any. She does. I thank her and leave. I have been riding for around twelve hours.

I'm in the motel now and am calling the bike shop. A cheery recorded voice informs me that they will be open tomorrow (Friday) but will be closed Saturday, Sunday, and Monday because of the long weekend holiday. I hang up. Maybe if I get there when they first open I can get it fixed in one day. Oh well, time to eat. I walk over to the convenience store near the motel. I purchase some milk. Yes, ladies and gentlemen, I will not go to the restaurant a mere fifty feet from my motel room. Instead, I will cook cold cereal and peanut butter sandwiches. Well, it's cooking to me. After, I shall try and find Rod's correct phone number and call him tonight. Not only is he not expecting me, but I may also have to stay with him for three days or so, if he lets me. I call his mother in Toronto and get the correct number. I call. No answer. I will try again in the morning.

July 31

I'm at the bike shop early. So early, in fact, that it's not open yet. I read to kill time. I still can't get a hold of Rod. The line seems to be perpetually busy.

The store opens and I walk into the shop. I'm approached by a man I presume to be the salesman. I tell him what's been happening with the bike. His brow furrows. I don't think he's heard this one before, or maybe it's my lame explanation, but it's pretty straightforward. Of course the bike is going into neutral, first and second this morning. Like when you get to the doctor's office and you don't feel sick anymore. He takes me over to the service department. I explain what's happening to them. I tell him it seems to be fine today but I don't trust it. I follow him out back to my bike. He tests the shifter and says it's a little sticky. He asks me some questions. I can only tell him what happened.

We go back into the service area where he retrieves a binder with a section on Yamaha recommendations. He checks any recall (on the bike) notices from Yamaha and there is something about my bike's make and model. Aha! It recommends replacing certain parts to do with the area in question. Free work, that is. We talk a bit and I explain my trip and blah, blah, blah. They have some calls to make

141

and parts to look up so I look around the showroom for a while. I eventually start talking to the salesman about my trip. A woman (who also works at the shop) joins our conversation. She tells me that she knew some people who did the same trip I'm about to do. They told her that the bugs were so bad when they were camping in Alaska that it would be the last time. I nod and make a face like, what can I say.

The service manager approaches me. He suggests I take my bike and come back on Tuesday after the long weekend. This way I'll have transportation. The parts they need to fix my bike won't be in until then anyway. I agree. I go outside and start getting ready to leave. The service manager and the mechanic come outside. They have changed their minds and think I should leave the bike here. They will look at the bike today or tomorrow. If they wait until Tuesday and then take a look at the engine it might be something different and we will have waited 'til Tuesday for parts for nothing. It would also be a waste of three or four days of my time. I agree totally with their reasoning and leave the bike here. I call Rod again but still the line is busy. The only thing to do now is arrive unannounced and, worse, totally unexpected at his doorstep. I hate that. I give the bike shop Rod's number.

I hop into a taxi and am off to Rod's house. He might not be home because he works ten days on and four days off. He could be in the forest somewhere evaluating a stream, for all I know. The taxi pulls up to his house. I see him standing underneath a carport, peering into a car engine.

I yell, "Hey, Rod!" He looks up. No reply. I feel uncomfortable now. I try again. "Sorry for just showing up like this but my bike has been having problems. Your phone was busy." Still no reply. He starts walking toward me. It isn't Rod. Oh, man.

"Hi, I'm Rod's roommate, Paul."

"Sorry, you looked like Rod from a distance," I stammer. "Is he here?"

"Yes, I'll go get him." He turns and walks toward the house.

I pay the taxi driver. Rod pops his head out of the side door. He looks like he was sleeping. I walk over and we shake hands. I apologize to the real Rod Drummond for showing up unannounced. He tells me not to worry about it. He says he's glad to see me. Rod and I have known each other practically all our lives. Our backyards connected and our mothers are friends. He tells me he is just starting four days off. He is going to Jasper with some of his friends and asks me to come along. Why not, I tell myself. I agree. I meet his other roommate, Dan. Rod suggests we drive around Prince George for a while. We drive by his work and the various shops.

Later on, around 3:00 p.m., the bike shop calls and tells me that they found nothing wrong with my bike. The area where the gear shaft is was pretty dirty but otherwise not broken. That's weird, I think to myself. They unfortunately broke a seal (an oil seal?) and don't have one to replace it, but tell me it will hold. Well, that puts me in a dilemma. Do I go to Jasper with Rod and his friends or continue with the trip? I have already agreed to go to Jasper, so I'll go there. Rod drives me to the bike shop. It costs $150-odd. I thank them and leave. They want to see me back on the road as soon as possible. They have fixed my bike in less than a day. That was very nice of them.

We leave for Jasper at around 6:00 p.m. The scenery is typically British Columbia—beautiful mountains and wildlife. I see a moose at the side of the road. It's a little later now and I see another moose, although this one is not as big. We've been on the road for a few hours now and the weather is turning nasty. It's raining very hard now and the visibility is getting low as the night begins to descend on us. It's kind of fun and scary at the same time. Rod and I listen to some of his cassettes. I haven't heard some of the music in years, which just adds to the drive, somehow. Rod's roommate and friends are about ten minutes behind us.

We all arrive safely in the town of Jasper, Alberta. We park the cars on a side street and go immediately to the Athabasca Hotel. There is a live band and lots of people drinking and having a good time. There are people in every nook and cranny of the bar. They have a DJ between sets by a reggae band. We leave the bar in the wee hours of the morning and, after talking with some of the other partyers, Rod and I go to the pickup truck. I will sleep in the open part in the back under the stars.

August 1

I wake up a little chilled and sore from sleeping in the back of the pickup. I didn't get rained on. We are up early and set out to find a good place for breakfast. After breakfast we do a little shopping for postcards and batteries and the like. Rod suggests we go to the Jasper Lodge where he used to work. Jasper is still the same bustling town I remember from a little over a year ago.

We arrive at the lodge, which is not that far outside Jasper. What a beautiful setting for a lodge. Mountains and a golf course. We walk through the monstrous entrance to the lodge. High ceilings and big main lobby. It manages to be elegant and rustic at the same time. Wooden chairs and a big fireplace add to the rustic side. I bet it cost a lot of money to stay here, though. They have lots of shops downstairs. We go up and out onto the outdoor patio, which has a spectacular view of the lake, which I'm sure is the lodge's private property. It looks like the guests at the lodge aren't in want for things to do. They have a golf course, swimming pool, horseback riding, bicycling, and various paths to walk on. We order lunch on the patio and spend the next four hours or so hanging out, talking old times and drinking on this beautiful patio.

We leave after a while and go to a bar where we were to meet the rest of the people we arrived with. For whatever reason, they don't show. We eventually meet up with them after Rod and I have been to dinner and another bar. They want to go to some bar or another, but I'm getting tired of bars and decide to see a movie instead. I will meet up with them at around 11:00 p.m. More drinking and loud music. I'm getting tired of the "party hearty" atmosphere. I'm not a prude; it's just that I burn out quicker now. We've drunk our share of alcohol in the last 24 hours.

I go to the movie theatre. The line-up is huge and I've seen both the movies anyway. I go to the truck and sleep and generally just sit there. I meet up with the gang at the bar. I have two or three drinks and watch the band and leave by myself. Back to the truck, which is becoming my home away from home. I can't sleep and spend the next four or five hours trying. I'm on the inside of the truck tonight, though.

August 2

I'm guessing it's around 6:00 a.m. I'm to meet Rod, Dan, and Mark at twelve noon at a coffee shop. I will kill time until then by going to breakfast and doing a little laundry.

I'm back in the truck now and reading a little. Oh well, I might as well take a nap on this cool August morning. I wake up to the sound of advancing film. Dan is taking my picture and I mockingly throw up my hands à la paparazzi. We all have a few laughs about Rod and me living in the truck. We also laugh at the fact that Rod has been introducing me to people as a Colonel in the KISS ARMY. We go our separate ways as Mark and Dan go back to their campsite. Rod and I decide to go back to Prince George this morning after a coffee or two.

August 3

Well I'm back in Prince George again. It's the next morning. We got back from Jasper yesterday, had dinner, watched a bit of television and then slept. Rod and I are in a local restaurant having breakfast, talking about the old days and some of the people we used to hang out with. After breakfast we go to the store where I buy some sunglasses. It's another nice day in Prince George.

I'm ready to resume my trip now. Rod told me I was welcome to stay longer if I wanted. I thank him but I'm anxious to get back on the road. I had fun going to Jasper with Rod and his friends, Dan, Mark, and Kim. Rod deserves a lot of credit, considering I pulled up out of the blue. It could have been awkward, but Rod always made me feel welcome. He takes my picture on the driveway. We shake hands and I thank him again for his hospitality. I wave and turn left off his driveway. I'm at a stop sign when I hear Rod yelling my name. I turn my head and see him coming towards me with my brand new sunglasses in his hand. Whew! Thanks, Rod.

I start out toward Dawson Creek, B.C. It's around 410 kilometres. An hour later, the fuel light comes on. I'm not as worried as I would've been at the beginning of my trip last year, although there aren't a lot of gas stations or settlements. Twenty minutes later I pull in to a kind of run-down gas station but I like it for that. A nice older gentleman asks me how I'm doing.

"Good, thanks, although I was a little worried I might run out of gas. I'm on reserve."

"Don't worry, there's plenty of gas around here."

"Well I'm not from around here, so I wouldn't know."

"Where are ya from," he asks.

"I'm from Ontario."

"Ontario, eh? Well, welcome to Canada."

I laugh hard at this, not expecting this jab at my home province.

"Canada doesn't start until the B.C. border."

Again I chuckle at his making fun of the east. He goes on to tell me a guy from Toronto lived here (I don't know where I am) and was always telling people the way they do things in Toronto as opposed to here. I tell him I'm also from Toronto but don't claim to know everything. We get talking about Alaska and I ask him if he thinks I should buy a gas can for emergencies. He says I don't need one. He then suggests that I get a plastic bottle if it eases my mind. He then fishes in the garbage and pulls out a plastic oil container. It holds one litre. It's the perfect size. He says I can go pretty far on a litre of gas since I'm riding a motorcycle. I agree and take the bottle. I thank him for his help and leave.

The scenery is pretty as I ride along a hundred kilometres outside Chetwynd. The mountains are pretty. I look up to my left and see a big forest fire that's burning in several spots on the side of the mountain. I can see helicopters carrying water containers on the end of long cables flying toward and back from the fire. I stop to take a few pictures. The helicopters look so small against the mountain and the smoke. I try and single out the helicopters and take their picture. I leave.

A few hours later now and I'm finally in Dawson Creek. YAHOO! Point zero of the Alaska Highway. I stop at a museum. I go to the gift shop and information centre (all in one) and buy a Mile 0 pin. I ask the info guy a few questions and then go back outside. I have my picture taken in front of a huge sign that says "World Famous Alaska Highway." A retired gentleman from Alberta took the picture. He tells me he worked for 40 years on an oil patch (I'll have to find out what that is). I tell him about my trip. We talk a bit more and go our separate ways, on our own separate journeys.

The mile zero marker is about 100 yards away from this sign. I ride over there. I stand in the middle of the road and take a picture of the tallish, thin, white marker. I buy a few postcards and sit and write them on my bike. Another friendly older gentleman asks me a few questions about my trip. I tell him I'm going to Alaska. He tells me that he used to deliver propane (he's retired now). In 1964 while on his appointed rounds he was told to go immediately to Anchorage, Alaska because they had a bad earthquake. He said it was 7.4 on the Richter Scale. Apparently it did a lot of damage to the town or city of Anchorage. The theatre was quite damaged as well (the name of which I didn't hear or he didn't say).

A few minutes later now and before I'm officially on the Alaska Highway, I will check my map. Well I think I'll stop at a place called Fort St. John. I'm checking the map when someone comes up behind me. He introduces himself as Brother (I instantly forget his name) from the Ontario chapter of the motorcycle gang (the name of which I would

147

rather not say). He asks me if I've heard of his motorcycle gang before. I say that I'm from Ontario and, yes, I have. He asks me about what I'm doing. I tell him all the places I'm planning on visiting. He asks me if I camp or sleep on the side of the road, or what. I tell him I will camp and use motels as well. He asks me if I want to go for a beer. I decline. He asks again, a little more persistently this time. I politely tell him that I'm in a hurry to get to Alaska and I'm a bit behind in my travel plans, which is true. He accepts this explanation and leaves.

I get the map put away, hop on my bike and I'm back on the road. A few seconds to go now and, YESS!! I'm on the Alaska Highway! I've waited years for this. I've talked about this with an old friend of mine (Nancy) four years or more ago. I didn't have a motorcycle licence, a car licence, a motorcycle, or anything when we talked about doing this, and now here I am. My dream has come true so far. It feels great. With luck and determination I am finally on the Alaska Highway. I will go another 50 kilometres or so, to Fort St. John.

Well here I am in Fort St. John. It took longer than I thought to get here. I stopped along the way to take some pictures. I will try for Fort Nelson tomorrow.

Part 18

It's a Rough Road to Alaska

August 4

I'm happy to report that it is another beautiful day. I go for breakfast at the motel restaurant. Afterwards I get packed up and go do some banking. Having done that, I get back on the Alaska Highway.

About forty minutes later I stop in a place called Wonowon for gas. There are two motorcyclists parked about twenty feet from the pumps. One of them comes over and introduces himself. (I forget his name.) He asks me if I'm headed to Alaska. I tell him I am. He suggests we ride together. I reluctantly agree. He introduces the other guy. Turns out he's from Thunder Bay, Ontario. The first guy, from Alberta, starts suggesting routes, places to stay, that he has a big tent, which would save us money on camp fees, where to stay, and so on. Although he seems nice, my internal alarm bells start going off. A little too helpful and pushy. I agree to travel with them for a while. I have the feeling the other Ontarian feels the same as I do, but neither of us verbalizes it. We depart from the gas station. The Albertan goes first, me second, and the other guy last.

It's not long before we start hitting patches of gravel and large stretches of dirt roads. We ride in staggered formation. We pretty much stick to the speed limit. On one particularly long stretch of gravel road, the Ontarian passes me. Shortly after this, the lead bike pulls in at a little diner. The other Ontarian and I arrive behind his bike. We have both cut our engines. We both look at the Albertan like, "Why have we stopped here?" The guy says that this place has great homemade pies. Silence. It takes us both a few seconds to compute this information. The other Ontarian says he's not hungry. I say I'm not hungry because I ate not too long ago. He then tells us that he'll catch up to us later, but if he doesn't, he says "God Bless." I could be wrong, but I find something distinctly wrong here. He was so persistent and quick to put us together and just as quick to say goodbye. I am relieved.

I'm 80 kms outside Wonowon and I see a female moose and her calf standing near the road across the highway. I stop quickly and take my pack off. They are looking at me now, a mere 60 feet away. I whip out my camera and as I stare through the lens, a thought hits me. What if mama moose gets mad? That could be bad for my health. I mean, we're talking about a moose here and it isn't running away, either, it's looking right at me. I don't think I would have time to put my knapsack on and start the bike with an angry moose charging me. I take a picture. They start moving to cross the road. I think the mama moose is spooked. I take a picture of them on the road. They are on my side now. They take another look at me and go into the forest.

I'm starting to see and ride over these gravel patches that are around eight feet long and stretch from one side of the highway to another. At this point, the highway is only two lanes. I seem to be running over them every twenty feet or so. They are man-made. Not long after the patches start I arrive at a construction site, where a worker tells me to stop. She gives me instructions on how to proceed. There is a truck ahead, spreading oil on the road. I'm to avoid the oil at all costs. A couple on a motorcycle followed the pilot truck onto an oil patch and wiped out. They were not hurt badly but they were extremely pissed off. Now the construction site is very careful when it comes to motorcycles. A motorcyclist is given a head start on the other vehicles. She tells me to take my time and to go around any oil patch. I thank her. Soon I'm given the signal to follow the pilot truck. I do so, slowly. The driver is careful. I take my time, avoiding the oil patches and pass through the site in one piece. I'm roughly 200 kms away from Fort Nelson, B.C.

The farther along the highway I ride, the less there seems to be of everything—fewer gas stations, settlements, traffic, and people in general. I'm about 40 kms from Fort Nelson, B.C. and there is a storm up ahead. I can see it raining, with lightning as well. As I get closer to Fort Nelson, it threatens to rain on me. I arrive in Fort Nelson. I have been riding (off and on) for 8 hours. I will stop here. The bike, by the way, is working perfectly.

August 5

It's overcast and cool this morning. I have breakfast and leave. It's chilly on the bike this morning. I stop and put on warmer gloves. I get going again and see some cows in a field—no, not cows, but buffalo. I stop and take a picture. There are about twenty or so.

A little while later (maybe a half hour or so) and it's raining hard enough for me to put on my rain gear. I start up again. What a difference from last year. This new rain suit (two pieces) keeps me dry and warm, something my other gear didn't. This cool and rainy weather reminds me of Eastern Canada and pretty much everywhere else I went last year. It's 30 minutes later. I come up to a construction site. The road is gravel. I take it easy. I go slowly for a few miles, and then the road becomes more mud than gravel. It continues like this for a bit, but then it's back to gravel again. It's gravel for about 12 kms.

I'm just approaching Summit Lake when I see a caribou on the side of the road. Soon after seeing the caribou, I come to a bridge that has a metal surface. It has a kind of thick metal mesh surface. When I'm in a car I love these bridges because it makes a humming sound like a B-52 bomber. As a motorcyclist, I dread them. It feels like riding across an ice patch, especially when the metal is wet. It feels like I'm going to wipe out as I ride across it. I pull into a combination gas station, restaurant, and curio shop in a place called Summit Lake.

I walk into the Summit Cafe. I'll have a quick coffee. Inside there are lots of pictures on the wall of the army and others during the period when they were constructing the Alaska Highway. I finish my coffee and go outside. I start talking to a motorcyclist and we compare road stories. While we are talking, another motorcyclist pulls in and goes to the gas pumps. He comes over to us after getting gas. He has what looks like a big dirt bike with his gear and a spare tire strapped on the back. He has come from the same direction as me. We talk a bit and he goes in for a coffee to warm up. I'm not the only one. He's from Wyoming. I pull out and wave to him.

A couple of minutes later I'm riding towards a corner. There are cars stopped. As I get closer I realize there are mountain goats or Big Horn sheep (I can't tell) standing practically in the middle of the road. I see a sign that warns me of this very thing. I pass the goats very slowly. I turn off the road just past the goats and get my camera out. I take a picture of this weird scene. I get back on the road. I come to an inside curve and go way too low. Before I know it, I'm riding over rocks that have fallen off the mountain. I'm going to wipe out—the bad accident I've been dreading is going to happen.

I bounce in the air off my seat. I look down at the rocks. I land back on my seat. There is a loud bang as I hit something. It jolts my head. I'm going to wipe out. My left hand bounces off the grip. I'm losing control. I re-grab the handlebar, scared to death. My eyes are bugged and I think my mouth is open. Somehow the bike comes to a stop and stalls. It all happens in a few seconds, but it takes a year. I breathe heavily and I am shaking, when I look down to see oil gushing out of the bottom of the bike. I think or feel that the back tire is flat. I'm not hurt. In shock maybe, but not hurt. The right side of my head has a slight ringing from that loud bang, which was a rock. I can still feel that loud noise in my head. The oil continues to flow from the bike.

I get off. The back tire is not flat. I bend down and look to see where the oil is coming from. It's coming out near a bolt or from the bolt hole itself. Whew! I thought I was going to fly over the handlebars at one point. It occurs to me that the trip may be finished if I've done any major damage I can't see. I'm also in the middle of nowhere. Now what? I could walk back to the Summit Cafe, but hey—that motorcyclist from Wyoming will be coming this way. He's going to Alaska same as me. I look for other damage to the bike but can't see any. I try the starter. The bike starts. I shut it off after a few seconds. Maybe all I need to do is tighten that bolt where the oil's coming out. That's a good plan, Dan, except you don't have any tools. The Boy Wonder strikes again. I guess I'll sit and wait.

About ten minutes later I hear him coming. There aren't any other noises out here. He comes into view and I flap my arms and flag him down. He gets off his bike just ahead of me. I tell him what happened. I ask if he has a tightening tool. He looks down at the area in question (the oil pan).

"You've got a hole in your oil pan," he says. I look and, sure enough, there's about a half inch wide and an inch long gash in the oil pan. He says I've got major trouble. He asks if I have any aluminium sealer. Never heard of it, I think to myself. I tell him I don't. He says he saw a sign saying there was a settlement or gas station a little ways back that said the place in question was two kilometres ahead. He says it's probably only one kilometre away now. I thank him for stopping. His name is Dave Nelson, from Wyoming. He suggests I get off the inside curve to a safer area. He then leaves to find the gas station (or whatever it is) and says he'll be back as quick as he can. It's around 11:30 a.m.

He comes back a few minutes later. There's a gas station over the next hill. He thinks they have a phone but isn't sure. I push the bike as Dave watches for traffic behind me. There are lots of big trucks on this road and I'm coasting along around five miles an hour. I'm on the bike coasting along when the road evens out for a bit, so I help it along with my feet. I'm doing a Fred Flintstone, trying to get up a small hill with feet power. Huffing and puffing, I get to the top of the hill. Dave tries to help but when he gets close to me I take it as a signal I'm going too slow and try even harder. I'm at the top of the hill now and, to my relief, it's steep and won't require any more Fred Flintstone type efforts.

I coast down the hill and into the parking lot of the gas station and motel. It's called the Rocky Mountain Lodge. I park the bike near Dave's already parked motorcycle. He says that, if he had the equipment, he could weld the hole. I tell him that it is okay, I'll call the Canadian Automobile Association and figure out what to do from there. I confess to him that I'm writing a book about my trip and would he mind if I used his name. He says he doesn't mind, and takes my picture. I tell him my name and thank him profusely for his help. He leaves, bound for Alaska.

There's a man working on the roof of the motel that I suspect to be the owner. I yell up to him and ask if he has a phone. He does, inside the little cafe. I call a 1-800 number. It connects me with an operator in Toronto. I explain the situation. She gives me a number for the British Columbia branch of the CAA. I call. After a few minutes of waiting a woman answers the phone. She, like the phone operators here and in Toronto, asks me if I'm hurt. To their relief (and mine), I tell them I am quite unhurt. She asks me where I am and what the address is. I turn the phone over to the owner of the place because I don't know either answer. I get back on the phone and she tells me a flatbed truck will be coming out to get me from Fort Nelson. When the truck arrives, I'm to ask the driver where would be the best place to get the bike fixed. I'm now to simply wait for the truck. I thank her for her help and hang up.

Well, there ya go. I will start waiting for the truck. This could have been a lot worse. I really thought I was gonna have a bad spill while it was happening. I can still feel the loud bang (if that makes sense) on the right side of my head. I had a little bit of a headache before the accident but now it's more pronounced. I'm at mile 397 of the Alaska Highway.

I'm spending my time reading or dozing just off to the left of the parking lot. I had my back to the cafe building when it was raining a bit but have again moved out into the open. I'm sitting, propped up against my bike on my bedroll and have a rock for a backrest and pillow. Because I don't have a watch, I can only guess at how long I've been waiting. The owner of the gas station tells me it's just before 5:00 p.m. I go back outside and wait. I try to read but I can't concentrate. I keep going over and over the accident in my head. I can still feel the odd sensation in the right side of my head. Is it part headache and part shock from a violent but brief episode? I can still hear that loud bang in my head. It's an awful and weird feeling.

I'm daydreaming when I hear a vehicle slow down to my right. A flatbed truck turns left into the gas station. The truck stops near me. The driver gets out. I say hello and I'm glad to see that he is not mad or grouchy. After all, I'm about to spend the next hour or two with him, riding in the truck back to Fort Nelson.

The back of the flatbed truck is lowered to the ground. We get the bike onto the truck towards the front. The flat part of the truck is huge and could easily have taken a car or two. He begins the securing process by putting a blanket on the seat. He then gets the canvas straps and starts that part of it. I help where I can but it's not much. I finally introduce myself. I shake hands with Ben. After securing the bike, we make sure my two big packs don't fall off the truck. We cover them with blankets and a canvas strap. I ask him where would be the best place to take the bike from here where they have a garage that could weld the hole in the oil pan.

"There is a Yamaha dealership in Fort Nelson," he says.

Can you believe that? Man, am I lucky. First Prince George and now Fort Nelson. When it comes to bikes, I am unlucky and then lucky. I wish I had some film in my camera. I ask him if we can stop at Summit Lake so I can go to the bathroom. He says he will. He adds that we'll go for a mile or two and see how the bike holds on the back. We set out for Summit Lake. We hit some bumps immediately and the bike barely moves. I'm a little bit nervous that it will fall off. Ben tells me he knows the road quite well as he used to drive trucks for years. He is a nice man and easy to talk to. He was retired when a friend (I think) asked him to drive trucks for the BCAA helping people (like myself) who get stranded or have accidents with their vehicles.

We arrive at Summit Lake at the cafe where I stopped to have a coffee about seven hours ago. I see a Harley-Davidson Road King parked in front of the restaurant. I had seen him ride by the motel/gas station earlier. I offer to buy Ben dinner, he declines but will accept a coffee. I hope this place sells film. I walk into the cafe and see the same waitress I had talked to this morning.

"Oh, you're the one Ben was sent to get. Didn't get too far, did you?"

She doesn't say it in a mean way or to embarrass me, she just states the facts. What could I say? It was true, I didn't get too far. I say hi to the owner of the Road King. I tell him I saw him go by earlier. We talk a bit. I order a burger and a pop for myself and a coffee for Ben. After finding out the coffee is for Ben she won't take any money for it. After using the washroom, I ask if they sell film.

"One hundred or two hundred?"

I shrug. She informs me that the 100 is fast film. I take the 100. I immediately load the camera. I go outside. Ben is adjusting the canvas straps that hold the bike in place. I take a few pictures of the bike on the truck. I ask him to take a few pictures of me with the bike and truck behind me, which he kindly does.

I get my food and talk to the Road King driver outside. He's from Vancouver on a week's holiday. I tell him if I had the money I would buy a Road King. He says he is selling this one soon. He will wait four or five years, then go on a bigger trip. He has a wife and kids. We talk about the metal bridges and road conditions in general. He tells me I will come across more metal bridges on the way to Alaska. I wish him luck on the road back to Vancouver.

Ben and I are on the road again. I see some of the scenery I missed when I came this way a while ago. He points out some of the older sections of the Alaska Highway that are no longer used. I was on a big stretch of gravel earlier and he points out how the old section was very twisting and turning. When it's finished, it will be a lot straighter and probably have more lanes. I look at my bike through the large mirror to my right. It looks absurd, perched on the back of this huge flatbed truck. It looks like a toy.

Ben and I talk about travelling and all kinds of things. It occurs to me that the heavy knapsack I carry on my back could have saved me from flying over the handlebars or off in another direction. I wonder if

I should tell my parents. I'm sure they worried plenty about me. This news won't help ease their minds. I will tell my mother it was a minor accident, which it was. I will tell my father nothing. He doesn't like motorcycles and has enough to worry about with an upcoming gall-stone operation.

Well it's a couple of hours later now and we are arriving in Fort Nelson. We turn left into what I assume is the BCAA centre. Ben gets on the phone to see if I can put the bike into the Yamaha dealership immediately. The shop is closed but he tracks down the owner at her home. She will come down to the shop and open it up for us. Is that a great gesture or what? The shop is two minutes away.

We pull around to the back of the shop with the flatbed truck. She is there waiting for us. I thank her profusely and tell her how much I appreciate her coming from home to open the shop. I tell her briefly what happened and about me having to go to the dealership in Prince George. She tells me her mechanic used to work at the same dealership. I shake my head at the coincidence. Ben lowers the flatbed and we guide the bike off it and into the shop. More luck. Dan (the mechanic) will be here at 7:30 a.m. She says I can drop by as early as I want after that time. I ask her if she noticed if the motel (which is about 100 yards away) is full. She tells me she hasn't noticed, but will drive me there.

I say goodbye to Ben and thank him. Julie drives me to the motel and they indeed have some vacancies. I thank her and she drives away.

August 6

I arrive at the shop around 8:00 a.m. Julie is there and she asks me if I would like a coffee. I thank her and help myself. I'm introduced to Dan, the mechanic, who is in the back of the shop. We go out to the service desk area and have a coffee. We begin to talk about the bike. He doesn't feel qualified to weld aluminium and do as good a job of it as he would like. Aluminium is tricky to weld. On the other hand, he doesn't want to do a patch job either, but feels this is the best way. I appreciate his honesty. He tells me the bike should be ready around

2:00 p.m. I tell him not to hurry because I have already booked another night in the motel. I leave.

I come back at around 2:30. My bike is sitting out front. I walk into the showroom and say hello to Julie. She says Dan is in the back if I would like to talk to him. She presents me with the bill. It's a mere $71. I am relieved. I go into the back where Dan is working on an outboard motor. I ask him if he found anything else wrong with the bike. He says he didn't, and even took the bike out for a ride to make sure. We go outside so he can show me the work he's done. He has completely covered the hole with a bonding or aluminium patch material. I go back into the shop with Dan and thank him and Julie for their help and kindness. I tell them I might drop by on the way back.

The bike feels normal as I ride away but let's face it, folks, after my little accident I'm a bit spooked. I go to a museum not far from my hotel where they have all kinds of artifacts and plenty of old vehicles inside and outside of the museum proper. Check it out if you are ever in Fort Nelson.

August 7

It's a cool clear morning in Fort Nelson, B.C. I have bought cereal, bread and cookies. That stuff, along with my trusty jar of peanut butter, makes for an okay breakfast. I also had the same meal for dinner last night. Oh well. I pack up and leave. As I ride along, I still am a little spooked. The sun and cool air rejuvenate me a bit, though. I will admit (part of being spooked I guess), I have lost a little confidence in my riding ability. I want to get past the point of my mishap. It's 9:00 a.m. I want to ride today at least until dinnertime. While riding, I practise evasive manoeuvres. Does that sound dumb? Anyway, I pick a spot up ahead on the road, then turn and miss it at the last second.

I run into some construction (gravel road) in the early going. I stop and take my camera out. I will try to ride and shoot pictures at the same time. I start riding again, with the camera resting between the seat and the tank. I take my left hand off the handlebar and grab the camera. It proves difficult to take a picture immediately because the shutter button is on the extreme right. My finger can't reach the button, so I use my middle finger, which works, but not that much better. I take a couple of pictures but it seems a little on the futile side, not to mention dangerous, on these gravel roads. A car passes me out of nowhere. I didn't see or hear it coming. I don't recommend this.

I stop at the Summit Lake Cafe to have a coffee. The waitress recognizes me. Makes sense. I've been here three times in less than three days. We talk a bit and I leave. I'm only a few minutes away from where I had my accident. Back on the road now and I'm coming to the corner where the goats were the last time. Sure enough, there are goats near the road. I slow down to find the spot where I went off. I look to my right now, scanning the side of the road. There it is, I see the tire skid marks in the dirt with a long streak of oil. I'm glad to get past it.

I'm approximately 22 kms from Summit Lake (the lake part of the area known as Summit Lake) when I see a deer at the side of the road. I don't stop, as I'm getting used to (but not totally) seeing wildlife. It's about a half hour later now and the landscape has turned into postcard material. The light jade-coloured river runs near me as I ride among the mountains. It's like this for mile after mile. I stop and take a few pictures. If I stopped and stared at all the views that are a feast for my eyes, it would take years to finish my trip. It's later now and I come upon the Lake Muncho area and am compelled to stop and take pictures. It reminds me of Lake Louise, in that it's a greenish lake surrounded by mountains.

I'm about 40 minutes away from arriving in a place called Watson Lake. (I think it's called the Gateway to the North.) I run into a gravel road/construction site. I'm getting a little used to these now, although this stretch of gravel road seems to go on forever. I pull into the Watson Lake district and I'm starving. I missed lunch. I have to get a watch.

I see literally hundreds of signs posted on poles in this one particular area. Well, there you go, it's a signpost forest. I seem to recall a woman at work (Linda) telling me about this. I get closer to the sign forest. I look at the signs for a little while and they're from everywhere you can think of, practically. I walk around for about ten minutes or so, but my hunger is such that I quickly leave and go to a restaurant. I will stay here tonight. I guess you've noticed I haven't camped yet. I won't lie; I'm avoiding it, because deep down I just don't want to. Why is that, you might ask yourself. Well, it just seems like a hassle and too much work for a bad night's sleep. Oh, by the way (I say this like it's not important, but it is), I'm in the Yukon Territory. When you say the word "Yukon" to yourself what kinds of images come to mind?

August 8

I again put on long johns, double socks and rain gear today. I'm set and ready to go at 9:00 a.m. I get on the highway. It's quite cool on the bike today and raining as well. Not too long outside of Watson Lake, say a half hour or so, there is a lot of construction. I'm given instructions to go slow and be careful. So far so good as I ride in the site. I'm coming up to a very muddy patch and I start to lose control. I put my feet on the ground to try and save the bike and me from hitting the mud. It works, barely. WHEW!!

It has occurred to me as I ride along that all the motorcycles I encounter are coming back from the northern direction. No motorcyclists have come up from behind me for days, it seems. Hmmmm. A couple of hours later I stop in the Teslin Lake area for gas. Another motorcyclist pulls in (from the opposite direction) on a BMW with Florida plates. I'm surprised by his English accent. He has big steel boxes at the back of the bike. He tells me he went as far north as he could. His name is Gavin. Among other adventures, he got a flat tire in Indiana and a speeding ticket in Alberta. I point to the steel mesh surfaced bridge that I just rode across. It's the longest I've been on so far, perhaps two or three times longer than average.

I tell him about the accident I had. He points to some steel guards he had put on the bottom of his bike. I tell him about trying to take pictures while riding. He laughs knowingly and says he has throttle lock which allows him to take pictures with his right hand. His BMW seems tall in the saddle to me. Gavin looks to be over six feet tall so he probably has no problems. We trade some more stories. He warns me about a cop about ten miles from Whitehorse at the bottom of a hill. He says he lives pretty far south (being from Florida) so he wanted to go as far north as he could. Gavin, like some other motorcyclists I've talked to recently, read a particular book about the highway. As far as I know (or can deduce), a motorcyclist or motorcyclists travelled on or gathered information on almost all of the roads in the north. I think the word "milepost" is in the title. I don't know why I'm mentioning this, but a woman told me I was brave to be doing this trip. I find these comments to be pleasing and perplexing at the same time. Am I brave? I don't know. We talk a bit more and go our separate ways.

I'm about 60 kms from Whitehorse and it's getting warmer. The sun feels so good and my hands and feet are grateful. The slower I go, the warmer I am.

I arrive in Whitehorse at around 4:00 p.m. I expected a frontier kind of town but I guess I'm thinking of Dawson City. They have an historic riverboat right when you get into the town proper. I go to one of the banks I deal with but it's closed. I grab a bite to eat and write some postcards near the statue of a miner and his dog. I go out to where the Klondike riverboat is and take a few pictures. It's here that I realize I have lost yet another pair of sunglasses. Oh well. I leave Whitehorse. It's six o'clock. I didn't find any cheap pair of sunglasses that I liked.

I'm not too far outside Whitehorse now and the scenery is breathtaking. They are not huge mountains but there is something about their low roundish shape and the way they kind of overlap each other to make a seemingly endless line of mountains. I haven't seen mountains like this before. It seems to me that it is an unusual landscape. The farther along I go towards Haines, the longer and straighter the highway seems to get. I keep coming upon long stretches of highway that gradually decline. I don't believe I've seen these long stretches in the Yukon so far. The mountain ranges particularly to my left seem never-ending.

161

They are not close to the road but are just different, somehow. I can't put my finger on it.

I'm about 5 kms from Haines. The mountains ahead are quite large, with snow-capped peaks. They remind me of the mountains in Jasper, Alberta. I will stay here tonight. I will try and see if I can arrange for a helicopter flight tomorrow.

August 9

A warm and sunny morning here in Haines Junction. I take the opportunity to clean my bike, which has seen too many construction sites. I'm starting to feel guilty about not camping yet. I shouldn't, I guess, but I do. At Haines Junction I have a choice. I can continue on the Alaska Highway towards Fairbanks or I can go into Kluane National Park and camp. I choose the Alaska Highway.

I'm on the road now. I've been travelling for a mere five minutes and, despite the time, it's cool at 10:00 a.m. I rode a mile or two into Kluane National Park this morning, then turned around. Now I have a case of the guilts for not going farther into the park. I do a U-turn and head back in the direction of the park. Maybe I will get a campsite today. I'm back in Haines Junction now, heading towards the park. I phoned a helicopter sightseeing company this morning. There is no sightseeing because the helicopter is somewhere fighting forest fires. As I ride along the road that will take me to the entrance to the park, I change my mind again and turn around. I just don't want to camp. I'm getting impatient now, as it's staying cool even in the sun. I stop and put on my thicker gloves. I put my small ones I'm wearing inside these.

It's around 12:30 p.m. and I see a sign advertising helicopter sightseeing. I look up ahead just in time to see a helicopter landing. I turn in to the parking lot. I am almost sure this used to be a gas station. I'm greeted by a fellow and inquire about a flight. They need to have a minimum of three people at $100 each for a half hour or $200 each for a longer flight. I could also pay the whole lot myself for $300 or $400 for a solo flight. There's no one around except me. He suggests I wait. I will.

We sit outside on a bench with our backs to the office. The sun is blazing down on us, which is great because, despite my two pairs of gloves, my hands are still cold. Are there any violins handy? My bike stands about forty feet away. He asks me if my Virago is an 1100. Aha!, I think to myself. I tell him he must know bikes to make such an accurate guess as to the make, model, and CC's of my bike. It turns out he has a bike of his own, a Suzuki Marauder 750. We talk about bikes for a bit. He invites me to look at his bike, which is in the old garage part of this former gas station. It's a great-looking bike. The seat, unfortunately, is cracked and split. He tells me that he can get it fixed in Whitehorse for a little over a hundred dollars. We go back outside to the bench. The pilot has wandered off with his dog. A female worker has arrived and we sit around and talk.

It's about an hour and a half later now and I think I'll give up and try another place. I no sooner tell him this, when a pickup truck with a camper on the back pulls in. Three people get out of the truck. With me as a fourth, the pilot is a fifth, that would be the maximum number of people. It turns out they have a complimentary flight coming to them but are going to get something to eat first. Oh well, I've waited this long, I guess I can wait a little longer. Back to sitting on the bench.

They return about 40 minutes later. I spend this time talking to Darren and the pilot and eating peanuts. I pay my hundred dollars. We all walk to the area where the helicopter sits. Darren (the guy with the bike) introduces all to Bob the pilot. He gives some instructions, including how to get on and off the helicopter correctly. We start walking towards the helicopter. I'm walking behind Darren and the three other people. He opens the back door of the helicopter and the three people pile in. So guess where I'm sitting. When I realize I'm sitting in the front beside the pilot, I get a slight twinge of panic. I've never been in a helicopter before. Let's face it, I wasn't too thrilled living on the 26th floor of an apartment building in Toronto. Looking down over the balcony railing gave me the willies. I climb into the front seat and of course there's a clear plastic floor or bubble at my feet. I tell myself that riding a motorcycle on the Alaska Highway is probably more dangerous than this. It calms me quite a bit. The only problem is, we haven't left the ground yet.

We lift off the ground and it's like floating at first. We start toward a lake at a fairly low altitude. So far, so good. Getting a little higher now. The trees look tiny as I look down at them past my feet. The pilot tells us information about the landscape over our headsets. I forgot to mention that we are wearing headsets so we can hear the pilot, and microphones as well, to ask questions. I can also communicate with the other passengers and hear their questions. To the left he points out some mountain sheep (I think they are). They are white specks on the mountain. We eventually come upon the Kaskawulsh Glacier, which is part of the world's largest non-polar ice fields. (I got that from a brochure.) There are slits in the ice fields that are quite long. There are also some holes that are pretty deep. I know I'm generalizing the information and I apologize for that. It's just so cool, flying in this helicopter, that the information you hear is secondary to the experience of flying in a helicopter for the first time and to the wonder that your eyes and brain are trying to grasp.

I take lots of pictures. It gets a little hairy when we start flying over mountains as opposed to beside them. Oh, I forgot. We hovered about two feet or less above a hole in the glacier. I love this. Okay, back to the mountains. We were flying over mountains and then we go into a dive, swooping down the center of two mountains side by side. What a rush! The pilot asks everyone how they're doing after this swoop and everyone is fine. We start back towards the departure point. As we approach the landing pad, it looks like a dot from up here. The pilot, having done this probably a thousand times, expertly lands the helicopter. Well, I have had my first helicopter ride and I LOVE IT! I ask the female worker to take my picture with the pilot, which she kindly does. We walk back towards the office. I buy a T-shirt and get ready to leave. Darren tells me to stop by on the way back, if I can. I might sound like a broken record by now, but they were all very nice to me. I go outside and the pilot is there. I ask him if he ever read a book called *Chickenhawk* about a helicopter pilot's experience in Vietnam. He tells me that indeed he had. I suggest how crazy it must be to try and pilot a helicopter while people are shooting at you from the ground. He shakes his head in agreement. I'm guessing he's thought about that scenario more than once.

I get ready and start out on the Alaska Highway once again. As I ride, I think about what I said to the helicopter pilot about being shot at while flying. My thoughts turn to my Uncle Bill, who was a dispatch rider in World War II. Sometimes it's hard riding a motorcycle with traffic and bad road conditions or, as in my case, just going off the road. One can only imagine (unless you've done it, of course) what it was like riding a motorcycle in the streets of the city or roads of the country while someone is literally trying to kill you. You are carrying a message or plans of some sort that the enemy doesn't want you to deliver. Any second a bullet could take you out. A moving target. I can only try to grasp the horror that my uncle felt seeing his best friend (Frenchy) get shot while serving his country as a dispatch rider. (They both were dispatch riders.) Sadly, his best friend did not survive. How bad would you be psychologically after that? Your nerves would be fried. I know mine would be. My Uncle Bill is in his late 70s now. I want to ask him about his experiences in the war but I don't want to make him relive the horrors unnecessarily. It's been my (limited) experience that a lot of veterans don't want to talk about it. Maybe I'll ask him, maybe I won't. Whether I do or don't, I will never forget what he did as long as I live, never.

It's a few hours later now and it's still chilly. After getting dinner I'm about 60 miles from the Alaskan border. For some reason it's a lot warmer now. I'm in kind of a plains region. I'm about 40 miles from the border now and running into a lot of gravel roads. It seems I ride over a gravel stretch of road every couple of minutes. It starts to rain but I don't put the rain gear on. I can actually see I'll be riding out of it soon. It rains harder. More gravel roads. I can still see where the rain stops, though. Ten minutes later and I'm out of the rain.

I arrive at a motel. I will stop now. I hope to be in Fairbanks, Alaska sometime tomorrow. I ask the desk clerk how far I am from the Alaska/Canada border.

"Nineteen miles."

So close now to one of my dreams. This whole thing started with me wanting to do the Alaska Highway on a motorcycle. Now I'm nineteen miles away from Alaska. Tomorrow my dream will come true. I will be standing on Alaskan soil.

I leave my hotel and ride over to a restaurant/grocery store. I can see a bunch of motorcycles parked outside the restaurant. Five of them are from Missouri. A couple of Harleys, a Honda Shadow, a Yamaha Venture. I start talking to another motorcyclist who's travelling alone on a late model Suzuki. He tells me he's had to jump-start his bike a couple of times. Sure enough, he tries to start his bike and nothing happens. I offer to help. I push his bike, he pops the clutch, and it doesn't work. We try again and this time it works. He rides away.

I walk over to the other group. One of the members of the group is washing her beautiful (and huge) white Harley-Davidson. Two others are working on the Yamaha Venture, which looks like it's having some electrical problems. I get the impression at first that they might think I'm a local. After all, I rode into the parking lot with no gear strapped to my bike or anything else indicating that I was a fellow traveller. That is, until I tell them about my accident and the flatbed truck. A member of the group says,

"Was that you?"

"Yes."

"You waved to us from the flatbed truck as we rode by."

"You were the group I waved to?"

"Yes."

What are the odds of bumping into the group I waved to from the back of the flatbed truck? I get talking to the rider of the Honda Shadow, which looks like it's from the mid-80s. He tells me the Shadow is a workhorse and has had no problems. I'm guessing the Venture owner wished he could say the same thing. I don't think this group is stopping here and I think I overheard that his headlight wasn't working. I wish them luck and leave.

Part 19

*Alaska! How
Sweet It Is!*

August 10

I step outside of my hotel room. So cool is it this morning that I can see my breath. It's raining, as well. I foresee a cold bike ride today. I'm in Beaver Creek, which I believe is the most westerly settlement in Canada.

The rain has stopped so I put away the rain gear. I get back on the road after checking out of the motel and getting gas. I ride along, knowing I'm within minutes of reaching Alaska by motorcycle. I pass Canada Customs for people who are coming into Canada. I have waited a long time to see those words "Welcome to Alaska."

I turn on a bend in the road and look up ahead, to see a building perched at the top of a hill. As I get closer I can see a brown sign. There are people standing near it. It could be the sign—YES! It says Welcome to Alaska. I've made it! I give a big WHA-HOO! I put my left hand in a fist and punch the air. I see a family standing near the sign. I quickly park my bike, grab my camera and walk really fast towards it. I ask the man (with his family) to please take my picture. He does. I ask for another for good luck. He takes the picture and I thank him again. I start walking towards my bike when I realize I forgot to get a picture with my Graphicshoppe hat on. I grab the hat and go back to the family. I offer to take their picture. They accept. After taking their picture I again ask if he would please take my picture with my lucky hat on.

167

Why did I call it my lucky hat? Oh well, it's my old company's hat anyway, I tell him. He takes a picture and we talk a bit. He and his family are moving back east after being in Alaska a couple of years.

I go back to my bike and then begin the ride up the hill towards the U.S. customs station. A border guard officer is already standing outside the office when I stop where the signs tells me to. He's on the tall side, with one hand on his hip. Are they armed? I'm guessing he might be. He gives me the signal to proceed. I get about five feet from him and cut the engine, coasting to a stop right beside him. I take off my gloves and sunglasses. I immediately ask him how he's doing. He says, he's doing good, and asks me how I'm doing.

"I'm doing great. I can't believe I've made it."

"Where are you going?"

"Fairbanks, Anchorage, and Homer."

"What is your citizenship?"

"I'm a Canadian."

He then asks me the standard questions about liquor and stuff like that. I say no to all of the above, which is true.

"What's in those bags," he asks.

I tell him what's in the saddlebags and backrest pack.

"What's in that big pack on your back?"

"I got all kinds of junk in there."

He chuckles when I say this and tells me I can go. I leave. It's a few minutes later now and I'm laughing and "YEE-HAWING" as I ride along in the LAST FRONTIER, as some people call it. I can't believe I'm actually here.

I'm about twenty minutes into Alaska now and it starts to rain hard enough to pull over and put the rain stuff on. I'm putting on the clothes when four motorcyclists from Iowa stop and ask me if everything is okay. I explain what I'm doing and tell them everything's fine. They go on to tell me they experienced a lot of rain in Alaska. A woman passenger says they went to the Arctic Circle. I'm not sure where that is in terms of where I am now, but it sounds impressive to me. When you hear the words "Arctic Circle" you probably don't automatically think of motorcycles. I thank them for stopping.

That's the great thing about travelling by motorcycle on the Alaska Highway, because generally motorcyclists will slow down and check to see if you're in trouble if you are stopped on the side of the road. I do the same. If I'm stopped, I wave at cars and trucks to let them know I'm okay, because it's not only motorcyclists who get concerned when they see a rider at the side of the road. There is a great sense of community, I find, on the Alaska Highway. Particularly with motorcyclists. There's almost an instant bond when you start talking to one. There's a buzz or energy in the air. I think the unspoken link or bond that we share is ADVENTURE with a capital A. A feeling we are doing something beyond ourselves. A shared excitement of a common dream, perhaps. When talking about bad weather conditions or roads, we nod knowingly and can't wait to tell our stories. I think it's like when you were really young and got a lecture from a police officer or ended up in the back seat of a cop car for something minor, and all they did was scare you a bit and let you go. Even though you were scared and angry at the time, you couldn't wait to tell your friends about it.

I arrive in Tok, Alaska without incident. The landscape is getting flatter and less mountainous. Leaving Tok now, just outside of it actually, and I'm on one of these incredibly straight and long stretches of road. The road stays this way for about ten miles.

Fifty miles outside of Tok and again a very long stretch of road. It's getting warmer and warmer, though. I wonder if it has to do with the gradual downward slant of the landscape and general flatness of the terrain. The highway is extremely good in most parts. I'm about 15 miles from Fairbanks, Alaska now. The highway becomes four lanes. I didn't expect this. It feels like I'm going into a big city. Maybe I am. I honestly don't know.

I'm in the city centre now and I'm lost. I was and am totally unprepared for the size of it. I see a large photocopy store (part of a chain of stores) and pull in. It's one of those stores that has everything. It has fax machines, photocopying, cards, pens, computers and, well, you get the idea. I fax the Graphicshoppe to tell them I have arrived in Alaska. From here I use their courtesy phone to look up a motel room.

I find the motel and it costs $108 U.S. for the night. YIKES!

August 11

I step out of my motel and start walking towards the restaurant for breakfast. Am I roughing it, or what? It's 41 degrees F., cloudy, and I can see my breath again this morning. I write postcards while I wait for breakfast and after breakfast. I promised to write a lot of postcards, especially from Alaska. After breakfast, I do some laundry and get packed.

I'm in a large bank. I'm inquiring about one of my credit cards that their ATM rejected. They tell me the magnetic strip is probably damaged. The woman suggests I go to my nearest branch and get a new card. Well, the nearest branch for this particular bank is probably over 500 miles away, maybe a thousand. I thank them for their help and leave. It's raining now.

I have just spent the last 40 minutes being lost. It's a talent, really. Well I'm finally out of Fairbanks and on the highway. At this point it changes from 55 miles an hour to 65. I don't go any faster, though, because the faster I go, the colder I am. Also, my head is itching like crazy. The scenery is nice, though.

I pull into a gas station. I'm approximately 9 miles from the town of Denali. A man at the gas station tells me that there is an L.L. Bean in town and they might have the warm gloves I'm looking for. My hands are freezing. I can't keep them warm no matter what I do. I'm in town now amongst the hustle and bustle. I cruise the strip of stores and restaurants, looking for the L.L. Bean store. I can't find it. I ask someone who works in one of the stores. They don't have an L.L. Bean here. I'm directed to an outdoors store.

Although it looks smallish on the outside it's got a lot of stuff inside. Lots of warm clothes for hiking and the like. I'm looking at the fleece gloves and inserts.

"How ya doing there, Captain?" a female voice says behind me.

It takes a few seconds to realize that she is talking to me. She helps me select a pair of fleece gloves. I'll put them on inside my rubber gloves. I'm back on the road again, trying this new combination of gloves and they are very warm. YESSS. The itching on my scalp drives me to the point where I turn off to the side of the road just at the end of the Denali town line. I get the idea that maybe my helmet is on too loose. Maybe it's the vibration of the helmet itself. I pull the strap as tight as I can get it without choking myself. I get back on the highway. I get up to highway speed and wait for the itching to start. It doesn't happen. Oh man, I can't tell you how good that feels, because the itching was driving me nuts. AHHHH.

It's a couple of hours later. After getting some gas, I take off my rain outfit and rubber gloves. It has become warm and clear. The temperature is pretty near perfect. I come across a strange little settlement that sells a lot of fireworks. In a small area there are three or four fair-sized stores all selling fireworks. I'm about thirty-two miles from Anchorage and I think I can see Mt. McKinley. It's huge and snow-covered, if that's the one.

I turn onto Highway 2. A few minutes later now and I check my rear view mirror and notice my sleeping bag is gone. It is normally perched on top of the pack that slips onto the backrest. I curse, then I begin to be relieved, and now I'm laughing out loud in my helmet. I'm laughing because I have no intention of going back to look for it. Oh well, I guess I can't camp now. Can you imagine my disappointment? HA! It's a few minutes later now and again I look in my rear view mirror, to see a huge truck flashing his lights at me. I pull over and get off my bike. I look at the trucker warily as he walks towards me. He has kind of a half grin on his face. I look at him with a touch of uncertainty and wariness, because I can't figure out why he wanted me to pull over. He picks up on this and immediately tells me that he saw my sleeping bag fall off. He tried to tell me further back on the highway but I didn't get what he was trying to do. I was beside a big eighteen-wheeler back down the road that I thought was pulling off the highway and didn't see me beside him, so I sped up. It was him.

I tell him it was extremely nice of him to make such an effort to alert me to the loss of my sleeping bag. He says he's been there. A fellow motorcyclist, I'm guessing. I don't have the heart to tell him I don't care about my sleeping bag. His concern and kindness compels me to go back and look for it. He gives me directions. He tells me that it fell off just as I was turning onto the highway. He adds that a car hit it and it flew off to the side of the road. I suggest it might be (hoping it would be) too destroyed to go back for. He assures me that it should be fine. Just my luck. I thank him for his help and kindness. I get back on my bike and begin to go back to the spot he's talking about.

Well here I am. I'm standing beside my bike and looking at the general area the trucker said the sleeping bag would be. I walk down the shoulder of the road, looking to my right mostly. Most of the terrain to my right is a swamp. Am I going to go wading in the swamp to look for it? Take a guess. If you guessed no, you are right. I'm only here because of sheer guilt that the trucker made such an effort to tell me it was here. For what it's worth (besides the swamp), I am honestly looking for it. After ten minutes and about a hundred yards, I give up looking for it. Oh well.

I'm on a three lane (on my side) highway going into Anchorage, Alaska. Anchorage, to my surprise, looks like a pretty big city. It's around 10:00 p.m. and the sun has just about set. I start looking for a hotel or motel. Everything seems booked solid. At one point I accidentally went the wrong way down a one-way street. After about forty-five minutes, I find a hotel for $126 U.S. for one night.

August 12

A gorgeous day in the city of Anchorage. My mental picture of Anchorage was wrong. I don't know what I expected, but it wasn't a big modern city. Oh well. I inquire about hot air balloon rides at the hotel travel info place. As far as they know, they don't exist in Anchorage. I will get an early start today. It looks like an ideal day for a ride.

172

I'm on the highway again now with my final destination being Homer, Alaska. If you have a map, try and find Homer just for the hell of it. Homer, Alaska means the end of the Alaska Highway for me. I began at mile 0 and Homer will finish it for me. I'm not too far outside Anchorage now and the highway is sheer rock on my left and water on my right. What a great place to ride a bike. I see a lot of people (on my right) stopped at a place called Beluga Point (or something like that). I turn in, hoping I'll be able to see a Beluga whale. I ask a man how long he's been here looking for a whale. He's been here over ten minutes and he hasn't seen a Beluga. Well, that's good enough for me. I get on my bike and leave. Oh well. Back on the road now, I stay behind the slower vehicles so I can see the scenery, composed of rock, water, and beautiful mountains.

I turn off on an exit that will take me to Homer. I'm 132 miles away now. The highway at this point becomes very narrow. The trees and plants come right to the road. It is a lot rougher on this part of the highway. The highway road surfaces were unbelievably smooth up until this point. The weather is still extremely clear and warm. A half hour later now and the countryside is getting flatter. My feet and hands are nice and warm. What more could I ask?

Seven miles from Homer I spot an R.V. in front of me with an Ontario licence plate. I pass them and wave. I see a lookout point and turn in. A beautiful view of the mountains and water. I see a couple pointing at some birds. I walk over to them. They are looking at a Bald Eagle who is riding the wind. The strange thing is that there are two or three black birds (crows or ravens maybe) harassing the eagle. Safety in numbers, I guess. They bother and bully the eagle so much, it gives up and leaves. I don't understand why the eagle just didn't turn on the other birds and attack one of them. Maybe even the mighty eagle has its enemies. I take some pictures and leave.

I breeze into Homer now and am quite mellow about the whole thing. Such a great day. The speed limits are low once you get into town. Well, as far as I know, I have ridden the entire Alaska Highway,

173

maybe more. The accomplishment of the people who built the highway is staggering. An engineering feat (I think I read this in Dawson Creek) that has not been matched since—taking only six months to build an estimated 1400-mile highway, under horrific conditions. I'm sure at times the conditions were appalling, given the terrain they had to work with and the weather. I believe it took over 10,000 (military and civilian) people to build it, starting in the summer of 1942. I tip my hat to everyone who helped build the Alaska Highway.

I ride out to the Homer spit, which probably looks like a giant thermometer from the air. There are people camped on the beach, there are lots of R.V.s, old hippie-type school buses converted into campers, older Volkswagen vans, and other ancient trucks. There are lots of shops and restaurants. I'm off my bike now and walking around. I come across a crowd gathered to look at some fish that are hanging on pegs. They are big with pure white sides. They look to be about 50 or 60 pounds. I ask a guy beside me what kind of fish they are.

"You don't know what kind of fish they are?" he asks, surprised.

"No."

They're halibut!

DOH! Well, I am in Homer, Alaska. I didn't realize halibut could be so big. I've been eating fish and chips all my life and didn't know what halibut looked like. Come to think of it, I am kind of hungry. I go to a grocery store and get some supplies and now I'll go to the fish and chip shop. Brother, is that me all over, or what? I get some groceries and then go straight to the restaurant. Now, after waiting for about ten minutes, my fish and chips are brought to me. They are delicious pieces of fish. They (the halibut) were probably caught yesterday or maybe even this morning. I go back to my hotel after lunch.

It's night now and I'm back on the spit. The mountains are just as pretty when night starts to fall. What is it about mountains?

August 13

What can I say, it's even warmer than yesterday. So nice a day in fact that I'm not wearing my jacket as I ride toward the spit to take a few pictures.

After taking the pictures I arrive at the local post office and mail a bunch of postcards.

Well I'm back on the highway with the destination of Anchorage. I will be taking the same route back because (as far as I know) there isn't another one. I pull off the highway after about five minutes because it just isn't warm enough without a jacket.

A while later now and I'm in a smallish town called Sterling, Alaska. I hope to get a postcard for my friend Jackie, who is from Stirling, Ontario. As you may recall, I stayed in Stirling with her and her grandparents. I turn into a place that sells maps and books. I get talking to the woman who works here. She says they had a terrible summer, weather-wise. They don't have a Sterling postcard. I ask her if she sells any books about motorcycling in Alaska. She doesn't. We talk a bit more and I leave.

I'm in Anchorage now. It was a nice ride with no spectacular incidents to report. I'm in what seems to be the older downtown part. One street (the one I parked my bike on) has a lot of street vendors, nice restaurants, lots of souvenir shops, and a federal building that was built in the early 1900s. I walk around a bit and look at the sights. I do this for an hour or so and leave.

I'm riding towards Fairbanks, Alaska now. Something I forgot to mention while I've been in Alaska, and that is how many road signs I've seen with bullet holes in them or dents from bullets that didn't make it through. There doesn't seem to be a pattern or any particular sign the people shoot at. Any and every sign seems to be fair game. I've also noticed that roughly half or more of the motorcyclists I've seen here don't wear a helmet.

It's 9:00 p.m. now and starting to get chilly. I'm going to keep riding for as long as I can. Another 150 miles or so and I hope to come upon a big town or settlement. It's 10:00 p.m. now and I'm freezing. The sun has gone behind the mountains. It's still light out but cold. I stop and switch to warmer gloves. I'm back on the road now. Minutes later I have a case of the shakes. I can't stop shaking and shivering; I'm so cold now. I keep telling myself that I'll see a motel or something soon. I slow down to a speed of 40 miles per hour to try and keep warm. The slower the better as I am really, really cold now. Half an hour later and I see a building that looks like a big log cabin. I ride past it, then turn around. I park the bike and go inside. They have a room. WHEW!

August 14

I can see my breath again this morning. I will try and find the Fairbanks Harley-Davidson dealership and buy a T-shirt when I arrive there towards the end of the day.

It's an hour later now and it is a great day. To what do I owe this luck? I talked to the waitress this morning at the restaurant part of the lodge and she said it has been the worst weather they have had in twenty years. Imagine my surprise. Another woman (who booked me into the lodge) said last night it usually stays light until 2:30 a.m., but not this summer. When I decided to go to Alaska, I wonder if everyone in the state had an involuntary shudder and didn't know why.

I'm in Denali again now. The little town part. I don't enter the National Park. I see a sign advertising helicopter rides. I park the bike in their lot and go in. I'm in luck. They have a helicopter tour leaving in an hour. It costs $185 U.S. but it is for almost an hour. I will get to see Mt. McKinley in the nearly cloudless sky.

After killing some time in the town, I'm back at the helicopter place. We are getting our boarding instructions. The helicopter I'm about to board is bigger than the first one. It holds three in the back and three in the front, which includes the pilot. I hope to get to sit in the front. The man who gives us these boarding instructions also tells us where we are to sit. We were all asked our weight, so I think he's sizing us up for balance. One man volunteers to sit in the middle in the back because he has no camera. He seems to be the only one. That was generous of him. I'm the last to be picked. I get the window seat in the front. YESSS! I'm sitting beside a woman with the pilot on the other side of her. It's a little cramped. The helper closes the door and I'm pressed up against it. Hmmmm. All I can think about now is that I hope he closed the door properly, because if he didn't, it's going to pop open at 3,000 feet. That could put a damper on my enjoyment of the flight, to say the least.

We lift off. I really like this. Again it feels to me like floating, not flying. We go in the direction of Denali National Park. There's huge white mountains in the distance directly in front of us. I'm about to ask the pilot if ...

"Yes, that's it."

He knows what I'm going to ask. It is indeed Mt. McKinley. It dwarfs the sea of white-peaked mountains before it. Even though we are still far away from it, you can see it's just a white monster of a mountain. Eventually we will get around 15 to 30 miles from it. It doesn't sound close, but it is when you are talking about the highest mountain in North America and (I believe) one of the highest in the world. We are lucky we have clear skies.

The pilot (Frank) gives us a lot of facts about what we are seeing but I don't pay too much attention. I'm too busy looking at all the scenery. I take pictures of the mountains and glacial regions. I love riding in helicopters now. It took me my whole life (up to about a week ago) to ride in one and I just think they are fantastic. He tells us about the different colours on the sides of the mountains. Some of the orangey colours are actually copper and other materials that make up the surface. We fly close to Mt. McKinley. He tells us that it's a very difficult mountain to climb because the temperature can plummet to -100 degrees F. (if I heard right) with the wind chill factor. I can't imagine climbing something so utterly unforgiving as this mountain looks. I take pictures. He shows us and tells us more things and, before you know it, the flight is over. I have my picture taken with Frank and find out from another passenger that he (the pilot) was in Desert Storm. I go to the gift shop and buy some pins and a video. I leave Denali.

I have 70 miles to go before I reach Fairbanks and there is a state trooper about 50 yards behind me. I had seen him earlier on the side of the road and slowed down, but he looked right at me. Now he's behind me. Luckily for me, I'm doing the speed limit or slower. I look in the mirror again and see he's flashing his lights. Uh-oh. To my relief, he does a U-turn and goes in the opposite direction.

Part 20 *Crossing Back Over the Border*

August 15

It's overcast this morning and I get a late start. I'm around twelve miles outside the junction that will take me to the Canada/U.S. border and the Top of the World Highway.

Highway 5 comes up fast. I turn left onto it and immediately the road changes from smooth to hard-packed gravel. For some reason, the surface of the road is a yellowish colour. The road is pretty good for awhile, then turns to loose gravel. It continues this way until I arrive in Chicken, Alaska. I get gas in the gas station/gift shop/service centre in Chicken, Alaska. I get a snack, look around a bit and leave. The road deteriorates almost immediately. I'm forced to go a lot slower. There are white-coloured rocks sticking out of the road. There are also grey patches in the road with sharp rocks in them. I try and avoid those patches as best I can. A large truck comes at me with a cloud of dust billowing out from its back. I almost have to stop completely before I can continue on. It is cool out, which is good. I'm almost always in the two lowest gears anyway, so it's not a problem. If it had been warm today I think my bike would have overheated. Another plus is, although it's overcast, it is not raining. To try and navigate this road in the rain would have been extremely difficult, in my opinion.

Some of the car and truck drivers slow down when they see me. Some don't. As time or road goes on, the road is getting narrower and narrower. I would hate to meet one of those big trucks or RVs on one of these narrow corners. Just up ahead I see a mini-van in the ditch. The people were headed in the same direction as me and somehow ended up in the ditch on the opposite side of the road. I slow down and ask the woman if she needs help. She tells me someone has already gone for help, thanks anyway. As I pass the van a man is squatting near the front of the van, looking a little sheepish.

I face another hazard when I get on a decent stretch of road and accelerate, thinking the road has gotten better. It hasn't. It's just a tease. I do manage to pass some RVs. This is tricky because, like me, they tend to drift according to the road conditions in front of them. I am again doing an Ace Ventura to get a better look at the road. I do this for most of the time for mile after mile. It seems to work. This road seems to go on forever. I think from Chicken it is 70 miles to the border. It feels like 700 sometimes. After a few hours of going really slow and fighting the road, I see a building at the top of a hill. I hope it's the border crossing. I get closer and … it is!

The border officer is already outside of the small office before I arrive. I guess there's not a lot of noise out here. He might have the loneliest outpost in North America. I pull up. He asks me how long I was in the States, what I bought, how much the things I bought amounted to. I answer the questions. Okay, I can go, he says. He goes back into the trailer home/office. Just as he gets in the office I think of a question. I raise my voice and ask him if the road gets any better. He tells me that it's paved. Oh man, music to my ears. Let's face it, I'm on a street bike that just wasn't designed for the 100 miles or so I was just on. A dirt bike, or one of those Paris/Dakar-type bikes which looks like a fancy dirt bike, would have been much better.

A few minutes later now and it feels so good to be on a smooth riding surface. It's not totally flat but after the road (did I say road?) I was just on, it might as well be sheer glass. Immediately you realize it's not called The Top of the World Highway for nothing. It's like riding on the top of an absolutely huge A-framed roof. To my right it is grassy and, although it's gradual and not a sheer drop, it's a long, long way down. I quickly become too confident on this highway. I force myself to slow down. It is a beautiful highway with great scenery but you can't take your eyes off the road for too long. The corners are narrow here as well. Steep climbs and quick descents. I would highly recommend riding on this highway, travelling by any means. It's unique. I have not seen a settlement or gas station since before I arrived at the border crossing. I have just arrived in the outskirts of Dawson City, Yukon. There was no settlement or gas station visible from the highway.

I follow the signs and descend into the outskirts of Dawson City. I come upon a line-up of vehicles. I'm not sure why we are all lined up— oh, I see, we are all waiting for a ferry. There's a fast-moving river to cross in order to get into Dawson City. I'm off my bike and a gentleman tells me it holds around nine cars. The ferry comes towards the bank in a kind of an arch (or skidding fashion) and kind of rams itself into the sandy bank. The cars and people in front come off. The cars and RVs quickly fill it up again. I'm daydreaming a bit when I realize there is a ferry-worker gesturing to me to get on the ferry. I ride on and squeeze onto the back. I can see the city as the ferry travels to the other side in its arch-like path. The river is running pretty fast. We beach ourselves on the bank. The ramp comes down. The ferry is free, by the way. I ride off the ferry and am greeted by history itself.

There's an old house just off to the left. It is abandoned, with overgrown bushes surrounding it. It looks like one of the original buildings from the goldrush days. Despite its deteriorated condition, it is beautiful, a jewel in the fabric of time. Like a wise old grandfather who, despite his age, has a respectability and presence. Tell me a story if you can, please, old house. To my right there is an old riverboat that looks like it's in the process of being renovated. I get closer to the centre of Dawson City. All the roads are dirt (so far) and the sidewalks are wooden. It's like the set of a Hollywood movie, only this is real, a kind of living museum, if you will.

181

I pull up near a hotel and go in. There aren't any rooms left in this hotel but she suggests I call the visitor centre. The visitor centre kindly hooks me up with a hostel that has exactly one bed left if I come over right now. I thank him and the lady at the hotel and jump on my bike and re-cross the river. The second left from the ferry area I go up a slight hill. I get to the gate. There's a black Russian motorcycle with sidecar to my left and an assortment of other vehicles. Past the gate there are tents and cabins and what looks like a central cooking area. I check in and then the operator takes me on a small tour.

Under a large carport-type structure there is a well-travelled bike from Finland. Man, is that person far away from home. Anyway, he shows me where the washrooms and showers and stuff like that are. I'm shown to a cabin. There is a single bed and two bunk beds. I get the top bunk of the first bunk bed on the left. There is no one here right now. There is no electricity or running water in this cabin. I start to store my stuff at the end of the bed. It turns out the motorcyclist from Finland is staying in this cabin. He arrives a few minutes later. I introduce myself. His name is Kari. He tells me all the places he's been on his bike (which is pretty much everywhere) and we trade stories about the road from Tok to the border. His time on that road was a lot quicker because he has one of those big dirt bike machines. I get the impression he's on a world motorcycling trip. He's staying in this hostel while he awaits some tires in the mail from Florida. I tell him I met a rider from Florida (Gavin) who went pretty far up north. He says he met Gavin up north. Small world. Now that I think of it, if he's ridden practically all over the world he probably had no problem at all with the road from Tok to the border. I bet he's seen worse.

I eventually get the rest of my stuff stored and my bike is now parked beside Kari's in the small carport.

I take the ferry back into Dawson City. I'm starving, because all I ate in Tok was a bowl of cereal, and in Chicken I had some small crackers with peanut butter in them. I usually only have two meals a day now. I take the ferry (without my bike) back to Dawson City.

I get off the ferry and start looking around for a restaurant. I walk along the wooden sidewalks with my boots clunking on the boards making a great sound. Dirty streets, a little bit muddy, this is what the old west must have felt like. To add to the cowboy feel of it all, I'm not the cleanest I could be. My jeans and denim shirt are slightly on the grimy side. I settle on a semi-pricey restaurant in the hotel that I originally went in when I first arrived. I order the prime rib. I feel like celebrating. Lucky for me, I get the last one. As more people come in they all seem to want the prime rib dinner and are very disappointed when told there is no more left. My dinner arrives and it's HUGE. Good thing I'm hungry. The dinner was delicious and I order blueberry pie and coffee for dessert.

I leave the restaurant and wander around a bit. I see the cabin Robert Service lived in, as well as Jack London's. They are quite small. I will explore more tomorrow.

I'm back in the cabin now. It has no lights and of course I have no flashlight. In true Klondike fashion, I bang my head on the beam in the ceiling. Some of my cabin mates start arriving now. One of them quickly falls asleep and begins to snore the snore of the gods. It drives me crazy. I can't sleep. At some point it sounds like he is going to die. He is snoring so long and so loud now I kind of wish he would expire. Just kidding.

August 16

I am the first one up. I immediately bang my head on the beam again, only harder this time. If I can't get a semi-private cabin I won't stay. I can't spend one more night with Sir Snore-A-Lot. I make a hasty exit with bacon and eggs on my mind. I also want to do some laundry today.

I ask one of the workers on the ferry where a good place for breakfast would be. A place called Klondike Katie's is suggested. After a brief time spent in a line-up, I am sitting and waiting for my breakfast. After breakfast, I begin the hunt for a laundry. I find it, but due to electrical problems it is not open. I will remain somewhat dirty for the rest of the morning. Oh well, I'm sure the miners and prospectors weren't exactly wearing starched white tennis outfits when they came into town. I will look grubby in true Klondike fashion. I'll go back to the hostel now and try and get a semi-private cabin.

Back at the hostel I'm taking a picture of the Russian motorcycle called a Dnepr. I also take pictures of the Honda belonging to Kari. I did manage to get a semi-private cabin. It has only one other bed and has not been rented as of yet. It cost me an extra 16 dollars.

I'm sitting at a picnic table when the owner of the Russian motorcycle strikes up a conversation with me. He rode on the Alaska Highway (the whole or most of it) in the middle of winter. Yes, you read that last line correctly. In −35 degree temperatures he rode on his Dnepr with sidecar. He tells me truckers were talking about him on their CB radios. He also had his picture taken by a newspaper, which made it to the front page. When I tell him about my cold hands problem, he laughs and rolls his eyes. I ask him how he kept his hands and feet warm. He tells me that he just kept wriggling them. I tried that and it didn't work. He will be going back to Alaska to get some new tires at a Ural dealer. Another (I believe) Russian type of motorcycle. He is wearing a green army sweater. I should have got one of those.

I go back over the river to Dawson City again to look around some more. I buy a ticket for the Gaslight Follies. I was lucky to get one of the few remaining tickets. The ticket seller tells me there is a tour of the theatre beginning in around ten minutes. I will take the tour.

The theatre is a replica of the original Palace Grand Theatre. The original theatre was torn down in the 1960s because it was deemed to be too far gone to be saved. The father of one of the ladies in our tour group was the conductor at the original theatre in its heyday. It is a beautiful theatre. It's smallish and charming with lots of wood. They did a great job of building this theatre. If you're ever in Dawson City, please check it out. There is an upper level as well as individual boxes. Also, there are small nicely-furnished rooms where the owner and stars would stay. The tour guide is dressed in period costume and is funny and friendly. The tour ends and I step back onto the street.

I have about four hours to put in. I'll walk around the streets some more. I'll take some pictures as well. It is sunny today and the city looks different in the sunshine. I think Dawson City looks better later in the day with an overcast sky. That was the way the city was when I first saw it, so perhaps that's why I like it that way. It is the 100th anniversary of the Gold Rush this year. It began in 1898. No wonder there are so many people here this weekend, or this summer for that matter. I also believe there is a reunion of sorts with people who are connected somehow with the past. So 100 years ago thousands of people came here to strike it rich. Some did, but I think most of them didn't. I am still wearing my usual outfit, which consists of jeans, denim shirt, long johns, etc. I will change for the theatre tonight. All clean clothes. I will leave for Vancouver tomorrow.

I walk around some more. I go back to the hostel and wash my hair in the sink and shave out of a plastic bowl. Roughing it, I tell ya! Oh brother, I'm getting all cleaned up for the show tonight.

I arrive at the theatre at around a quarter to eight. I walk inside the theatre and am shown to my seat. I think about my theatre co-workers back home. Well, well, I had forgotten that Joey Hollingsworth was in this production. I don't know him personally, but he was in a show called *R.S.V.P. Broadway* at the Winter Garden Theatre. I saw that show many times (well, because I worked there) and I hope he does some tap dancing in this show too.

The show starts off with a piano player. Then there are the other characters—a Mountie, the miner-type guy, the prude, the pretty girl, etc. I won't tell you the whole show. All I can say is, come up to Dawson City and see it for yourself. Joey Hollingsworth did indeed do some tap dancing in the show. He was great, as were all the members of the cast.

I'm out in the lobby now and the actors have started to come out and meet the audience. Joey comes out as well. He graciously signs some autographs for some children. After five minutes or so I introduce myself and mention I work at the Elgin and Winter Garden Theatre Centre (in Toronto). I tell him how much I enjoyed his tap dancing in this show and *R.S.V.P. Broadway*. We talk about *R.S.V.P.* (as he signs some more autographs) and this show. He is a very positive person. He got very good reviews for *R.S.V.P.* and will be going to New York City to work on Broadway (not *R.S.V.P.*) We talk some more and I shake his hand. I called him Mr. Hollingsworth a couple of times and he insisted I call him Joey. I like that. A class act.

I'm in Diamond Tooth Gertie's, not too far from the theatre. It's a gambling casino. I have spent five dollars' worth of quarters in the slot machines. I have ten $1 tokens left but can't get near the machine (it's quite busy), so I cash out and leave. It was fun, though. They have a live show going on. Back on the road tomorrow.

August 17

I say goodbye to the hostel. Unfortunately, it's raining. I begin on the journey to Whitehorse. The fog or clouds have moved into the hills. I can only see about thirty yards ahead. I'm about twenty kilometres on the road to Whitehorse when I keep getting the feeling I'm going the wrong way. I stop and check my map. Well, I'm going the right way.

I pull over a little later because I *must* be going the wrong way. This feels like the Top of the World Highway. Well let's see, now, according to the map … I AM GOING THE WRONG FREAKING WAY!! DUMB! I went 43 kilometres the wrong way.

I'm going back through Dawson City now. I am finally going the correct way. It is still raining. The first thing I notice outside of Dawson is that the leaves are changing colour. A sure sign that fall is on the way, along with cooler temperatures.

I'm 150 kms outside of Dawson now and the fuel light comes on. I have about 20 kms until the next settlement. No problem. I pull into a gas station a little while later. I stop beside the gas pump. A worker comes up to me and says, "No gas, I'm sorry. Our electricity is out. A tree fell on our power lines. It could be hours before someone comes to fix it." He points. Indeed, the tree had broken and fallen onto the wires. I ask him about the nearest town or gas station. He says the nearest gas station (if I heard him right) is 70 kms away. That's way too far for me. I would simply not make it. What shall I do? What would you do? I'll wait. Maybe the power company will get here sooner.

I sit in the rain for a while and ponder my fate. One car or vehicle after another pulls up to the gas station, to hear what I've heard. Eventually I'm invited into the garage to get out of the rain. The two guys running the gas station look to be in their late teens. They tell me that today is a holiday in the Yukon. Also, there is a big forest fire possibly coming this way. Apparently thousands and thousands of hectares of forest have been destroyed and more are still burning. Man, did I pick a bad time to be here.

One of them offers to siphon gas from his truck to get me on my way. My faith in human kindness has been strengthened on this trip. After several tries and a bad taste in his mouth, I offer to help. He declines. After a few more tries he's ready for me to give it a go. I ask him how to do it. I have never done this before. I ask him the technique. He tells me it's ok. He tries a couple more times and the gas starts to flow. I thank him very much, pay for the gas, offer to pay too much for the gas and leave. It's 70 kms to the next gas station. I get back on the road and can smell the forest fire almost immediately. At about the 35 km mark the fuel light comes on. I will try and go as far as I can before switching to the reserve tank.

Well, I make it to the gas station and am now in a lineup for the pumps. The lineup starts to move, but my bike won't start. I try again. No luck. I guess I'm out of gas. Elementary, my dear Watson. I fill the tank. It still won't start. I look at the instrument panel, it tells me nothing. I look at the choke lever; it's wide open. I rode 70 kms with the choke wide open. Way to go, Dan, geez.

I will stop at a town called Carmacks or the first motel I see. I'm cold, wet, and hungry. I'm also out of dry gloves. I think I left a pair of gloves in Dawson City.

I arrive in Carmacks and go straight to a hotel. A couple on motorbikes from Alberta are here. A Honda and what looks like a Midnight

Maxim from the mid-eighties. The woman of the couple is standing just inside the lobby. She tells me they have closed the road to Whitehorse because of the forest fire. I ask her if all the rooms are taken, she says no, but I had better hurry. I do hurry and get one of the few remaining rooms. A half-hour later, the hotel was fully booked.

August 18

It is mostly sunny this morning. I stop at a local gas station in Carmacks. Apparently there was a telephone pole across the road. Maybe it was the pole and the fire. I say both, because the hotel desk clerk confirmed the motorcyclist's story about the road being closed due to the fire. Oh well, pole or fire, I was staying anyway. I get back on the road and, despite the sunny patches, it remains cold. My hands are freezing. I stop to switch gloves.

I'm 80 kms away from Carmacks and I can see the smoke from the forest fire burning on both sides of the highway just up ahead. I ride another few minutes and take pictures of the smoking, blackened forest. The smoke is floating across the road up ahead. There is still the odd pocket of forest where the forest floor is still smouldering. What an awful and eerie sight a recently burnt forest is. If anything were left alive in this forest I would be very surprised.

I'm 50 kms from arriving in Whitehorse and my hands are so cold it's driving me nuts. As soon as I'm in Whitehorse I will buy some mittens or snowmobile gloves, or something. It's about a half hour later now and I'm in the information centre in Whitehorse. A man at the centre gives me directions on how to get to a Yamaha dealership in town.

I arrive at the dealership a few minutes later and ask the counterperson if they have any snowmobile mittens. She tells me that snowmobiles have heated grips now, so they don't need the big heavy mittens anymore. She says they have muffs that fit over the entire handle grip. I've seen them in Toronto on bicycles. At this point I'm willing to try anything. After a lot of searching she and the mechanic find them.

They might be difficult to put over and around the clutch and brake covers, so the three of us go outside to take a look. The muffs have a nice lining inside. They are black inside and out. The mechanic slips them up and over the levers up to the mirror stem. It looks kind of weird, but it works for me. I go inside and pay for them. She had said earlier in our conversation that she was surprised my hands were cold with the fleece and rubber combinations. She goes on to say that women usually complain most about cold hands. I tell her I have small hands (which I do) and low blood pressure (the jury is still out on that one). I thank her and we both go back outside. The mechanic has finished. It looks funny; everything (starter buttons, signal buttons, horn, handgrips, etc.) is covered up. It looks like my bike just grew big floppy ears. I thank them both and leave. I can't see what I'm doing (handwise) so it's hard at first to find the various switches by feel. I'll get used to it. It is one thing, though—WARM. With a capital W.

I arrive in the Teslin Lake district and get some gas. They also have a restaurant. I'm sitting in the restaurant when the couple from the hotel in Carmacks come riding in for gas. I leave Teslin Lake with 277 kms left to ride before arriving in Watson Lake, where I'll spend the night. The muffs are still doing their job. The leaves are turning colour in this part of the north as well.

I arrive in Watson Lake without incident.

189

Part 21

If I'm going south, this must be B.C.

August 19

I get a late start under partly sunny skies. I turn left onto the number 37 highway going south. As soon as I get on the road I have a feeling it's going to be rough. Some highways are just different immediately and number 37 is one of them. There are no painted lines on the road and it's narrow. There are lots of twists and turns. It looks like one of those roads you see on television with car rally drivers going at insane speeds. Turns and curves you have to slow down quite a bit to execute. If the whole highway is like this, it's going to take me a long time to ride its 700 km length until I get to the junction.

The weather is nice. The road is fun to ride on. Small hills, speed up, slow down and repeat. It's kind of like being on a rally. I arrive in a place called Jade City for gas.

I'm ten minutes outside Jade City and I have continued to go downhill.

Seventy kilometres later and I'm still descending gradually to some flatter plain, I guess. It has turned into dirt roads for a while now and now it's hard-packed.

I'm again on loose gravel and it has remained this way for a couple of hours now. I feel like I've been fighting the road for hours. Watching the road that's directly in front of me rather than thirty or forty yards ahead. It reminds me of the highway from Tok, Alaska to the Top Of

The World Highway, although it's not as bad. It seems to take forever to get anywhere.

I'm riding along, singing songs in my head. I'm finally clear of the dirt road. I see an older Toyota Landcrusier at the side of the road, bent and crumpled. The owner or owners' possessions are strewn all over the place. I slow down to see if anyone is in the car or nearby. No one. I hope they're all right. It looks pretty bad.

The scenery is and has been great. Mountains, streams, and lakes. Oh yeah, I forgot to mention, a little while back I came upon a car stopped on the corner of a road. As I approached, I realized they were looking at a black bear that seemed to be not much older than a cub. I did not stop as I passed them, fearing mama bear was close by.

It's later now and I'll take the first motel I see. The sun is setting and throwing shadows on the road—the kind of shadows that make it hard to determine what is a shadow and what is a pothole or bump in the road.

It's 9:00 p.m. and I find a motel. I'm in a place called New Hazelton.

August 20

It's a nice day here in New Hazelton. I get an early start. I arrive in Smithers, B.C. and see a Harley-Davidson dealership. I pull in and take a look around. There's a new bike here I have never seen before. It's called a Harley-Davidson Nightrain. It sure is black, all right. Almost everything that normally would be shining and gleaming is also blacked out. I get talking with a Harley rider from Wisconsin, U.S.A. It turns out he went to Homer, Alaska and pretty much every other place I did. We talk a bit about Highway 37. In his opinion, there was one section that was so bad, it couldn't even be called a road. He says they just got a tiller-type machine, dug up the road and left it that way. I don't remember this particular stretch but it was pretty bad at times. We also talk about the Tok to Top of the World Highway. He and his passenger did that long stretch on a huge Harley (I think he is riding

191

an Ultra Classic), *and* in the rain. He must be a helluva rider, in my opinion. What a nightmare it must have been. I wish him luck and leave.

I continue on. I have to admit I'm a little bored today. It happens sometimes. The weather is perfect but I'm in a kind of retracing-my-steps-back-to-Vancouver mode. This part of the trip is pretty much over for me. I will again visit my friend Rod in Prince George. As I ride along, I daydream about maybe starting my own motorcycle company one day. What if I were to win, say, $15 million in the lottery? I could start a very small motorcycle company. I could manufacture maybe two models of say 25-50 of each. Which is funny because (as you know) I know next-to-nothing about motorcycles or business. Would that stop me? No. I think about what they might look like and a possible ad campaign. What colours they could come in. That kind of stuff. I have many, many hours to think of such things, with at least eight hours a day on the bike.

I'm just nearing the centre of Prince George. I stop and remove the handlebar muffs. It's just too warm now for them. I'm also wearing all my northern get-up. I will call Rod's work and see where he is.

I'm now waiting for Rod at the pub. When I'm back in Burnaby I'll figure out (try to) how much I spent (a lot) on this part of my trip and what I have left for the second part. I would like to see three things in the States—Redwood trees, the Grand Canyon, and Graceland in Memphis, Tennessee. I hope to be in Burnaby by tomorrow.

August 21

It's a really nice day here in Prince George. I get an early start. I want to be back in Burnaby today, which could take nine hours or so. I stayed at Rod's house. He insisted I stay there even though he has the flu.

On the road now and it's getting warmer. Despite that last sentence, I'm still wearing the usual. I have done this route at the beginning of the trip, so the road won't be a problem.

I'm forty kilometres out of Cache Creek. I'm descending into a valley. A blast of warm air hits me at the bottom of the hill. What a difference—it feels like it just jumped ten degrees. I'm in that region I mentioned before with brownish dry mountains that feels like a desert. Not long after, I'm going through a tunnel. For some reason, I'm just not thrilled with tunnels. It changes everything. It feels too closed in and loud. I'm about a half hour's ride from Hope, B.C., and the mountains are particularly pretty here. A sea of rolling shades of green. They feel a lot closer here, because they are. There are some incredibly deep valleys here and sheer drops.

I'm in Hope, now, in a phone booth. I call my sister Pat. My brother-in-law Don answers.

"Hi, Don."

"Dan. Where are you?"

"I am in Hope."

"Well your friend Dawn is really worried about you. When will you be home?"

"In a couple of hours."

I call Dawn. She's going to kill me. She has called practically every hospital from Vancouver to the Yukon (22 in all), to find me. I told her on Sunday I would be back to Vancouver in a few days. I totally miscalculated. When I didn't show up in Vancouver on Wednesday, she began to get very worried. She also called the R.C.M.P. and asked them to keep an eye out for me. She talked to one hospital and asked if they had a Dan Murphy admitted there. She was told they had THREE Dan Murphys. Dawn gave them my date of birth and they didn't match. Today is Friday. Geez, I feel so bad listening to Dawn recount how frightened and worried she was for a couple of days. I should have called her. She's glad I'm alive and again is going to KILL ME! I don't blame her. I apologize many times. She called everybody.

On the way to Vancouver, a couple from Alberta ride past me with the exact same bike as mine. How many of these things did Yamaha sell in 1993? I arrive in Vancouver without incident.

August 23

I'm telling my father about my financial plans concerning the trip. I explain that my friend Dawn will be putting $250 on each of my cards while I'm on the road. This will help me keep my head above water financially (for a little while anyway), which is great of her. My father says,

"Put me down for a thousand."

"Wow, thanks, Dad."

Well that was a generous and unexpected boost. I will pay it back eventually. (I heard that!)

Part 22

*Back to the
Bike Hospital*

August 26

As I approach the Horseshoe Bay ferry I am pondering several things. First and foremost being the state of my father's health. He has undergone a gallstone operation. Apparently it went well. My father is 72 years old and (I guess) an operation at that age can be risky. I'm also still going over finances in my head and, thirdly, I'm wondering if I'll have a chance to meet Sean MacMahon's father, who lives in Burnaby as well. I ride up to the pay window and hand over 24 dollars. Not bad. She tells me to go to a certain lane number. I do and, as I guessed, it is for motorcycles, of which I am the only one. I shut the bike off and go join my sister's family, who are Pat, Don, Danny, and his friend Max. They came here in their car.

I come back to my bike a half hour later and see I'm no longer the sole motorcyclist. The two couples on identical Harleys are from Florida. They rented the bikes in Seattle instead of riding their own Harleys all the way here. After a while I start reading my Stephen King novel. Eventually we are given the signal to ride on.

I spend my time on the ferry reading a motorcycle magazine and talking with my companions. One of the stories is about the author of the article taking a ride (a long time dream of his) on a Vincent Black Shadow, a bike that has become legendary for its speed and beauty.

There is a list of things you should do before riding a Vincent and one of them is to say a prayer. I thought that was pretty funny.

I disembark from the ferry and ride to a prearranged meeting place. We are eventually met by Ria, my father's friend. I follow them all to my dad's house. As we arrive, I am surprised to see him sitting on his porch, looking like a million bucks. I expected him to be bedridden and frail. I hug my father and tell him how good he looks for someone who recently had an operation. Most people would say he looked good no matter how bad he looked (I would be one of those people) but in this case it was true. I will try and contact Sean's dad tomorrow.

August 27

Sean's father returns my call from Victoria where he's working. He might be too late to meet me. It is, after all, a work week and he is on the other side of the island. I will call him later in the day and see how his schedule is. I will visit my dad again and look around downtown Parksville.

It's later in the afternoon now and I call Sean's father, Dave. He won't be home until late and he's going sailing tomorrow. He asks how long I'm staying. I tell him I'm leaving tomorrow so we'll have to make it another time. Oh well, sometimes these things work out and sometimes they don't. We both tried and that's the best we can do.

Waiting for the rest of them to finish a mini-golf game, I'm out in the parking lot, well, bored. I had played here yesterday (it was fun) and the place was like a mini-golf Mecca. I start to check the tires on my bike for stones wedged in the tread—always good for hours of excitement. I begin with the front. No stones but, hello, a crack. Then I spot a small chunk about to come off the tire. Some more small splits. I guess I should get a new front tire. It has about 23,000 kms on it. Let's go to the back tire and look—oh, I guess I'm looking at two new tires. This back one is kind of baldish.

Back in Vancouver now, I ride along the Barnett Highway on a perfect day. Can you guess where I'm going? If you guessed the bike shop, you are correct. My home away from home.

I'm in the service depot now, telling them about the recommendations book I saw at the Prince George Yamaha dealership. I mention the problem I had before of not being able to go below third gear and the recommendations book talked about that part of the bike. He hasn't heard of it (the area in question, gear area) but will call the Prince George dealership. I also mention the oil seal I was too impatient to get fixed on my way back through Prince George. The dealership (Prince George) had said they would fix it all for free but I didn't hang around. It was closing night of my friend's play the next day as I was coming back through Prince George and I didn't want to miss it.

So in this round of bike-fixing we are talking about: two new tires, a new front light bulb, a new oil seal, an oil change, and possible free work on the gear shift stuff. Plus a total drain on my wallet. KA-CHING! The tires alone cost $290. Let's not forget labour. They will call me on Monday, two days from now.

September 2

I have just gotten off the phone with the bike shop. The work that was under fix-free-of-charge, a kind of recall notice, was actually to do with the starter and not gear area. I have talked to other Virago owners in the past (and non-Virago owners) and they would invariably ask me if my starter was giving me trouble. I guess Yamaha got wind of this, realized they had a problem and told all dealerships to fix it for free and send them the bill. Which in my case was exactly what happened, even though I'm not the original owner. With parts and labour, I got about 300 dollars' worth of work for free. My bill is around 500 dollars. Let's see, that makes a total of around 900 dollars since my plane landed in British Columbia over a month ago. Oh well, that's life. On the financial front, I have around $3,000 (CDN) left on my credit cards. I will leave for the United States in a few days.

September 3

I'm waiting at the bus stop, helmet in hand. This particular bus (the 160) will take me to Port Moody where the bike shop is. A nicely dressed woman sits beside me on the bench. Maybe I should strike up a conversation with her. I decide not to. She asks me if I know how often this bus runs. I tell her I'm a visitor and don't know. I deduce (à la Sherlock Holmes) she might be on her way to a job interview and ask her if she is. She tells me she's on her way to a funeral. So much for deductions. I apologize. She tells me her friend was killed in a motorcycle accident. Oh, man. I ask her how old he was. He would have been 35 in November. Same age as me. He got in the accident and succumbed eight weeks later from his injuries in the hospital. She said he wouldn't have wanted to live anyway, his accident was that horrific. He had no wife or children but a lot of friends. Cold reality creeps back into my world. I tell her motorcyclists, like new recruits in a war, tell themselves it won't happen to them, that somehow we won't be the ones to die, it will happen to someone else. I tell her about my trip and she thinks it's a great idea. The bus comes a few minutes later. Her name is Sue.

I'm on the bus now and I can't help thinking about motorcycles and death. I'm about to get off the bus. Sue is sitting by the back door. I tell her (I don't know why) that I'll be thinking about it all day now. She says she shouldn't have said anything. I tell her it's ok. She wishes me good luck and tells me to be careful.

I'm in the bike shop now. My bill comes to $513. He tells me I got a lot of free work done courtesy of Yamaha. I tell him I will be riding across the desert in the near future. I then ask him if I should give the bike a rest once I'm in the desert after a few hours. It is air-cooled, after all. He says that I should give it a break every once in a while and clean the air filter. I thank him and leave. It is Thursday today; I will leave for Washington State on Saturday morning.

Part 23 *Onward and Southward*

September 5

I'm up at 7:00 a.m. I want to leave by 9:00 a.m. I hope I don't forget anything. I actually wasn't going to bring the tent when I was thinking about my trip yesterday. I was getting ready for today's departure and I thought to myself, "Why should I bother bringing the tent? Who am I trying to kid?" In the end, though, if I'm ever in a survival situation I will need a tent. Shelter is pretty important in a life or death fight for survival. I start loading up the bike. There isn't a cloud in the sky today.

After showering I finish packing and go outside. Pat, Don, and nephew Dan are waiting for me to get a picture taken. I was again welcomed here with open arms and am grateful for that. After the picture taking, I hug them all and leave. So warm is it as I start out, that I don't wear a jacket. My denim shirt is untucked and I'm sweating underneath my helmet. It's 9:00 a.m.

The U.S. border wasn't that hard to find. I'm in a fair-sized lineup to go into Washington State. It occurs to me it is the Labour Day weekend in the U.S.A. as well as Canada. The line seems to have stopped moving completely. I look at the front of the line just in time to see about five border officers come walking quite fast out of their little building towards a jeep. I look for a bit, but lose interest. I look around to see a woman waving at me. From her car she asks me where I'm going. She has recognized my Ontario licence plate. I tell her (or yell

199

over to her) some of the places I'm going. She says that's great. She asks
me how long I've been on the road. I tell her a month. I realize immediately that's wrong (I guess I was thinking in total number of days,
which is still wrong) but don't feel like yelling over a long-winded
explanation. She and her friend think that's great, what I'm doing. I
thank her and her friend. A few minutes later I pull up to the border
guy and cut the engine. From what I saw back in the line, these guys
are checking pretty thoroughly. He asks me my citizenship. I start taking out my wallet. He doesn't want to see my identification. He asks the
usual questions. He then walks directly behind me (about 6 feet). He
stands there for about twenty seconds or so and then comes up to me
and says I can go.

I'm now in the U.S. The highway in this part of Washington is quite
pretty. Lots of trees and the odd mountain thrown in. I'm surprised the
speed limit is 70 miles per hour. I thought it might be 55. I remember
some big ad campaign saying something like "55 Stay Alive." Oh well.
I couldn't have asked for a better day, though.

I ride along thinking about redwood trees and singing songs in my
head. After a while the highways start to look all the same to me. I stop
for food and spend about ten dollars in total. Three hours later, I get gas
in Castlerock. It's a name I've been seeing for a long time, due to being
a fan of Stephen King's, and because of the movie company of that name.

I'm in the state of Oregon now. It's 4:15 p.m. Although I've been on
the road now (off and on) for 6 hours, it doesn't seem that long. I'm just
about in Salem. I have a feeling I've overshot the point where I was supposed to turn towards the coast and hook up with the Pacific Coast
Highway. I stop in Salem and check my map. Doh! I have missed the point
where I should have turned towards the coast by a couple of inches on the
map. Although it does look like I picked a good spot to stop and check.
There's a highway leading directly to the Pacific Coast Highway. I ask a
local man for directions and he gives me good and simple directions.

Not long after leaving Salem the highway turns into a beautiful
green tunnel, kind of. The trees are close to the road and hang over me

as I ride. They block out the sun to make the tunnel effect more real. The weird thing is, when a patch of sun does make it through, I'm temporarily blinded as I ride through it. I spend a lot of the time (in the sunny parts) with my left hand up to my helmet to shield my eyes or I won't be able to see what's going on. I'm about fifty miles away from arriving in Newport, Oregon. I will be at the ocean then. I see a sign advertising a Ripley's Believe It Or Not museum. I immediately think of a very touristy part of Niagara Falls I visited that had a Ripley's museum I went to as a child. I will try and get a motel in Newport.

I'm just approaching Newport proper on the Pacific Coast Highway. This highway is as beautiful as everyone says it is. Great-looking shorelines and ocean scenery. I guess the constant pounding by the ocean makes for some great-looking terrain. As I drive into Newport it becomes clear I probably won't find a motel or hotel. Everything seems booked. A lot of No Vacancy signs. I spot one motel that has rooms and stop to check it out. They have one room, and it's pricey. A guy just brought back the key to the very room I'm thinking about taking and said he didn't want it. I'm getting a rare bad feeling about this motel. He suggests another hotel outside of town and then says the railroad people sometimes stay there, though. What does that mean? Is it some kind of veiled warning? Sounds like it to me. As if to say, "I recommend it but don't say I didn't warn ya." I call the hotel anyway and only half listen to the directions because there's a pretty good chance I'm going to go right past it. He shows me the map and tells me I could try Corvallis about an hour's drive inland. I thank him and leave.

It's getting dark as I start off for Corvallis. The highway I'm on (20) is hilly with some sharp corners. Now it's dark and the road is quite a challenge, with no street lights. I begin to wonder if all the cars in front of me are also going to Corvallis for the same reason I am. I arrive in a place called Philomath. I see a motel with a vacancy sign. I pull in, book a room. It's only 45 dollars. I started out this morning at 9:00 a.m. and it is now 8:30 p.m.

201

September 6

I get up and get quickly back on the road to Newport. Not a cloud in the sky. I missed a lot of the scenery last night because of the dark. This road also has the tunnel-like feel to it. Some of the trees actually touch each other from either side of the road above me. The branches hang low over the road in spots. It is a pleasure to ride on this road.

I'm in Newport again. I'm down at the wharf, looking at the boats and fishing vessels. There's a seal—oh, make that two seals swimming among the boats. I look up and away to see a large bridge. It's called the Yaquina Bay Bridge. I take a picture of it. Why, I don't know.

I have some breakfast and look around a bit. I get back to the main drag and ride around, not caring if I get lost or not. I see a beautiful old house that says Green Gables Book Store. I park the bike and walk downstairs into the bookstore part. The place is deserted. A woman appears from a door somewhere. I say hello and tell her I was in Prince Edward Island last summer and saw the Green Gables house. She tells me she's a retired librarian and the Green Gables name seemed like a good one. She asks me if I'm looking for anything in particular. I decide to get the second Green Gables book, what the heck. I don't seem to be reading much of the book I bought. Besides being a bookstore, the house is a Bed and Breakfast as well. We talk a bit more and I leave.

I ride around for a few minutes and see a sign saying there's an historic lighthouse nearby. I find the lighthouse. It is in fact the Yaquina Bay Lighthouse. It was built in 1871. I walk up the stairs and go in. The lighthouse is white with brown storm shutters. The tower part (with the light in it) is red and white. I am greeted near the inside of the front door by a volunteer. She offers to let me put my heavy backpack in the corner. I am grateful for her offer. I make a small donation to help preserve the lighthouse. I walk around the house and see the old-fashioned kitchen and the other rooms. On the third floor is a tiny room with a small single bed where the lighthouse keeper could keep a close eye on the light part of the house. The lighthouse, oddly enough, was only used for three years. A bigger one was built, so they stopped using this one. It got to the point in 1946 where they were going to tear it down. It was saved and restored by residents who formed the Lincoln County Historical Society. I buy a few postcards, thank the volunteer for her kindness, and leave.

I get back on the 101 South highway. The scenery reminds me of the Cabot Trail in Nova Scotia. I stop now and again to take pictures. The roads are in excellent condition. There are also a lot of state parks along the water's edge.

I'm passing through a place called Oregon Dunes and they have, well, some nice-looking sand dunes from what I can see. I see a lot of dune buggies in the area. There are also 4x4s with small flag stems with flags at the end. I approach an old bridge just outside a place called North Bend where I will stop for lunch. It's 4:00 p.m.

It's 6:40 now and I'm in Brookings, Oregon. I'm beginning to wonder when I'll be in California. A little over an hour later and I see the Welcome to California sign. I look ahead and see what looks like a border-crossing station. Sure enough, there is a border officer standing with clipboard in hand. I cut the engine and coast towards him. Before I even stop he says thank you and waves me on. The trees start to get bigger almost as soon as you get into California. I will stay at a motel near Jedediah Smith State Park and see the redwoods tomorrow. I find a motel in Crescent City. The desk clerk gives me directions and tells me I'll see trees so big they'll block out the sky. Sounds good to me.

September 7

It's a little cloudy today but I must say I'm pretty excited about seeing those redwood trees. I get my bike (after eating breakfast) and am now riding on the 101 North to highway 199. I turn onto 199. A few minutes later now and the trees are already bigger. Not the huge kind you can drive through yet, though. Up ahead I see a pretty big tree. The trees are blocking out the clear, blue, sunny sky and shafts of sunlight are poking through onto the road. Oh man, such a beautiful sight! Postcard material for sure. I wonder how old this tree is. A couple of hundred years, I'm guessing.

I turn onto South Fork Road and it becomes a gravelly surface and quite narrow pretty quickly. I wouldn't say there was room for two cars, one and a half maybe. The plants near the road all have a fine layer of dust on them for about twenty feet into the forest. The trees pretty much block out the sky. A little later now and I pass a sign, the state park sign, I think, and I guess I should have made a right turn. Oh well. I ride quite slowly on this road. A sign up ahead says Single Lane Only. Well, there ya go. It's a single lane road for traffic going both ways. They weren't kidding. I can't see what's around a lot of the corners at all and stop dead to wait if the coast is clear. Sometimes the road goes right between two trees and is barely wide enough for a pick-up truck. I creep around the corners at five miles an hour.

The trees are huge. I ride among the giants now. I have a feeling there are bigger ones somewhere. I did think, however, that all or most of the trees would be the size of the kind you drive through if they cut out the middle. I honestly thought tree after tree would be that monstrous. I must say, I was a little disappointed at first because I had a set idea of what a redwood forest would look like. They are still big and impressive. I turn the bike around and start back towards the sign I passed. I stop and take a picture of an enormous stump of a redwood tilted towards the road.

Eventually I get to the turnoff for Jedediah Smith State Park. I get to the parking area and park my bike. I leave my big knapsack, the one on my back, beside my bike and start walking down the trail. After about thirty feet I stop. I can't leave the knapsack back there. All my writing and all kinds of other stuff are in it. If someone steals it, there won't be a book. On the other hand, it's pretty heavy to be walking along the trail with. I start walking back. As I get closer to the parking area I spot a big tree to my right. I walk up to the redwood and touch it. I have touched some of the other big trees too. I guess a lot of people do that. I take a picture and get back on my bike. There was an information centre on highway 199 not too far from here. I'll go there and ask about more big redwoods.

I'm at the information centre now. I'm talking to a parks officer, ask him if I've seen the biggest trees. He starts to give directions for the way I just came from. He tells me the trail I didn't take because of my knapsack has a pretty big tree there. I ask him if some of the trees I did see could be two or three hundred years old. He tells me some of the redwoods I saw were more like 1200 to 1500 years old. WOW!!

I ask him where the trees are I can drive through. I tell him I've been seeing that image, of a car driving through a redwood tree, all my life. He tells me there are some you can drive through but they are privately owned and there is a charge to drive through them. He gives me a map where I can find other big redwoods and the privately owned ones. I thank him, buy a few postcards and leave. I will go back through Cresent City to get to Klamath where the redwoods are that you can drive through.

Not long after going through Crescent City now and the highway, 101 South, is just great. Lots of trees, and the roads are in great condition. I'm on yet another motorcycle dream ride. I would encourage any motorcyclists, or whatever you drive, to ride this scenic highway, 101 South. Not too much time passes before I arrive in Klamath where the drive-through tree awaits me. It's not hard to find. I ride up to the woman and give her the $2 price. She gives me a small info pamphlet, which I put in my pocket. I ride away from the booth and up a steep grade and, geez, a steep and narrow turn. I feel like I just passed some kind of riding test. I see the tree and it is indeed drive-through. I park my bike and take a picture. Just then, a guy in his mid-teens runs up to me and asks if I want my picture taken near the tree. He asks me if I "just ride all over the place." I answer by telling him some of the places I've been. I thank him for offering to take my picture. He suggests I get the motorcycle in the background as I stand in front of the tree. He takes the picture and I offer to do the same for him and his family. They decline. I get back on my bike and go through the tree (the wrong way, apparently, oh well) and retest my driving skills on the way back down. I'll get back on the 101 South now.

The officer in Jedediah Smith State Park gave me a map and told me there was a big redwood tree in the Prairie Creek Redwoods State Park. I'm riding through the park now and (again) it is just pure pleasure on a motorcycle. It's not long before I see the signs saying Big Tree. I park the bike, get out my camera and follow a short path to the Big Tree. Well, they weren't lying, that is ONE BIG TREE. It is 21.5 feet wide and 300 feet tall. Just a monster of a tree. Considering you could probably wrap your arms around most of the trees in your area quite easily, I wonder how many people it would take, joining hands, to surround this tree. How many generations of people have gazed upon it in awe because of its immense size? It would be the king of the forest in a children's story, I bet.

It's a little cool as I'm about to enter Eureka, California. I ride through the town. Just outside of Eureka I stop for lunch. After lunch I pull on my fleece pullover. Two minutes on the road now and the sun has come out in full force. It's getting hotter and hotter. I quickly pull off the road and take off the pullover. It is very hot now. Even the wind is warm at 60 miles an hour.

I arrive in a place called Ukiah at around 6 p.m. I will stay here and go to San Francisco tomorrow.

Part 24

Out of the Trees and On to Other Famous Sites

September 8

I mailed out some postcards and faxed the theatre. Morning chores, you know. Another beautiful day in California. I go to a local motorcycle shop here in Ukiah for some motorcycle oil. I don't want a repeat of last summer. I get the oil and look at the bikes for a bit, and then leave.

I'm riding along the highway now just outside of Ukiah. I see some vineyards. I'm guessing I'm in California wine country. How do I come up with these startling insights? The vines are green (no kidding) like the trees or the hills, but the grass or brush is brown. I'm not a wine-drinker. Maybe I'll take one of the wine tours or something.

I'm about 50 miles from San Francisco in a slight traffic jam. Suddenly a cube van in front of me slams on the brakes and skids a bit to the right. I am following too close and have to brake hard. PHEW!

The closer I get to San Francisco, the bigger the highway becomes. I'm almost at the Golden Gate Bridge now and it is quite chilly. It must be the fog or something. There is a quote that goes something like this: "The coldest summer I ever spent was the one I spent in San Francisco."

I'm pretty close to the bridge now. Of course I've been hearing about it and seeing pictures of it all my life. It's pretty big and shrouded in fog as I cross over it. I think I can see Alcatraz Prison. I want to go on a tour of it if I can. I begin to follow the signs for Fisherman's Wharf. I find it and the parking lot attendant lets me park my bike for free. I walk towards a building with an Alcatraz Tours sign on it. There are lots of people everywhere. I see a sign that informs me I won't be able to take the tour until 11:45 a.m. tomorrow. It's almost a full day away. Well, so much for that. I don't feel like hanging around until tomorrow. What to do, what to do?

I start walking back towards my bike. I come across a tour company offering tours of San Francisco. Well, that's handy. A two-and-a-half-hour tour. I pay my 22 bucks and get on. We start out at Pier 39, I believe. The guide/driver is quite funny; and starts hinting almost immediately about a gratuity we might possibly give him at the end of the tour. He talks about Alcatraz and trolley cars. I tend to look more than listen, so I don't take in a lot of what he's saying. Sorry about that. We are looking at the architecture of the buildings and particularly the old houses downtown—Pacific Heights and like areas. The guide tells us some of the houses (which are stunningly beautiful) go for millions of dollars when sold. They all seem to be jammed together on these hilly streets. If I had that kind of money, it would be worth it to me. They use all kinds of wild colours. Some of them are pink and bright yellow. Some of the grey ones with the white trim kind of remind me of a wedding cake. Some of the entrances to the houses are very pretty.

We stop near the Golden Gate Bridge, which is actually red. Apparently, when they first coated the bridge with a kind of reddish primer colour the public liked it so much they insisted it be kept that way. Well, that explains a thing or two as I look at the red Golden Gate Bridge. It cost some 35 million dollars when it was built (I forget when), which was an immense sum at the time. I'm constantly looking at the houses the guide points out and every other one I can see. He points out a bookshop and then a bar Jack Kerouac used to hang out at. The tour ends. I think I'll leave San Francisco now. I don't want to go to or even near Los Angeles at all. I will get lost and the gangs there will use me for target practice.

I get back on 101 South. After stopping for gas, I resume going south and smack into a traffic jam. I'm behind a big truck and we are crawling at five miles per hour and then stopping, and it continues like this. It's 5:00 p.m. I see (for about the fifth time) a motorcyclist riding up the middle of the stopped traffic and, incredibly, when traffic is moving. Eventually it clears. Not long after the land becomes very flat. A lot of farms in the regions of Salinas, Gonzales, and finally (for me so far) Soledad. On a financial note, I have about 900 American dollars' worth of credit left on my credit cards. Which translates to around nine days left of my trip, I think.

September 9

Well it's cloudy this morning but, what the heck; I'm in California. I get some gas, which is becoming a pain in the neck. I'll explain. First thing is that you have to pay in advance for your gas, so now I'm guessing how much I need. Secondly, the nozzle has a rubberized accordion-like thing around it so the gaseous vapours don't escape into the air. Which is fine, but the thing is, you have to shove the nozzle all the way into your tank in order for the rubber accordion thing-a-ma-jig to tell the gas pump to let the gas flow. In other words, if the accordion bit isn't crunched up, you don't get gas. Whoever invented this gave little or no thought to motorcycles, in my humble opinion. Of course, because the motorcycle gas tank isn't very deep, the nozzle keeps telling the gas pump to shut itself off. Oh well. I'll try and make it to the Grand Canyon today. I get back on the good old 101 South. After a while I stop in a place called Bakersfield for lunch. After that, I catch the 46 highway east. I wrestle with another gas pump a little later and get on the 58 East highway. Brother, is it hot. The scenery is brown hills and little greenish trees or bushes dotting the landscape.

Although the speed limit varies from 55 to 70 miles an hour, I'm getting tired, regardless of the speed limit. A very strong wind is hitting me from the right side. All the eighteen-wheelers are passing me. I don't have enough energy to keep up with the flow of the traffic. I think the people who pass me in the cars are curious or concerned as to why they are going twenty miles an hour faster than I am. They look in the rearview mirrors at me and begin talking to the passengers. Maybe they think I have white line fever or exhaustion. Well, they are right about the exhaustion part.

I see a sign saying Historic Route 66 is the next right. I'm on it for about a mile when I stop for gas. I'm back on 66 now and the area looks rundown. A lot of the houses are for sale and more than one is abandoned. It has a used-to-be feel about it. After about 16 miles, I see a sign saying Interstate 40 left. That was quick. I thought Route 66 would be a lot longer.

It's a half hour later now and I see another sign for 66. OOPS. I thought it seemed a little short back there. The desert can be quite pretty in its own way. I stop in Ludlow to give the bike a break. The engine is unbelievably hot. I take a few pictures of the desert while I wait. I don't think I'll make it to the Grand Canyon today.

As the sun starts to set behind me the desert becomes golden. The shadows going across the hills are fantastic. There's a storm brewing up ahead. I'm about 60 miles away from Needles. I see a flash of lightning up ahead. WOW! It looked so great. It's cooling off a little now.

I get caught in the rain just as I arrive in Needles.

September 10

I leave at 10:00 a.m. It was quite warm an hour ago, so today will probably be hot. I start out again on Highway or Interstate 40 east. I'm ten minutes into the day's journey when I hit the Arizona State line. I didn't expect to be in Arizona so quickly, for some reason. The scenery hasn't changed much but the speed limit is now 75 miles per hour. There are more eighteen-wheelers than cars for as far as I can tell. It's a little cooler on the bike today, though, which makes it just about perfect.

It's an hour later now and I'm in a place called Kingman, Arizona to get some gas. They have the old-fashioned pumps. It's the little things, someone once said. I pull away from the gas station with the sun shining brightly in my eyes. It's shining in my eyes that way because my sunglasses are lying on the road somewhere. Oh well, I didn't like them anyway, they were too big and uncomfortable. I stop and get some new sunglasses. It's an hour later now and the landscape is getting greener. Lots of land for sale here in Arizona. There are some vast flat parts on this stage of the highway.

I'm in Williams, Arizona for gas and food. The junction to start heading towards Grand Canyon is not far from here. I buy a couple of postcards. I will write them in the restaurant.

I'm on highway 69 now, going to the Grand Canyon. It's a little chilly so I more or less maintain the 65 mph speed limit. I have around 60 more miles to go before I reach the Grand Canyon Village. It seems some of the flat parts of the land go into the horizon. I want to try and book a balloon ride over the Canyon but the guy back in Williams (who I bought the postcards from) hasn't heard of any.

I arrive in Grand Canyon Village around three o'clock. I ride down the main street and see a sign proclaiming HELICOPTER RIDES. Oh hey, a helicopter ride over the Grand Canyon would be so great, wouldn't it? I think so. There is also an IMAX theatre here in the village. I get a brochure about the helicopter rides and travel a mile or so up the street to the helicopter place. I park my bike and, WOW; they have a lot of helicopters here. Man, this place is busy. I go into what looks like a little airport terminal. They have a gift shop and coffee bar. I step to the counter and a woman gives me a price list. I agonize over the cheap and not-so-cheap flight costs. I decide on the $154 flight. I am told to watch a safety video right after I'm finished paying. I stand on a scale flush with the floor. I didn't notice it before. For curiosity's sake I ask them how much I weigh. It turns out I'm 162 pounds. I thought I weighed about ten pounds less than that.

I have about twenty minutes to kill before I have to go into a waiting area. I look around a bit. I go to the gift shop. At the appropriate time I go into the waiting area. The helicopter pads are in full view and you can see people getting on and off the helicopters. My name is

211

called. I'm shown to another place to wait. I ask how many helicopters they have. I'm told they have 23. Man, that's a lot of helicopters. Millions and millions of dollars' worth, I'm guessing. A man and a woman soon join me. A few minutes pass and then we are told to follow the ground crew. We go to an already-running helicopter. We stand with our backs to the helicopter and a ground crew woman takes our picture. It's a four passenger (plus pilot) helicopter. For the first time I will be sitting in the back seat. Brett is our pilot's name, he informs us, after we are safely strapped in by the ground crew. We put on our headsets and hear music.

We lift off and fly over a veritable sea of trees. For some reason we are not going very fast. As we get closer to the edge, the music changes. The Grand Canyon awaits. The triumphant music is timed to our clearing the trees and over the Canyon. I'm laughing as we go over the edge of the trees and into the Canyon. Ah, showbiz.

The Canyon is so huge and deep I can only shake my head in awe at its magnificence. The facts about the Canyon have now replaced the music. I can't hear what the facts are, so I reach up and turn up the volume. I still can't hear it. I crank up the volume again. Nothing. I follow the cord of the headset to the panel and, OOPS, I've cranked up the volume on the headset that the guy beside me is wearing. He doesn't seem to notice. I find the correct knob and my headset is already at the maximum volume. It doesn't bother me. It's enough just to see the Canyon walls with their orangey-red surface. I take pictures like crazy, and then for some reason my camera dies. The film won't advance. What could be more perfect than my camera dying over one of the most scenic places in the world?

Surrounding the Canyon the land is so flat. The Grand almost seems like a line of upside down mountains. I've seen a lot of flat expanses of land leading up to the base of tall and mighty mountain ranges, but not a flat landscape leading up to the King of all Canyons. Try and picture a mountain range upside down and hollowing going into the earth. Some of the walls and big rock formations in the centre look like ancient stone walls built or carved out by people time has forgotten. They look almost like temples. We fly over another large forest and more of the Canyon. Well, before you know it, our time is up and we begin flying back to the Heliport.

The flight was worth every penny. I retrieve my knapsack and helmet the counter people kindly stored in their office for me. I pay for the picture (10 dollars) that was taken at the helicopter before we took off. It's a big picture and turned out well.

It's a little later now and I'm sitting in the IMAX theatre's showing of Grand Canyon Hidden Secrets movie. I love IMAX theatres because the screens are so huge. The film begins. It shows some of the early inhabitants, explorers and modern day activities you can do in the park and Canyon, which is kind of the same, I guess. Of course there is some awesome footage of the Canyon itself. Tomorrow I will go to the Grand Canyon National Park.

Part 25

Viva Las Vegas!

September 11

Unfortunately, it's raining this morning. I will go into the park today anyway. I pack up my stuff and check out of the motel. The park isn't too far away. I ride up to the spot where you pay to get into the park around 10:00 a.m. I'm wearing my rain gear for the first time since leaving British Columbia. I pay ten dollars and ride towards the Canyon. I see a sign saying EAST RIM RIGHT. I turn and spot a lookout point. I stop, get off my bike and stand at the edge of the Canyon, which is enclosed in fog. I can see nothing of the middle or bottom of the Canyon because of the fog. I decide to go to the information centre.

I walk into the info centre and sit down to look at the stuff I was handed at the gate. I then walk up to one of the info people and ask her if I can expect the fog and poor visibility to be throughout the park. She answers in the affirmative. Well, that's good enough for me. So I walk out of the centre. It is raining even harder now. I will go back to Williams and then to Kingman, where I will head north to Las Vegas.

There must be motorcycle package tours around here. I see groups of riders and the vehicles that pull the trailer, in case one of them breaks down I guess. I think they are all riding Harleys, which is great, fine, nothing wrong with that. The only problem is that the guy driving or pulling the trailer just passed me TOO FRIGGIN' CLOSE! You'd think the guy would know better. What an idiot.

I'm halfway to Kingman now and the rain has stopped. It's quite warm and sunny. It's around 2:00 p.m. when I arrive in Kingman. I pull into a restaurant parking lot and take off the rain gear. Oh, what the heck, I'll have lunch. I notice the motorcyclists here don't wear helmets. After lunch I'm on my way to Vegas. It's around 100 miles from Kingman.

It's about an hour and a half later and it's getting really windy. The fierce wind is blowing me around. I'm leaning to my right (into the wind) almost constantly now. I can see a storm brewing up ahead. As it starts to rain there is a motorhome in front of me, and an 18-wheeler behind me. Wow! What the … ouch! It's raining so hard it feels like hail. The motorhome in front of me is slowing down, which is fine by me. The combination of heavy rain, wind, lightning and spray from the motorhome is making it hard to ride and stay in control. I look in my left mirror and all I see is the front of the 18-wheeler, pretty much. The truck driver has decided that the motorhome and I are going too slow. I'm practically in a tropical storm and the trucker behind me couldn't care less. I want to give him the finger, but decide against it—he's only about 20 feet behind me and could crush me like a bug. I can't believe this guy. My blood starts to boil. He doesn't let up until we catch up to the slower traffic ahead. Man, what a jerk. I pull off the first chance I get. He looks right at me. I again suppress the urge to give him the finger. As I ride along I see a place I can stop to see the Hoover Dam, but I can't be bothered now.

Not too much later I'm riding towards Las Vegas. Once in the city, I celebrate the momentous occasion by spending the next hour being lost. I find a motel. I will go to the Las Vegas Strip (not a stripper bar, in case you didn't know) or the main street tonight.

Not trusting myself to find the Desert Inn, I take a taxi. I walk into the lobby and inquire about tickets for Dennis Miller. I'm told to wait in a standby line. After waiting about half an hour with the other standby people, we are allowed in to sit at the back. Two jugglers open for Dennis Miller and they are very funny and expert jugglers. Alas, I don't

215

remember their names. Not long after, Dennis Miller comes on. Even though I'm sitting at the back, he is quite visible. He starts making me laugh right away. I think he's an extremely good stand-up comedian. His rants are particularly good. He makes some bizarre references to 1970s people and events that are funny. The shows ends and I'm very glad I got to see him.

I walk around the Vegas Strip, which is so beautiful at night. The entrance to Caesar's Palace is beautiful. I will try and find a car collection tomorrow.

September 12

I wake up pretty early and decide to walk to the Vegas Strip. It looks easier to negotiate in the daylight. I walk across a bridge, then make a loop underneath. There are people living underneath this part of the bridge just a short walk from all the glitter and gold. In no time at all I arrive at the Harley Cafe. It has a humungous Harley bursting through the wall above the entrance. I ask the people behind the counter if they ever heard of a motorcycle museum. They never heard of it. Oh well. Next I'll go to Bally's and see if I can get a ticket for Louie Anderson's show tonight—another great stand-up comedian. I've actually seen his show before. I feel like laughing, so why not see a comedian? Well, I'm in luck because I just managed to get a ticket for a seat four places from the stage. Sometimes it pays to go it alone, I guess. Now I'm off to the Imperial Palace to see the car collection.

I'm now at the Imperial Palace and have just paid for my ticket to the car collection. One of Marilyn Monroe's cars is here. Old Cadillacs from the 1930s, an old Harley-Davidson with a sidecar and a whole room full of Dusenbergs. One of Hitler's cars is here, the second I have seen on my journey. I saw the other one in Ottawa. There are some cars that former United States presidents used. Packards, Lincolns, old fire trucks and it goes on and on. Army trucks as well, and a gift shop to end it all off. I haven't seen a lot of car museums but this is easily the best I have ever seen.

I next walk towards Caesar's Palace, the most beautiful hotel here, in my humble opinion. I walk into the shopping mall part of it and it is impressive. I love the blue sky and white clouds that are painted on the ceiling. When I walk down the hallway it feels like the clouds are moving towards me. I stop to see if it is some kind of projection. It is an optical illusion. I ask the info centre if they have a Warner Brothers store. They do, which is great because I have been dying to see one. I love the Bugs Bunny cartoons especially. I'm given a map and start walking towards it. I stop at a store selling all kinds of music, sports, movie and Americana memorabilia. I could drop a bundle in a store like this, if I had a bundle.

I arrive at the Warners store. There's a big screen at the back of the store showing a Daffy Duck and Marvin the Martian cartoon. I love the cartoons they appear in together. They have shirts, pens, cells from animated films, like Batman for instance, watches, hats, and lots of other cool stuff. I find myself just watching the cartoons on the big screen. I eventually look at a Bugs Bunny pocket watch for 90 dollars. It's tempting, but I still might make it to Memphis, although you never know. I see a display of great-looking pins. I buy a couple of Supermans, Batmans, a Scooby-Doo and a couple of Bugs Bunny ones. I look around a bit more and leave.

I see a sign in the mall advertising a 3-D ride. It's called *Race for Atlantis*. What the heck. I buy a ticket and wait in line. We're all in a dark room with elevated ramps leading up to the entrance of the ride. The room has music, lights, and a mist rising from the bottom. Eventually we're allowed in (some of us) and are handed 3-D headsets. We are given some brief instructions and are told we must win the race. We then go to another room where we buckle ourselves in. It starts. The graphics and 3-D effects are amazing. It's wild, like being on a cosmic roller coaster. All kinds of things are just about to hit us as we are hurled at what seems like 200 miles an hour. People are screaming, particularly the girl beside me. This is so much fun. It's scary at the same time, like you're sitting in the nose of a jet plane and the pilot has gone insane. It ends too quickly for me but it was worth it. If you get to Caesar's Palace, check this out.

It's a little after 8 p.m. and I'm at a slot machine in Bally's hotel and casino. I'm up 110 dollars. A few minutes later I'm up 75 dollars. Time to cash in because I don't want to be late for Louie Anderson. I get my money and go into the theatre. Well, I'm actually five seats away from the stage, which is still fantastic. I get talking to a couple from Detroit. We start talking about the weather yesterday. I tell her it felt like it was hailing at one point. She tells me she heard it was hailing yesterday. A-HA!

The show begins with a young comic named Johnny (I didn't get his last name), who talks about being a third-generation Mexican-American. He takes a lot of heat for not being able to speak Spanish from other Mexican-Americans and Mexicans alike. He keeps us laughing until Louie Anderson comes on. With little fanfare, Louie comes on. He is gracious in his praise of the opening comedian. He starts to talk about gambling. A guy two seats away from me at another table is laughing so hard at the gambling jokes Louie is telling he is practically choking. Louie talks directly to the audience, asking various people what they do for a living, where they are from, and that sort of thing. He is very funny and has a sharp mind. Some people in the audience are celebrating birthdays and he sends a bottle of champagne to the lucky people. He gives other people free signed T-shirts with his Life with Louie character on it. The show ends and I realize once again I have seen one of the greats.

I go back out into the casino and promptly lose 40 dollars at the same machine I had only hours before won around 110 dollars. I leave about 35 dollars ahead. I go see a movie and then go back to my motel.

Part 26

Crossing the States, Eastbound

September 13

I check out of the motel. I ride down the Vegas Strip, looking for a place I could buy a map of the United States. I can't find mine. The Las Vegas info centre suggests I try a certain chain of stores, which I do.

I ride out of Las Vegas on Highway 15 North. Just outside Las Vegas on 15 it is quite desolate. I guess it was the kind of scene or route I was expecting when I arrived a few days ago. I guess I thought it would be Vegas Strip and that's it. Well, kind of, anyway.

I'm an hour and a half outside Vegas, heading north still, and I have come across this huge valley and mountain range. There's a big patch of green, lush land around a small river. Two minutes later I come across the town of Mesquite, which is quite pretty, with casinos like a little Las Vegas. A little outside Mesquite it gets quite rocky and mountainous. I've somehow ended up in Arizona again. Oh well, this part of Arizona is starting to look Grand Canyon-ish. The rocks and some of the mountains are a kind of reddish-brownish colour. The river is also the same colour. The colour of the earth reminds me of Prince Edward Island.

Later I see a sign saying Zion National Park take next exit. I keep riding for a few more seconds and pull onto the shoulder. I have a feeling I know something about the park called Zion. Something tells me I should go to Zion. Oh, by the way, I'm in the state of Utah now. As I ride towards the park, it feels like I'm riding on the moon. No, that's not right. Like riding on Mars.

I enter Zion National Park at 3 p.m. The scenery is unbelievable as soon as you enter the park. To the right across from the Visitor Information Centre is a monstrous red mountain. Even the road has a reddish colour to it. I leave the info centre and start slowly weaving my way up higher now. I have to stop and look at these red stone mountains against a cloudless blue sky. Every turn of the head is a new feast for the eyes. I get back on the bike and am still ascending the mountains. I am stopped by a park ranger. She tells me I'll be delayed for a few minutes waiting for traffic coming from the tunnel in the opposite direction. No problem. I can look at the scenery and give the bike a chance to cool down.

We wait maybe about ten minutes and then are given the signal to proceed through the tunnel. I'm first in line. I enter the tunnel. No other traffic. Hey, this is a long tunnel. Not bad, as tunnels go. I come out and the rocks and mountains look so different here. Some are red and some are yellowy-white with what looks like wrinkles. It kind of looks like a close-up of an elephant's skin or like whipped taffy that stayed whipped.

After about three hours, all I can say is, go to a library and try and see some pictures of Zion National Park or, better yet, go to Utah itself.

It's a couple of hours later now and I have a feeling I'm way past the turn for Interstate 70. I pass a sign with something to do with Butch Cassidy on it. I find a motel in a place called Big Rock Candy. I can't find it on the map but I think I overshot the highway 70 by a few hours' worth of miles.

September 14

Well, it turns out I'm twenty miles from where Butch Cassidy used to live. I'm also in a different time zone, an hour ahead. I'm glad to report I haven't gone past highway or Interstate 70, as a fellow motorcyclist told me this morning.

I'm back on the road again. It's a flawlessly blue-sky September day. It's 11:00 a.m. and I'm approaching a place called Salinas. I see a sign proclaiming NO BULL NO SERVICES FOR 110 MILES. I'm glad I didn't miss it. I will definitely stop and get gas here.

I'm 80 miles (or is it kilometres on my tripmeter? – oh well) away from Salinas and the scenery is beautiful, riding between big rocks, then green foliage and red rock. I can't help but think of Mars. I'm approaching Green River which, if I read the sign right, is the Watermelon Capital of the World.

I'm in a place called Fuita and am also in the state of Colorado. I try my remaining credit card and it's not working. It has only worked once since this part of the trip started. If it continues this way, my trip will be shortened. The only place it worked was in a casino in Vegas. I have about 50 dollars in cash, another hundred in a chequing account and maybe 1,000 dollars credit on the card. We'll see how it goes.

I'm 150 miles from Denver now and the highway is just a pleasure to ride on. High mountains and a river to my right. I'm going through a tunnel now that is extremely well lit. Which makes a big difference to me. I eventually arrive in a place called Dillon. I get a motel and start calling friends and relatives to tell them I'm still alive.

September 15

I wake up and look out the window to see a towel hanging off my bike. It is not mine. I parked beside a motorcycle last night; maybe he or she left it for me. I go downstairs and ask the front desk if there are any messages for me. She tells me the maintenance man left the towel on my bike for me. Well, that was nice of him. I wish he were around so I could thank him. I leave the motel and go to a bank. No go at the bank. Credit card not working. I go back to the motel and pack up. Oh, I talked to the maintenance man and thanked him for the towel. He told me he doesn't want people using good towels to wipe off their bikes. After talking with him for a few minutes I discover he is a former motorcyclist.

221

I leave Dillon at 10:30 a.m. Another great day in the good old U.S.A. I arrive at the outskirts of Denver about an hour later. I look for a City Centre sign to direct me downtown to see about my credit card. Well it's ten minutes later and I never did see the sign. Oh well. One thing about banks, they are pretty much everywhere. I start passing signs for the Denver Airport. Minutes later, after all the mountains and rocks I've been seeing lately, I'm just outside Denver and the land is as flat as a pancake. Lots of farms and vast plains. In fact on the map it says GREAT PLAINS in big letters.

I stop for gas in a place called Limon. Why don't I just call the 1-800 number on the back of the card? I find a phone booth and do just that. I tell the operator my dilemma of my card not working. She checks my account and says I have 600 dollars in credit left. She tells me to go to a bank and get a cash advance. I thank her and hang up. I thought I had more than that. Well, 600 Canadian adds up to around 350 or 300 in American money.

I get back on the highway and start doing some calculations in my head. I quickly pull off the road to think a little more clearly. I look at the map. I don't think I can afford to go to Memphis. I've got maybe $200 in Canadian money and $300 in U.S. funds. If I get $350 U.S. from my credit card, I'll have a grand total of about $750 U.S. If I go to Memphis I will probably arrive back in Toronto flat broke. I can't do that. It's not fair to my family and friends, in my opinion. It will be close financially anyway whether I come back home with a couple of hundred, depending on the bank or not. They might refuse a cash advance. Who knows. I'll go straight to Lexington, Kentucky, then straight up north to Ontario. I'll still get to see a lot of states this way.

Almost 4:00 p.m. and I see a Welcome to Kansas sign. The scenery hasn't changed much. Plains, farms, cows, and the birthplaces of people I can't remember or don't know.

It's a few hours later now and the sun is setting behind me. I have set my sights on Salina, Kansas. As I ride across the plains of Kansas it occurs to me that people ask if I get lonely on my trip. Well, yes and no. No, in that I don't linger too long in any one place so there's usually something new to see. Even in the city I live in I will sometimes go to movies and restaurants by myself. It is not that I don't have friends, it's just that it doesn't bother me to go alone or it is not a given I will have a bad time just because I'm alone. Now we get to the yes-it-does-get-lonely part. It usually occurs when I see a couple who are crazy about each other and looking at each other like, well, you know how they look at each other. Maybe they haven't been going out that long, what my friend Dave calls the honeymoon stage. I think to myself sometimes I wish I had a woman looking at me like that. It would have been nice to write letters to a woman who loved me and vice versa. I will have lost a potential girlfriend or two because of the trip, but that's life.

I'm on a newly paved road now and it's almost pitch black. I'm experiencing the perfect temperature thing again. I have no sense of temperature because it is perfect. The bike has a steady hum to it. I have gotten my second wind and the stars have come out. I'll try and explain how I feel right now. Have you ever been out for a walk on a summer's evening, the temperature is warm but not hot and there is no wind, or just the slightest hint of one. You're in a good mood and walking at a slow pace. All seems right with the world. That's how I feel right now. The steady hum of the bike, the stars, road, and temperature have all come together under the Kansas sky.

It's later now and the perfections of the night have faded a bit, as my wrist is burning and my hamstrings are aching. I'm riding in one lane because of construction, which is going on for mile after mile. I worry a bit about hitting a piece of wood, animal, or whatever. Especially large objects from the various construction sites along the way. I can hear Rod Serling saying this in my head perfectly. He says,

"I present to you a man riding a motorcycle, alone, under the watchful observation of a Kansas sky. With only a small headlight, painted lines on the road, and perhaps the stars themselves to guide him. He fears the fear of all late night travellers. The fear that an object will pick this moment in time to lie in wait for him. If so, he might never reach Salina, but end up instead in (pause) *The Twilight Zone*."

I can hear it perfectly in my head.

I arrive in Salina. I make a right off the highway towards a motel and then a left and - hey! - Ah GEEZ - I'm on the ramp for some other highway heading north, apparently. I'm trying to find an exit when the fuel light comes on. Which is perfect because there's nothing in sight. I turn off the highway and switch to reserve. I'm at a junction. I go in the direction of the 81 South sign. It is twelve miles to Salina, a sign informs me. Whew! The I-70 East ramp comes up too fast for me and I go right past it and onto the shoulder. I stop and turn, then get onto the ramp. I get back to Salina without further incident. I get a motel.

September 16

After checking out of the motel I'm riding now towards downtown Salina. The desk clerk at the motel gave me directions to the banks. I park in front of a bank and go in. After a couple of minutes in a lineup I stand before the teller. I explain to her what my bank in Toronto told me to do, which was to try and get a cash advance. I ask her for $250 U.S. and hope the card or the procedure will work. It works. WHEW! We talk about my trip a little. I leave the bank. Well, there ya go, the last of my credit.

On the I-70, I kiss my fingertips and touch them onto the painted words and poppy on my gas tank, then the Royal Canadian Air Force pin on the lapel of my leather jacket. I do this little ritual at least once a day. Superstitious? Who, me? Just because I do this little ritual every day and wear the same T-shirt and denim shirt at the beginning of each stage of my journey? Well, let me just say that I wasn't superstitious until I started riding a motorcycle.

A few hours later and I'm approaching Topeka, Missouri. There's a toll booth up ahead. I stop at the toll booth and she gives me a card. I ask her what I do with the card. She tells me I'll pay a toll booth in

Kansas City, $1.75. Ok. A little later now and I exit the highway and am confronted with another toll booth. I guess they don't want you to leave the highway without paying. I stop at the toll booth and the officer and I stare at each other. What do I do? He asks me for my card and asks for 75 cents, please. I'll get another card when I get back on the highway. After getting gas in Lawrence, I again ride up to the same booth and am given a card. I will pay $1.25 when I get to Kansas City.

Boom-chaka-laka-laka-laka/-boom-chaka-laka-laka-laka hey-hey-hey/I wanna take ya higher/baby-baby-baby/take ya higher

I'm singing that song, "Gonna Take Ya Higher" (I think that's what it's called) by Sly and the Family Stone. I'm bouncing my head up and down and moving to the music. I'm approaching the Kansas City toll booth. I have the $1.25 ready. Toll booths are a bit of a pain on a bike but, oh well. I go through with a minimum of hassle. With that done, I ride towards Kansas City. There's a detour for the I-70 so I have to pay close attention to the signs. I pass over a bridge. I keep following the signs for fifteen minutes or so and—BOOM—I'm in Independence, Missouri. I didn't expect to be in a new place so soon.

I'm nearing Boomville and it occurs to me this part of the state (Missouri) looks a lot like Southern Ontario. Lots of hills and farm and just the general feel of it, like parts of Ontario. It's kind of weird. I arrive in Fulton, Missouri and call it quits for the day.

September 17

I depart from Fulton, Missouri in the rain. It's still warm, though, so it's a comfortable kind of rain. I'm back on the I-70. The green colours of the farms and trees look great in the rain.

I'm about twenty minutes away from downtown St. Louis. I'm looking at the billboards to see if there are any bike shops in the area. It has stopped raining, which is good, because the highway has turned into a big 5-laner. There's a car about twenty-five yards ahead of me. I look to the right and see more billboards. I look straight ahead and see about a four or five foot aluminium ladder directly in my path. I have no time to swerve. The first thought that enters my head is, I will be going down. I don't think of it as a frightened kind of thought, but as a fact. I hit the ladder and I look down as I do this. My front wheel hits the ladder and bounces up in the air at a right angle, the ladder goes right and hits my right foot. The next second my back wheel hits the ladder, a quick bounce and it's over. I look to see if my front tire is going flat. It's not, as far as I can tell. I'm lucky. I had hit the top left corner of the ladder, which I can see now as the best possible place. If I had hit it at a different place, it could have gone very bad. What should I do? Should I stop and move it?   No way, too dangerous.

I'm still trying to decide what to do, if anything, when I see the exit for downtown St. Louis. I take it. Once off the highway I begin to look for a phone booth. I can at least call the police and tell them about the ladder. I see a big sports arena but no phone booths. I keep riding around the streets, looking. St. Louis has some beautiful old buildings. Oh well, forget the phone booth, I'll try and find a cop instead. I'll pull up beside a police officer and tell him or her my story and then they can radio it in. I'm riding around for a few minutes when I see a cop just up ahead. He makes a turn and I follow. He makes more turns, but I can't get near him. Well, back to the phone booth hunting. I keep riding and still can't find one. What gives? I stop and ask a hotel valet attendant where the police station is. Take the first right and keep going, are the directions he gives me.

I eventually find it after mistaking a kind of police academy type place for the central police station. The new recruits or trainees gave me directions to the station. I walk into the building to see a police officer sitting at a reception desk. I tell him what happened on the highway (after he had to deal with a prisoner who managed to get released without his plastic wristband being taken off, he was concerned how this could have happened). He asked me if I was hurt. I tell him I'm not hurt. I ask if there's somebody he can call so that another motorcyclist doesn't hit it as well. He tells me he'll call the proper department. I tell him it was about twenty minutes outside of town. He says he'll call the proper authorities. I thank him and leave. I think about the Rod Serling bit I did in my head the other night about the fear of hitting something at night. Well, it almost came true. It was in the daylight, mind you, but I could have ended up in a different dimension, if you believe in things like that.

I get back on the highway and eventually enter the state of Illinois around a half hour later. The weather is pretty much the same. It will rain for a while and then stop. The scenery is pretty much the same. I don't say that in a bad way. I like looking at the farms. A lot of times there is an old pick-up truck or a car in a field or by the farmhouse. Sometimes they have beautiful old cars just sitting in their driveways.

I arrive at the Indiana State line without incident. Less than an hour later now and I have stopped in Cloverdale, Illinois for the night. It's 5:30 p.m.

I sit in my motel room and there's a cold feeling in my belly. I now have time to think about hitting the ladder today. Fear creeps into me and it sits coldly in my stomach. I can't help but think of the "what-ifs." What if I had hit the ladder dead on? I try not to think about it but it's there just the same.

September 18

I want to get an early start today, so I leave at 8 a.m. The sky is somewhat cloudy but it's not raining. I have a pleasant morning ride into Indianapolis, Indiana. I stop in the downtown area. I didn't see a pay phone so I walk into a cigarette shop after parking my bike. I have to find a bike shop because my oil warning light is coming on more frequently. I need some oil. I ask the counterperson if he could tell me where a telephone booth is. He tells me there isn't any around. I ask him if he has a phone book, which he does, but I can't use his phone. I check the book and find a Yamaha Kawasaki dealership on Post Road. I ask him if he knows where that is. He tells me to go straight for around 9 miles. Sounds simple enough.

227

Well, it wasn't quite that easy but I did manage to find the shop after asking a couple of people. I walk into the shop, which is fairly large. It has a carpeted showroom floor and lots of bikes. I tell the guy at the counter what's been happening with the oil light. I tell him it stayed on for five miles this morning. He suggests we go and take a look at the oil level. We get outside and I tell him that to my embarrassment I have not mastered the art (art?) of putting my bike on the centre stand. I feel silly, but it's true. I have put my motorcycle through enough. Trying to use the center stand would be cruel and unusual punishment, for the bike and me. I always feel like it's going to fall over whenever I try. I don't know how many more pick-ups I have in me. Does the word hernia ring any bells?

Anyway, he easily puts it on the center stand. I tell him the oil level window is probably dirty. Which (in case you didn't know) is located near the bottom of the engine. He bends down and sees it is too dirty and goes to get a rag. He comes back, cleans the window and declares the oil level to be fine. He goes on to say the sensor may be in the wrong spot right now, where the oil may not be making its presence known. Something to that effect. I tell him I'm a little paranoid about oil levels because of last summer's major repairs. He assures me they are fine. We talk a bit about my trip. Another bike shop employee joins us. As we're talking, a motorcycle goes by with the rider not wearing a helmet. He tells me helmets aren't required, and eye protection either. I tell him of the Alaska law requiring only the passenger to wear a helmet. I thank them for their help, look around the showroom and then leave.

I'm back on the I-70, with the bike shop guys' directions. As I ride along I think about the whole helmet law debate. In the last two or three states I could have ridden without one. I have a feeling, knowing my bad luck/good luck way of things happening to me, it wouldn't have been a good idea to go helmetless. I will explain. If I had ridden without a helmet I would probably have had an accident but not injured my head but broken my leg. Good luck I didn't hit my head; bad luck that I broke my leg. Which all equals: trip over. I have ridden in the odd parking lot without a helmet, to park my bike or get gas and, I have to admit, it did feel kind of good. However, it's not a feeling I would trade for a scrambled brain. Of course, there is the theory that some bike accidents are so horrific, helmet or no helmet, it doesn't make a difference. I don't want to risk my head on a dumb minor accident, though. Well, that's just my opinion.

I arrive in the state of Ohio at 11:30 a.m. I start getting hungry and stop for lunch. According to my bill (for lunch), it's 1:40 p.m. My watch reads 12:40 p.m. I guess I entered another time zone along the way.

Well I'm back on the highway. I've been on the road around fifteen minutes when I see signs saying Neil Armstrong Space Museum next right. What a stroke of luck! I follow the signs to the museum. The building (part of it) looks like a planetarium. I park the bike and start walking towards the building. I come alongside a couple. I'm in a talkative mood. I tell them I didn't know the place existed and also about the letters, A.A.C. I had painted on my tank which stand for Aldrin, Armstrong, and Collins. We talk about my trip a little. The woman blurts out that maybe I'll ride a motorcycle on the moon one day (DooDooDooDoo, DooDooDooDoo Twilight Zone theme here). The first motorcyclist on the moon one day, I say, and smile.

I pay the entry fee and they kindly let me put my knapsack in the cloakroom. There are all kinds of pictures of astronauts, including Neil Armstrong of course. Lots of different painted pictures of Neil by various artists. Lots of miniature planes. There's a real plane hanging on the wall. It's the plane Neil learned how to fly in. Some space suits. Well, just all kinds of stuff.

I walk into a dark domed theatre—well, a planetarium I guess. The show starts a few minutes later. It's the history of the space program to the recent past. I look at some more artifacts. I walk by a computerized flight-simulator. There's a man just landing the Space Shuttle sitting there with hands on the controls. A voice tells him he did a good job and should think about a job at N.A.S.A., kind of thing. He is rated on his performance in different areas and stages of his flight. He gets out and I get in. I start the simulator. The voice tells me the objective, which is basically to keep the Space Shuttle inside or near a diamond-shaped guide, if you will, and then land the Space Shuttle safely. I get a practice run at keeping the shuttle steady and in the diamond. I do ok, but not great, either. I start at 16,000 feet. I begin. I'm trying to keep it near the little diamond-thingy the best I can. I push down way too hard on the stick and am now way off course. I then overcompensate. As we near the runway I'm at two hundred feet and the little diamond shape is nowhere in sight. If there are any other people on board this flight, I think they should start praying. I'm all over the place and, seconds later; I crash the Space Shuttle *Columbia*.

I'm given an animated analysis of my flight, complete with the crash. The voice then actually tells me not to quit my day job. Too late. I look around some more. I then buy some pins and leave.

It's 5:00 p.m. and I'm passing by Toledo, Ohio. A bit of a traffic jam due to construction prevents me from avoiding rush hour traffic. Well, it's twenty minutes later now and I have just crossed the Michigan State line. I'm now in the State which will get me to Ontario, Canada. A little over a half hour later I enter Detroit City. Every time I looked at the map of the United States (after realizing I would be going through Detroit) I vowed not to get lost here. When I was growing up, Detroit City had the worst crime and murder rate of any other state, to the best of my knowledge. If someone had told me when I was around 13 years old that they were going to Detroit City, I would have looked at them like they had lost their minds. I apologize to the people of Detroit, but that's what I thought.

I start seeing signs now for the Canada Tunnel. There's a tunnel to Canada? I never heard of that. I follow these signs for the Canada Tunnel. The signs say something like Lodgeway Canada Tunnel North. I follow them. It's twenty minutes later and I haven't seen the word Canada in that time. Guess what? I'm lost in Detroit City. I should have stayed on the I-75. I can't go off highway 10 North now, who knows what section of the city I'll end up in? I keep on 10 until I reach what I consider the suburbs. I turn into the parking lot of a pizza place. I walk in the pizza place and ask the man behind the counter how to get back to I-75. A woman in a postal uniform stands beside me. They both want to give me directions. I tell them not to take offence, but I don't want to be in Detroit City at night. The woman tells me no offence is taken. She knows what I mean. The counter guy starts writing out directions and tells me it's real easy to get back to I-75 but I'll have to go back downtown. He starts drawing a map. I really don't want to go back downtown. The woman beside me tells me to meet her outside because she believes the route he's giving me is too complicated. He finishes drawing me a simple but detailed map. I thank him very much but don't think I'll use it.

I walk outside and the woman is standing beside my motorcycle. She thinks the route is too complicated. Unfortunately, she can't remember the best way to get back to Canada. She has done it before but can't remember. She says she lives across the street and she has some maps. I tell her that won't be necessary. I get out my map (oh boy, here we go) and see there's a highway 69 going right to Port Huron, Ontario. Once you're on it, that is. I ask her if 69 is north or south of here. She doesn't know. She again offers to get some maps for me and I can stand in the driveway if I want. I tell her it's ok, I get lost all the time. Which makes no sense at all as a reply to her offer. I tell her I will eventually hit 69 East back to Ontario. She tells me it might be south of here. She still wants to get the maps. Although she seems nice, I can't trust her, which is sad. This is how people disappear. A seemingly innocent gesture can turn into the last time you're ever seen. I think she starts to sense I don't trust her and gives up. I thank her and tell her I will be all right. I don't think she believes me, neither do I. I will follow the other guy's directions after all, but keep my eyes open for highway 69.

I'm back on highway 10 South after getting briefly lost after leaving the pizza place. Oh, man. I'm dreading going back downtown. It's going to be dark by the time I get there. I'm not on 10 South long when I spot a sign reading 469 East. I just manage to get over to the proper lane. I start seeing signs for Port Huron. WHEW! What a relief. I can't begin to tell ya. Going back to downtown Detroit would have been a nightmare. Not too much later I start seeing signs like FOLLOW 469 FOR CANADA PORT HURON.

It's dark now as I pull up to the Canada/U.S.A. border customs booth. I am asked the usual questions. I'm allowed back into Canada. I ride to a phone booth and call my friend Audrey. She's not home. I'll go to Hamilton (where she lives) and see if I can stay with her tonight. I get on the highway and after a while I stop seeing signs for Hamilton. I start seeing signs for Toronto. I must be on the wrong highway. Ah, now I see, I'm on the 401 and not the 403, which would take me to Hamilton. Geez, not twice in one day, and in my home province, even.

I get off the highway and take a smaller secondary one going south towards Hamilton. It's around 10:30 p.m. This highway ends and I can go either left or right. Hmmmm. I think Hamilton is west, so I'll turn right. I'm in a place called St. Thomas now. I see a motel and pack it in for the day. I call Audrey. I tell her I got lost (I doubt she is surprised) and I'll see her tomorrow. We'll talk in the morning and she'll give me directions. I check into the motel. What a day.

Part 27 *The End of the Line*

September 19

After getting directions from Audrey, I'm on the road again. I get a kick out of seeing the Ontario licence plates. I forgot to mention that last night. I will be in Hamilton in about an hour. The trees are pretty, with their fall colours.

I arrive at Audrey's without getting lost, although I didn't exactly follow her directions to the letter. I have not seen her in well over a year. We spend the day catching up, looking at pictures from my trip and so forth. Before too long it's time to leave. She gives me directions to get onto the Queen Elizabeth Way and I arrive in downtown Toronto without incident.

I ride by the theatre (where I work, or used to) and see a couple of ushers and a cop at the door. The Toronto Film Festival is on. Our theatre is one of the venues they use. I ride around to the back stage door and park the bike. Jose, the back stage security person, is standing outside having a smoke. He asks about my trip, so we talk about my trip for a few minutes. I then ask him to use his walkie-talkie to call down to the front of house office and tell them that someone's coming down to see them. I ask him to do that without telling them it was me, so I can surprise them. I love surprising people. I walk downstairs into the lounge and bump into Grant, Karen, and Mike, who are bartenders at the theatre. We exchange greetings. It's great to see them. As I walk to the bar room office, Lori sees me for a milli-second but it doesn't register, as I walk immediately in behind someone else. Lori, Rene, Kelly, Bruce and Eric are there. Lots of hugs and a few tears. I walk around the theatre surprising people. They are Sean, Catherine, David, Jessica, James, Suzanne, Sylvia, Kevin, Lorraine and Rob. They don't recognize me at first, which makes it even better, because it's so dark in the theatre. I go back downstairs and am given some shifts to work from Lori. I'm lucky there's some stuff coming up at the theatre. I say goodbye to them and leave. It will take about a half an hour to get to my mother's apartment.

I'm almost at my mother's apartment now, where the trip officially started. I make a right turn onto her street, down for a bit, then left. I ride to the almost exact spot where I had said goodbye to my mother when the trip first started. I back into a spot and cut the engine. I did it. I fulfilled my dream. The dream was to go on a big motorcycle trip, particularly the Alaska Highway. There are no greetings for me here at the end of it. There's no parade, no party. Of course not, but in my mind just a little *Fanfare for the Common Man*, Maestro, if you please.

Afterword

I stand and watch, as the tow truck driver makes preparations to lift my motorcycle off the ground. I sign a piece of paper absolving him of any liability should the bike fall out of the sling it is to be transported in. I ask him if car drivers have to sign the same piece of paper. They do not. Why is my bike in need of a tow in the first place, you may well ask. Well, a few days after coming back from the trip I decided to wash my bike. Which I did. Unfortunately, I used an S.O.S. pad to clean it with. As you may have guessed, I scratched the hell out of my paint job. What was I thinking? I should have known better. Anyway, the next day I rode my bike to the store. When I got out of the store the bike did nothing when I pushed the starter button. It eventually started and stalled a couple of times. Well, I managed to ride it home. After that, however, it would go no farther than six feet and sometimes no distance whatsoever before it would stall. Maybe some water got into the electrical system when I washed it. I called the bike shop and told them the story. They said it sounded like an electrical problem. I will have it stored and then have it fixed in the spring. When I can afford it.

* * *

I would like to take this opportunity to thank you for reading my book. My dream initially was to ride a motorcycle the length of the

235

Alaska Highway, which I did. I then expanded the trip to include other places. I didn't get to all of them, which is the way things go sometimes. I coulda planned a little better, I woulda had more money if I'd planned and budgeted, and I shoulda learned to read a map perhaps. In the end, though, that's all coulda, woulda, shoulda talk. I hate those words. Did I make mistakes? Absolutely. Am I around $15,000 in debt? Yes, I am. Would I do it all again, knowing what I now know? In a minute. I fulfilled my dream, that's the important thing. I hope you can fulfil yours as well. Maybe you've been afraid to open a restaurant, take a flying lesson, change jobs, and discover your dream job perhaps. It could be that you think people might laugh at you. Is starting a toy car collection your dream? Why not start one? You may not even have to quit your job like I did. Maybe your dream involves a night course in psychology. You don't have to drop everything, disrupt your family, or whatever. Take a small step towards it, is all I ask. Then keep going, if that's what you really want. Take some steps, get a plan and . . .

GO AFTER YOUR DREAM!

Acknowledgments

I would like to thank the following people and organizations for helping me directly or indirectly with the trip or with this book:

The whole 1970s era; ABC's *Wide World of Sports*; Mutual of Omaha's *Wild Kingdom*; *The Undersea World of Jacques Cousteau*; *The National Geographic* TV show and magazine; *Canadian Geographic* magazine; Laura Bevacqua; David Brenner for writing the book *Soft Pretzels with Mustard*; Mel Brooks, Bugs Bunny, Jim Carrey, Daffy Duck, Warner Brothers cartoons, and the Marx Brothers for showing me that wackiness is an art form; CAA (Canadian Automobile Association); BCAA; Gina Chiarelli; Paul Christie; Dan Drummond, Rod Drummond, Roy Drummond, and Norma Drummond—my second family; Chris Durham; Margaret Eder; The Elgin and Winter Garden Theatre Staff '93, '94, '95, '96, '97, '98; Kelli Ewing; Don Ferrari; Dan Murphy-Ferrari; Tammy Fortunado; Vanessa Gangaram; Scott Gibbon; Cindy Graham; Rick Gregory; Jackie Hadley and the Hadley family; Sherry Hoerster; Catherine Ryan Hyde for writing *Pay It Forward*, and Lainie Curry for suggesting I read it at the perfect time; Tim Hortons; Nancy Huff; Larry Legebokoff and the Legebokoff family; motorcyclist Dave Nelson from Wyoming who helped me after the accident; Lori Maclean; *Mad Magazine*; Sean McMahon; John Murphy (my late father); Dawn Murphy; Kelly Mudie; Chuck Norris for writing the book *My Secrets to Inner Strength*; Goldy Notay; Tony Pearce; Dave and Pam Reid and the Reid family; Chris von Rosenstiel; Melanie Spurio; Genevieve Steele and the Steele family; Soula Taskas; Rene Redhead-Tinney and Harlan Tinney; Audrey von Troost; Wayne Utley and the Graphicshoppe staff '95, '96, '97, '98; Kevin Virtue; Sonya Vandermeer; Barb Wollocot; Barb Yakura; the Yamaha dealership in Prince George, B.C.; Julie at the Yamaha dealership in Fort Nelson, B.C and Ben from BCAA for getting me there; James Loates and his staff at VISU*TronX*.

ISBN 1553950068-2